INTRODUCING CHILDREN

TO THE

WORLD

LEONARD S. KENWORTHY

Associate Professor of Education, Brooklyn College

INTRODUCING

CHILDREN TO THE

WORLD

43323

In Elementary and Junior High Schools

HARPER & ROW, PUBLISHERS

New York, Evanston, and London

CONTENTS

PREFACE

"The elementary schools that will make the greatest contribution to life in the next generation will be those schools that are related to the world community, yet are firmly anchored in their home communities." [1]

For years that sentence has been on my mind. I have reflected on it, talked to others about it, read materials which might clarify it, conducted discussion groups, workshops, and classes on it, and experimented with methods and materials which would apply it to real life situations.

Finally I have gathered these experiences into a book in order to share them with fellow educators. There have been numerous chapters in other books and several pamphlets on introducing children to the world, but as yet there has been no volume devoted exclusively to this topic as it affects elementary and junior high school boys and girls. It is hoped, therefore, that this book may serve a special function in the area of education for international understanding.

Since this task is so enormous, the book is exploratory and suggestive rather than comprehensive and definitive. The field is too new and too broad for one person to cover it in an exhaustive way. It will take years of research and experimentation before we are certain as to the best ways of developing world-minded boys and girls. In the meantime it is hoped that this book will stimulate many persons to work in the broad field of education for international understanding.

Attention is given to the place of homes, churches, libraries, museums, the mass media, and other agencies of society, but the focus is on the elementary and junior high schools. The work of senior high schools has been omitted because it would take another volume to explore methods of introducing boys and girls of that age

[1] Educational Policies Commission, *Education for All American Children* (Washington: National Education Association, 1948), p. 279.

to the world and because the subject matter organization of most high schools would demand a different form of treatment than the one used here. Such a volume is being planned as a *Bulletin* of the National Association of Secondary School Principals for the fall of 1956 under the title *International Understanding through the Secondary School Curriculum.*[2]

Many persons have taken some part in the preparation of this book. Among these are my pupils in elementary and junior high school classes, student teachers and other college students with whom I have worked, my colleagues at Brooklyn College, in UNESCO, and in the School Affiliation Service of the American Friends Service Committee, fellow members of committees on international understanding, participants in workshops and international seminars, the authors of many books, and a large number of friends. To all these persons I am grateful.

Special thanks are due to Ruth Tooze, Director of the Children's Book Caravan and co-author of *Literature and Music as Resources for Social Studies;* Constance Carr, editor of *Childhood Education;* Mary Esther McWhirter, director of the Educational Materials for Children division of the American Friends Service Committee; and Margaret Cormack and Helen Brell of the Education Department of Brooklyn College. The librarians of the children's divisions of the Forty-second Street Library in New York City and Teachers College, Columbia University, have been most helpful, as has Miss Glenora Edwards, librarian of the Teacher Education Room at the Brooklyn College Library. Three students who have helped from time to time on the laborious task of checking bibliographical data are Hilary and Arlene Gold and Sandra Sherry. I am deeply indebted to all these persons.

In this volume I have used some ideas which I have developed elsewhere. This is true of materials drawn from *World Horizons for Teachers* and my two chapters in *Teaching World Understanding,* edited by Ralph Preston. Other ideas derive from articles I have written for *Childhood Education, The Chicago Schools Journal, The Clearing House, The Junior Red Cross Journal,* and *Social Education.*

I am especially indebted to the H. W. Wilson Company for help

[2] Leonard S. Kenworthy, ed.

obtained from their *Educational Film Guide* and their *Filmstrip Guide* on the visual materials cited.

The materials for children cited throughout the book are listed in complete bibliographical form in Appendix B, plus some material not mentioned in the chapters. Appendix A contains materials of special interest to teachers and Appendix C lists organizations in the field of education for international understanding. Most of the materials cited are recent and available from publishers; a few materials referred to are no longer on sale, but are still available in libraries.

Anyone who has worked with children will realize how difficult it is to classify books as to grade level. Readers will want to consult other lists than the ones for the grades they teach, especially to locate books for slower or faster readers in their groups.

It is my hope that some suggestions as to aims, experiences, and resources will help elementary and junior high school teachers, parents, and other leaders of children in their efforts to introduce boys and girls to the world. I am hopeful also that some of the studies which are suggested here will be undertaken and some of the needed materials produced.

This book has not been written with any thought that international loyalties will replace national loyalties. It has been prepared with the conviction that these two are complementary rather than contradictory. Our boys and girls must be educated in loyalty to the highest ideals of our own country and to the world community. If these aims are kept in mind, children will discover that the welfare of the United States and the welfare of the world are inextricably interwoven. A refinement of loyalty to our nation and the development of loyalty to humanity are top priority aims of education in our times.

Just prior to the entrance of the United States into World War II I had the honor of serving as Director of the Quaker International Center in Berlin, helping a few of the victims of Nazi persecution to leave that ill-fated land. While there I saw how every agency of Nazi society had been utilized to promote diabolical purposes.

After the war I had the privilege for nearly three years of serving on the secretariat of the United Nations Educational, Scientific, and Cultural Organization in London and Paris. There we wrestled with the problems of how an organization can stimulate and promote international understanding without interfering in the jealously guarded sovereignty of nations.

From these and other experiences I have learned how much easier it is to mobilize the forces of society to foster intolerance and hatred than to promote respect for and cooperation with one's world neighbors. No matter how difficult the job of introducing children to the world may be, however, it is the most important task of education today. This is an assignment for everyone. It cannot be limited to the schools and to teachers, although they must provide leadership.

Occasionally persons who undertake this task will be labeled idealists, internationalists, globalists, and visionaries. Actually this business of preparing children to live in the world community is the job for *realists*. Isolation is impossible in our interdependent world. It is no longer a question of whether we should prepare children to live in the world community; they will either live in a world community or not live at all. Education for living in the world community is the condition of our survival. The questions today are what kind of community it will be and how we can prepare children to live in the global society which is already here.

LEONARD S. KENWORTHY

INTRODUCING CHILDREN

TO THE

WORLD

Whether we realize it or not we are all actors in the great drama of our day, the drama of the integration or disintegration of man.

—EDMOND TAYLOR, *Richer by Asia*

Now, for the first time in human history, there is no spot on earth where the innocent may find refuge. No ark will keep us afloat; no Bamboo Grove, where philosophers may meditate—is immune from the barbarian's bombs; no foreign land is itself free enough from the threat of oppression to give safety to the oppressed. And no havens of refuge exist, like the monasteries of the Dark Ages, which the barbarians would respect. Since the rise of fascism, violence has become unqualified and universal; and it is civilization itself—not this patch or that patch of civilization—that is threatened with ruin.

—LEWIS MUMFORD, *Faith for Living*

Man has become too powerful and the earth has become too small to allow him the unwise use of his power. He has to choose either the great decay or the great embrace. There is nothing in between.

—ROBERT ULICH, *Conditions of Civilized Living*

A society is possible in the last analysis because the individuals in it carry around in their heads some sort of picture of that society.

—LOUIS WIRTH, in Karl Mannheim's *Ideology and Utopia*

People are not just driven by situational pressures; they are also pulled by idealized goals set by their culture.

—CLYDE KLUCKHOHN, *Mirror for Man*

The whole is never attained, but only by pursuing the whole can we make heroic gains.

—ROBERT M. MacIVER, *Toward an Abiding Peace*

There are three main drives behind the revolutionary changes sweeping across Asia. They are nationalism, communism, and regionalism. Of these, nationalism is the oldest and still the most powerful.

—CARLOS ROMULO, in *The New York Times*

There has probably never been a time when so many people in so many parts of the world were not only looking for guidance, but were themselves eager to make their contribution to the building of a new order.

—E. H. CARR, *Conditions of Peace*

Education for the Twentieth and Twenty-First Centuries

Most of the boys and girls in our elementary and junior high schools today will live until the end of the twentieth century, and a large proportion of them will live well into the twenty-first century. Parents, teachers, and other adults working with children need to keep that fact constantly in mind and to ponder its meaning as they prepare boys and girls not only for life today but also for the next fifty to seventy-five years.

Just what kind of world it will be when these children come into control no one dares to predict. There are, however, many indications of the enormous changes that will take place in the years and decades ahead.

An Air Age World

We are immersed in an air age and today's boys and girls will mature in a world which is more and more influenced by that fact. Even our concept of the world has to be changed. When some readers of this volume went to school they were told that the diam-

1

eter of the earth was around 8000 miles. Today children are taught in air-age geographies that the diameter of the earth is around 9200 miles, since the air ocean which extends beyond the earth's surface is now a real part of the earth. Who is to say how much greater the world will be in a few years, with all the explorations into outer space?

Other shifts are also needed in our thinking about our globe. At present commercial planes have a cruising speed of around 325 miles per hour, but new planes soon to be released will have a cruising speed of 500 miles per hour. The world's record speed, established in 1955, now stands at 822 miles per hour. Regular air routes have been started across the Arctic and soon such travel will become commonplace.

Helicopter transportation from skyscraper cities to planned suburbs seems just around the corner. A reputable science editor has written recently about the possibility of passenger rockets powered by atomic energy that will take people anywhere in the world in an hour. Interplanetary travel is now a subject for serious research by scientists.

Each new invention precipitates changes, and the airplane will undoubtedly change our world in the years to come even more than it has already. It will increase travel, alter trade and commerce, influence the distribution of population, open up new areas of the world, assist agriculture, demand more international unity, and increase international controls. Our globe increasingly becomes a world community.

A World of Atomic Power and Automation

Even more revolutionary changes are in store as a result of the splitting of the atom and the incredible changes brought about or predicted by the rapid expansion of automation.

Atomic energy has become the double-edged sword of science, capable of destroying mankind and also capable of creating a better world for all the inhabitants of this earth.

David Sarnoff, head of the Radio Corporation of America, says that electric light will be "freed" in the future from its glass bulb prisons and that homes and cities will be lighted by a new kind of "cold light"—produced by materials that glow when an electric currcnt passes through them. This means, for example, that television sets in the future will probably be no thicker than a picture frame.

Atomic power for homes and factories is another probability in the near future; atomic electricity was produced in a private utility company in upper New York State as this chapter was written. Experiments are being conducted into the uses of fissionable materials for a wide variety of peaceful purposes. These range from the production of power to the production of food and the reduction and cure of many diseases.

Meals in the future may be prepared in a matter of a few minutes. Complete meals, already cooked and frozen, may be dropped from freezers into stoves equipped with atomic power. The food itself may even be prepared artificially, using the sun's energy as plants do.

Already there is an amazing variety of machines and devices run automatically. Refrigerators defrost themselves, clothes and dishes are washed by robots, telephone calls are made by weird machines which respond automatically to the flick of a few fingers on a dial. In industry, oil refineries are almost completely robotized and giant electronic computing machines "think" for human beings. It is now possible to dial telephone calls across the continent, to keep all records of large industries on magnetic tape, to provide automatic translations of materials written in foreign languages.

A Revolutionary World

Since World War I, more than 650 million persons have won their independence. Many millions more are now demanding freedom to order their own lives. There is a relentless revolution under way in many parts of the globe—a revolution which may be resisted temporarily but not arrested permanently.

Already Asia has moved toward the center of the world stage and Africa is poised for its entry into the limelight of freedom. The political center of gravity has shifted from Europe to other parts of the globe and will move more rapidly in the years ahead.

Nor is this world-wide revolution merely political in nature. Simultaneously a social and economic revolution is under way. The people of the world who have lived and are still living in poverty, disease, and illiteracy are claiming the birthright of every human being—a decent standard of living, good health, good food, education, and self-government.

Moreover, the racial supremacy of the white people of the world is challenged and colonialism bitterly attacked. The colored people of the earth have at last discovered that "all men are created equal" and are demanding that white people practice what they preach. The white people of the earth have to learn to live as a minority, albeit an important minority, in this world of many colors.

A World in Conflict

Our world is in a conflict over political and economic ideologies which will continue for many years. In his volume on *Education in a Divided World*, James Conant predicts that this basic conflict will continue for at least the next half century.

Many assume that the conflict is between two worlds—the one Communist and the other free. Actually there are several ideologies competing with one another, ranging from the Russian form of communism on the one extreme to fascism on the other. In between there are several political and economic forms of society, with democratic socialism in one form or another in a larrge number of nations and our own form of democratic society and welfare or competitive capitalism in the United States.

In this context, destruction of unprecedented proportions is one possibility in the years ahead. Already the armaments race is under way and the search for deadlier weapons rushes on.

A World of Four and a Half Billion Neighbors

Tremendous strides have been made in recent years in reducing infant mortality and in lengthening the lives of men and women. Medical discoveries have made it possible to wipe out many of the dread diseases which previously destroyed millions.

This means a rapidly expanding population, with a world of four and a half billion persons predicted by 2030.

Probably there are no greater world problems to be solved in the immediate future than those of food and population. Agriculture may well undergo a tremendous transformation as far-reaching in significance as the replacement of horses by tractors has been in the past few years in our own country.

Scientists are now at work on hormones which will hold back the blossoms in the spring to prevent damage by late frosts or to speed up their maturing in the autumn. Seeds are being produced which can be planted in pellets containing stimulants, insecticides, and fertilizer. Men and women are experimenting on food to be produced in factories instead of farms. Research is under way into the use of desert areas like the Sahara and jungle regions like the Amazon as sources of food for the enormous expected population. Investigations may lead to the extraction of a boundless supply of raw materials from the sea.

A Cooperative World

Meanwhile, less spectacular but tremendously important discoveries are being made by social scientists in understanding large cultural groups as well as smaller and more primitive ones, in probing into the formation and change of attitudes, in investigating the processes of communication, in studying how groups function, in measuring public opinion, in probing the causes of tensions and means of lessening or eradicating some of them, and in analyzing other aspects of human activity. A new science of human relations is developing, which might revolutionize the world if applied in the period just ahead.

On the world scale there has been a tremendous development of international social and cultural organizations, ranging from the Boy Scouts and Girl Scouts to the World Confederation of Organizations of the Teaching Profession, from Rotary International to the World Council of Churches, from the League of Red Cross Societies to the International Confederation of Free Trade Unions, and scores of others.

In the governmental field there has been a steady increase in recent years of international organizations. Typical of these are the Benelux Union, the North Atlantic Treaty Organization, the Organization of American States, the Arab League, the South East Asia Treaty Organization, and the British Commonwealth and its economic arm—the Colombo Plan.

At the top there is the United Nations, the most ambitious inter-governmental organization in the history of man. Its specialized agencies are even more inclusive in their membership, including more nations than the United Nations itself.

Whether the future will bring more regional governments and a world government no one can predict, although the trend over the centuries has been toward larger and more inclusive governmental units.

These are some of the changes under way or contemplated. Others will certainly come in the next few decades.

Some Implications for Education

The implications of all these changes for education stagger the imagination. Today's boys and girls will be inhabitants of a global world by the latter half of the twentieth century and the early parts of the twenty-first century. In the words of Ralph Barton Perry, they are going to live "in a greater world, embracing the whole earth and its inhabitants, and their lives must be organized in the same pro-portions."

In the years just ahead there seem to be two general directions in which mankind may move. It can move toward world suicide or toward world society. It can move toward world chaos or world com-munity. Mankind stands today at a great crossroads of history, con-fronted by a deep and momentous decision as to the direction it will take.

The schools of the United States are bound up in this decision. If the choice is toward mass annihilation and world suicide, our schools might as well be closed now and boys and girls turned over to the experts in destruction from whom they can learn the latest devices for killing their fellow men in other parts of the globe.

If, on the other hand, the decision of mankind is to extricate itself from this fate and to move toward a better world community estab-lished in peace, justice, and freedom, then the schools will have a tremendous role to play. They will be called upon to produce a new kind of individual—a person with world horizons, capable of living effectively in a world community of from three to four billion neighbors.

Such an education would not replace education for local and national citizenship. It would refine the loyalty of our citizens to their community and their nation within a community of the world. Such an education would not denationalize pupils; it would extend their loyalties to humanity. It would do this in terms of complementary or supplementary loyalties, adding loyalty to mankind to the already existing emphasis upon loyalty to the family, friendship groups, community, state, and nation.

Even if the world remains in turmoil with a series of crises for years to come, boys and girls will need to be better enlightened about the world in which they live than at present. They will have to make the decisions as citizens which will vitally affect themselves and their children, as well as millions of other persons around the globe. In business, in politics, in labor unions, in churches, and in other groups, today's children will have to make and carry out policies which will affect world events and in turn be affected by them.

A port-hole view of the surrounding nations will not suffice. Children will need to have a cockpit view of the entire world. They will need a planetary perspective.

The returns are not yet in on how humanity plans to face the future, but world community has come—a community full of confusion, conflict, change, crisis. But also a community promising many form of cooperation.

Educators are realizing that this revolutionary world demands a new look in education. They must become pioneers again, experimentalists, revolutionaries in the best American educational tradition. Even though they are beset with problems of where to teach and who is to teach, these pioneers are beginning to consider what needs to be taught to prepare boys and girls for a rapidly changing world. They have begun to assume that children are already living in a world community and must have the necessary type of education. They have begun to realize that education must be used as an instrument of international understanding as well as of national unity.

The effort to achieve such a world-centered education seems staggering, but it is not impossible. In fact there is historic precedent for the schools of the United States to accomplish the seemingly impossible.

A little more than a hundred years ago the people of this nation caught a vision of a democratic society. They decided to implement this dream by launching a tremendous national experiment to develop generations of Americans from a motley assortment of children from many parts of the world.

The school was selected as a center for this experiment. Many of the prerogatives held by the home and other social institutions were shared with the school. As a result, the schools of the United States developed into a different kind of institution from the schools of other countries. They became laboratories for learning the democratic way of life.

This could not have happened if the citizens of this country had not wanted it. The majority of parents and other adults *did* want this experiment to succeed. They allocated large sums of money to the schools. They made public education free and compulsory. They demanded local control so that they might supervise what was happening to their children. They rated teachers high in social prestige.

There was, however, opposition to such a program. Often it was strong; sometimes it was even violent. But the will of the majority prevailed and the schools went about their task. By and large they were successful in achieving their goal. Millions of boys and girls and their parents became Americans. A whole continent learned the basic lessons of democratic living. The American way of life developed and was expanded.

Nearly every foreign commentator from de Tocqueville to Denis Brogan has singled out this "Americanization" process as the dominant and distinguishing characteristic of public education in the United States. It was a unique experiment in history and the school was its focal point.

Other institutions helped, of course. The home played its part. The church was enlisted; clubs and community organizations helped. But none was as important as the school.

Today the people of the United States are confronted with an even greater decision than they faced in the early 1800's. World events have catapulted our country into world leadership. We can relinquish that leadership and slide down the toboggan of history into relative unimportance or oblivion. Or we can accept the challenges of our new position and prepare our people to assume world leadership wisely and well.

If we take the latter course, every medium of education will need to be geared to this tremendous task. Every technique of learning will have to be employed. Every insight we have or can develop will have to be made available in promulgating such a program of world understanding. Every individual whose background, training, and talent qualify him for leadership will have to be enlisted, and thousands more trained.

Twice in the last half century Americans have proved what is possible when the entire nation is mobilized for war. Astonishing results have been attained. If the United States as a whole realizes what it means to live in a global society and to assume leadership in that world community, a similar mobilization for peace will be needed. In such a mobilization the schools may not play as important a role as they did a hundred years ago in the process of Americanization. Since that time, the public library, the museum, the press, radio and television, farm and labor groups, civic organizations, and women's clubs have all become potent educational agencies. Some of the responsibility of education for international understanding will fall upon these agencies of society.

But the school should remain in the forefront. It is the one social institution primarily concerned with transmitting and transforming the culture.

If the American people become informed about the need for an education which prepares children for life in the world community, they will not only approve radical changes in our curricula, they will demand that the schools provide a new and up-to-date education for the twentieth and twenty-first centuries. The pressures on the schools will then be for more and better education about the world rather than less as is occasionally the case today.

The purpose of the schools in this country has always been to help children and youth to use the past in order to live effectively in the present and future. If the schools live up to that purpose now, educators will need to sketch in broad outline the kind of world we live in today and will live in tomorrow. Then they will need to develop a comprehensive, cumulative program to help boys and girls to live in this changing world.

Today's frame of reference is not broad enough. Just as the glass in colonial homes was imperfect, giving people a distorted view of the outside world, so our curricula today give children a distorted view. Architects have broadened the frames of windows in modern homes and inserted perfect or near-perfect glass in "picture windows" so that more of the outside world is visible and more perfectly seen. We as educators have also to put broader windows into our schools, with more perfect glass, so that they are in reality windows on the whole world.

A curriculum for the twentieth and twenty-first centuries can as yet only be sketched in broad strokes. But the general outlines are increasingly apparent. Briefly stated such a curriculum should help children:

1. to learn about the earth as the home of man and other living things;
2. to be introduced to the people of the world with their many similarities and their many differences;
3. to learn about the many ways of living on this planet and some of the reasons for the wide variety of modes of life;
4. to learn about the world as a place of fun and beauty;
5. to gain an elementary understanding of the interdependence of the peoples of the world and what can be done to promote better relationships;
6. to learn about the division of the world into nations and cultures, a few of the values adhered to by different groups, and some of the problems arising from these divisions—to the end that better adjustments can be made in the years ahead;
7. to realize the conditions under which people live in various parts of the earth and to become sensitized to the need for better standards of living for all the people of the earth, in larger freedom;
8. to become effective democratic citizens of their local communities and of the United States, while understanding other forms of government around the globe;
9. to acquire an elementary knowledge of the major religions and value beliefs in the world today and to learn to respect persons whose views differ from their own;
10. to know something about the long struggle of mankind to replace

conflict with cooperation and to develop a desire and the simple skills to participate effectively in building a better world.

Such are the major goals for our schools in the years ahead as wise, dedicated, imaginative, informed teachers and administrators, school board members, and parents introduce boys and girls to the world community in which they are actually living.

Such goals are not the dreams of internationalists, idealists, globalists, visionaries. They are goals based on the realities of life in our times. They are goals for survival in the interdependent and explosive world of our day. They are today's application of the Judaic-Christian ideals on which our nation was founded. They will be difficult to achieve. But they are vitally important if we and our world neighbors are to live happy and fruitful lives together.

I think the most important single thing which can be taught to our school children is the fact that they are not only citizens of the United States, but belong to the society of the world.

—LEVERETT SALTONSTALL, to the Committee on International Understanding of the National Education Association

Human hope is based in part on the negative belief . . . that nothing in human nature makes war inevitable. It is founded even more firmly on the positive belief in the ability of the educational process to condition human nature in such a manner that a decisive proportion of the people of the world will want a peaceful world and will explore all possible means of achieving it.

—*Education for International Understanding in American Schools*

I believe that nothing less than a complete recasting or reorientation of our educational system can promote peace, can save mankind from annihilating wars. But what is needed cannot be covered by the timid approaches of the average educational reformer. Reform means that you take existing elements and reshuffle them into a more satisfactory pattern; you revise the curriculum, raise the school age, build new schools. But that is not what I mean: I mean a complete transformation of the methods and aims of education.

—HERBERT READ, *Education for Peace*

The world cannot stand another global war and the thing to prevent such a tragedy is education.

—DWIGHT EISENHOWER, to a UNESCO Seminar, 1948

The building of peace on earth will be the task of the next generation. The world will be what the children of the next generation make it, but the upbringing of that generation is our own responsibility. If we have the courage, the determination, and the imagination to free our children from many of our taboos, many of our own anxieties, and many of our unfounded fears—if, in other words, we succeed in giving them true maturity and a strong feeling of world citizenship—we can be sure that they will grow into a happy and peaceful world. The responsibility lies with each and every one of us. I can think of no greater field for earnest, determined work. Whatever helps our children to grow up to be mature, compassionate, tolerant, and worthy citizens of the world must be of interest to each of us. We have our chance now. It is the last time we may have it.

—BROCK CHISHOLM

Chapter 2

Characteristics of an Effective Program

A few years ago Salvador de Madariaga asserted that the world used to be like a wide and deserted road over which a picturesque stagecoach passed now and then, whereas today it is like a crowded thoroughfare with a continuous stream of high-powered automobiles. Furthermore, he said, these autos seemed to be interdependent, so that when one driver pressed his foot on the accelerator, many other cars rushed forward as well as his own.

Unfortunately too many schools in the United States today are producing drivers for yesterday's stagecoaches through archaic curricula rather than educating drivers and pilots for the latest model automobiles and airplanes through modern, globally-oriented curricula.

If we are to produce new kinds of men and women for a new age, we need to remodel and revise our curricula. Perhaps nothing short of a drastic revision of experiences for pupils from nursery school through college will produce the desired outcomes, as the English educator Herbert Read suggests on the opposite page.

In the light of our contemporary world and the world which will probably emerge in this century, the following seem to be some of the most important characteristics of an effective program for boys and girls.

Begin Programs with Young Children

Children learn their prejudices early in life. Prejudices are picked up from the tone of voice of parents in speaking about people of other races, religions, or nationalities, by threats of punishment for playing with certain children, by the methods of discipline used in homes, by the contacts children have in their neighborhoods, and by a score of other influences.

Richard Rodgers and Oscar Hammerstein expressed this idea when they wrote that you have to be taught to hate, in their song, "Carefully Taught," from *South Pacific*.

Any program for developing world-minded Americans must bear in mind the importance of these early years and start in the home and in the preschool and primary grades.

This does not mean an extensive program about the world, but it does mean an emphasis upon helping children to feel secure, to feel that they belong, that they are important. It means that young children must be helped to channel their aggressive impulses into socially useful tasks. It means that competition must be minimized and cooperation accented. It means that apathetic children need to be observed and assisted in becoming alert, active members of their peer groups. It means that the overaggressive must also be studied and the reasons for their hostility understood and overcome.

Although important at every stage of development, this mental hygiene approach is most needed in the preschool and primary grades. Only children who can accept themselves, with all their strengths and all their limitations, can accept others.

Howard Lane summarized this approach when, speaking to a UNESCO seminar of teachers a few years ago, he said that "if we are to build One Peaceful World, we must revolutionize the status of children in the neighborhoods of the world."

Programs in world-mindedness cannot stop there, however. Until recently it was thought that no teaching about the world should be carried on in the early years at school. Most schools still cling to that outmoded theory.

Actually, any careful examination of the lives of young children will reveal that the world impinges upon them even before they go to school and certainly in the preschool years. Some children have been born abroad or have lived in other countries in these early years. Some of them have relatives who are abroad in business, government, or military service. The adults around them are reading newspapers, looking at television programs which include the world, and discussing world affairs. Many children visit the wharves or airports. There are celebrations of U.N. Day or Week in the school or community. Often there are people from abroad in their neighborhood or shops with "foreign" goods in them. The movies give them another view of the world—although not always a correct one.

In these and other ways children today are being introduced to the world early in life. The schools have a responsibility to help make this introduction a correct one, carried on in an atmosphere of respect, understanding, and interest. As Delia Goetz has phrased it in her excellent booklet for teachers, "World understanding begins with children."

Encourage Program at Every Grade Level and Throughout the Curriculum

World-mindedness is not a monopoly of any grade level or of any subject field. Any effective program needs to include a wide variety of experiences for every grade and every group of children no matter what their ability is. All children are going to live in the world and all of them need an introduction to the world-wide society as well as to their own community and nation.

In the early years these experiences will occupy only a small fraction of the time in schools, and most of the teaching in this field should be incidental. Children may meet someone from abroad and share experiences with him or her. They may sing songs or play games which they understand vaguely are from another part of the world. They may celebrate a holiday or take part in a school-wide program relating to some phase of international understanding. Such experiences may be indirect, but they are important to world understanding.

In the primary and intermediate grades units of work which children normally undertake can be expanded to include the world community. The study of food, transportation, clothing, home and family life, communication, and a score of similar topics should be examined locally, nationally, and internationally, even though the emphasis will be upon the local community aspects.

Special units could well be developed for these grades, such as Pets Around the World, Hats Around the World, and Fun and Beauty Around the World.

By the fourth or fifth grades children usually begin to understand a little about other countries. At this point a study of nations similar to ours can be started. There is certainly interest in the strange and unusual, but whether children should be introduced first to nations which are as different from ours as China and India is open to question. To this writer it seems far wiser to start with countries like England, Australia, New Zealand, Canada, the Scandinavian countries, Hawaii, the Philippines, and others.

By the sixth or seventh grades, children are usually ready to cope with countries which are more complex from our point of view. They are also ready for a more thorough study of international conflict and cooperation.

By the time they reach the eighth or ninth grades they should be ready for a study of countries which are more different from ours, for a deeper examination of some of the problems of the world, and in some cases even for an introduction to the concept of culture.

At all these various points extensive use should be made of the library, of assembly programs, clubs, plays, films and filmstrips and other audio-visual materials. Often school-wide projects can be introduced and action programs included.

Such an all-inclusive program is mentioned in a recent issue of the magazine Affairs, issued for the parents of pupils in the Oak Lane Country Day School in Philadelphia. In conjunction with their affiliation with La Maison d'Enfants de Sèvres, the kindergarten children were painting pictures and collecting their favorite Golden Books to be sent abroad, the first grade was collecting photographs of trains and making place cards to send to their friends in Paris, the second-grade children were selecting one personal possession which they thought their opposite numbers in France would enjoy, the fourth, fifth, and sixth grades were writing to pen pals, and the junior high school pupils were making tape recordings of songs and poems to send abroad. This seems a fine example of a program which permeates the entire school and should be cumulative in its effect.

Base Program on Knowledge of Child Development and the Learning Process

Gradually school curricula in the United States are being adjusted to the findings of psychologists regarding child development and the learning process. It is high time that programs devoted to developing world-mindedness were similarly constructed. Basic aims of the program for all levels should be determined and appropriate experiences for different levels of maturity need to be outlined with enough flexibility to meet the differences from group to group and school to school. The ten basic themes outlined in this volume are one attempt to suggest some of the major aims of a program introducing children to the world. The experiences suggested in each chapter devoted to these ten aims are based so far as possible on what we know of the interests and capacities of children at various stages of their development.

Since this is the first broad attempt to develop such a program, it needs to be carefully examined by competent persons in the fields of child development and the learning process, and every improvement possible suggested.

Psychologists are agreed, for example, that holidays and celebrations are especially meaningful to young children. This should mean that programs for developing world-mindedness emphasize such days as Pan-American Day, World Children's Day, United Nations Day, and holidays observed in many countries, such as Christmas and harvest festivals.

Social psychologists believe that action projects are important in developing attitudes, so that learning takes place in the hands as well as in the head, so far as these two can be separated. This accents the need for all kinds of creative activities and service projects, especially of a shared nature, in programs for international understanding.

Again, self-interest is a strong element. The Germantown Friends School has made use of this theory in its third grade where the children all had pictures taken of themselves and their houses and sent them to their affiliated school in France, together with short accounts of themselves written by the children, asking for similar materials in return.

The potent influence of audio-visual approaches is vouchsafed by most authorities on learning and should give administrators and parents another clue to programs for international understanding.

Among the many other findings which should be applied to this broad field of world-mindedness are the following: changes take place best when the total group is involved; old views should be accepted with equanimity and persons should be encouraged to air and examine their beliefs; attitudes can be changed at any age but probably are changed most easily in the young. These and other equally important facts in learning and attitude formation and change could revolutionize most programs relating to the world, making them far more effective than they are today.

Complement Program with Studies of the Local Community and the United States

The study of the world is not a separate subject to be added to the curricula. Neither is such a study intended to replace or even minimize studies of the local community or of the United States.

Education for loyalty to the United States and to the world are complementary aims in American education today.

For example, children should be taught to admire such national patriots as Washington, Jefferson, Jackson, Lincoln, Wilson, and Roosevelt. And they should also be taught to admire such great leaders of humanity as Gandhi, Einstein, Kagawa, and Schweitzer.

Occasionally persons interested in the world scene give the impression that their world-mindedness rules out interest in local and national affairs. Such persons need to make it clear to their students and to the adults around them that they are concerned with all three, and they should seek to develop the interest of their pupils in all these major communities.

Utilize a Variety of Resources

There is no one way to promote world-mindedness. If there were, the task would be simple. Some children become interested in the world through people, some through books, many through films and radio and television, some through service activities, a few through stamp, doll, or coin collections. There are scores of ways of interesting people in the world community and any program along these lines should be broad enough to include a great many types of activities.

If such a program is developed by many persons with their own special interests, it is more likely to meet the needs of a great variety of pupils. In many instances parents and pupils can make suggestions or participate in planning curricular experiences.

One of the biggest advantages of the unit method of teaching is the fact that it encourages a variety of approaches and thus is more likely to provide for individual differences.

Include Practical Action

A danger in almost every program in education is the risk of too much verbalization. This can be a special weakness of any program in world-mindedness. The world community seems at times so remote and so large that it is difficult to see what children can do about it.

Any successful program in introducing children to the world, however, should include action projects. These may range from exchanges of art and international correspondence to helping a displaced family or contributing to the care of an orphan child in a distant country.

Wherever possible these projects should be ones in which people share rather than merely give to some worthy cause. Where children can make the things they send abroad or earn the money which they contribute, better learning will take place.

Administrators and Boards of Education should examine the service projects carried on in their schools to see if one or more of them take into account this new dimension of the world community and to see that new types of action projects and new organizations are given a fair hearing for "drives," along with well established organizations.

Promote Program Cooperatively with the Community

The task of developing world-minded boys and girls is too large for the school to undertake alone. Furthermore, the school is not equipped to do certain things which other community agencies can perform. It should be a part of any school's philosophy to work with community agencies, introducing children to these groups or institutions which they can use all their lives and in which they can be active participants in later years.

In rural areas schools should be working alongside the church, the 4-H Club, the Farm Bureau, and other organizations in helping to promote world-mindedness. In towns and cities there are more churches; Y.M. and Y.W.C.A.'s; local branches of the American Association for the United Nations, the Foreign Policy Association, the League of Women Voters, the Association of University Women; the Girl Scouts, Camp Fire Girls, and fraternal organizations; and settlement houses and community centers with which the schools should be working. Local libraries, art galleries, and museums are also rich resources upon which the school should draw, while state libraries and state universities can often be helpful in the loan of books and audio-visual materials. Radio and television stations also need to be kept in mind as allies.

Cooperation with these community agencies should not be one-way. Boys and girls can contribute to the agencies in a variety of ways. Class scrapbooks can be given to local libraries or hospitals, programs or "spot announcements" can be prepared for radio stations, plays and panels arranged for churches and civic and fraternal organizations, and help given to various groups in city-wide programs and drives.

Through such cooperation children can learn many skills, feel themselves a part of their own community, and in a small way contribute to the formation of public opinion.

Teachers, too, can cooperate locally, contributing to organizations and in turn winning support for programs of world-mindedness in the schools. No program of world-mindedness can be effective if it does not have strong local support. Therefore administrators and teachers have a responsibility to interpret what they are doing to parents and others in order to win such support.

Use Experimental Approach and Include Appropriate Evaluation

The promotion of world-mindedness in schools as a central aim is new. There is not yet sufficient knowledge to determine what are the most effective experiences for children at different age and maturity levels. Teachers and administrators need therefore to look upon such programs as experimental. They need to follow with keen interest their own experimentation and that of others by noting the growth of pupils through various methods and materials. They also have a responsibility to share their findings in publications and in conferences with other educators.

For those who are interested in experimentation and evaluation there are many opportunities. Teachers need to keep records of pupil reactions to books, films, filmstrips, and other materials. They need to develop simple tests of attitudes and skills. They need to prepare new materials such as are suggested in this volume and to try them out in classroom situations. Education for international understanding needs to move from the missionary stage to the evaluation stage; teachers have an obligation to undertake experimentation and evaluation.

Typical of the needed experimentation is the UNESCO project on Education for Living in a World Community. Started in 1953, it is a voluntary project in which schools from twenty countries are taking part. Each school has selected a project related to the rights of women or the Universal Declaration of Human Rights, or the study of a country other than its own. One of the most promising aspects of this project is the evaluation which the schools have to undertake. Several forms have been suggested by the UNESCO secretariat, including tests of knowledge, attitude scales, group discussions, essays, and individual interviews.

Tentative forms for the attitude tests towards other countries include four approaches. Items from Part I include the following:

A Strongly agree	B Agree	C No Opinion	D Disagree	E Strongly disagree

1. They work hard.

5. I would like to have them as guests in my home.

19. I would feel uneasy with them if I were alone.

Typical items from Part II include the following:

1. I would let them visit our country.

8. I would be happy to have one as a very close friend.

Sample items from Part III indicate more general attitudes toward people of other countries. A few of the items follow:

2. In a large city, people of different nationalities should live in different districts.
Strongly agree ( ) Agree ( ) Uncertain ( ) Disagree ( ) Strongly disagree ( )

14. Some nations are naturally warlike.
Strongly agree ( ) Agree ( ) Uncertain ( ) Disagree ( ) Strongly disagree ( )

In Part IV pupils are asked to write an A if the statements apply to *all* individuals of the nationality name, an M if the statement applies to *most* of the people, an F for a *few*, and an N for *none*. A few items chosen at random are:

1. They are hardworking
7. They have funny eyes
19. They are trustworthy
20. They are stupid

Organizations in the United States interested in promoting world-mindedness could perform a much needed service by developing and perfecting such instruments.

Secure the Support of School Administrations

Little can be accomplished without administrative support and much can be done if there is enthusiastic administrative sanction. Even in the most democratic organization the top brass controls the stop-and-go signs for curriculum work.

There are many ways in which administrators and school boards can assist in promoting fine programs about the world. They can hire teachers with foreign experience or persons interested in promoting world-mindedness. They can encourage and in some cases assist their teachers to travel or study abroad. They can bring into a school system for short periods specialists in various phases of world-mindedness as consultants. They can encourage teachers to study in summer or in extension courses some phases of the world. They can interpret to the community the school's responsibility and enlist the support of the public in such programs. They can release teachers from time to time to work on curriculum projects in this field or lighten their teaching loads for such extra work. They can allocate funds for equipment for programs in world-mindedness.

As in all other phases of curriculum development, administrators have a tremendous responsibility to encourage programs in world-mindedness and to educate teachers who are world-minded, not forgetting that they, too, can grow along with their teachers.

Develop World-Minded Teachers

In the final analysis curriculum changes are carried out by classroom teachers. Fine bulletins, excellent equipment, administrative sanction, and community support are important, but nothing happens unless teachers are vitally concerned. The teacher always remains the keystone in the educational arch.

Unfortunately many of today's teachers were trained in a period when the world was not of major importance to Americans. They were educated before the days of World War II and the hydrogen bomb. Their world is all too often a parochial one and they are too frequently provincial in their outlook.

The writer has already devoted an entire book to the subject of *World Horizons for Teachers* so that he will not elaborate in detail the needs of teachers in this vast area of preparation. Perhaps it will be sufficient to incorporate here a list of the characteristics of world-minded teachers. These characteristics, outlined in the 1954 Year-book of the National Council for Social Studies on *Approaches to an Understanding of World Affairs* are guideposts. No teacher has passed all of them. They are goals toward which many alert teachers are moving.

In brief, the world-minded teacher is on his way to becoming:

An integrated individual, skilled in the art and science of human relations, and conscious of the wide variety of behavior patterns in the world to which he may have to adjust;

Rooted in his own family, country, and culture, but able to identify himself with the peoples of other countries and cultures;

Informed about the contemporary world scene and its historical background, and concerned about improving the conditions of people everywhere;

Convinced that international cooperation is desirable and possible, and that he can help to promote such cooperation;

An intelligent participant in efforts to improve his own community and nation, mindful of their relations to the world community;

Clear in his own mind as to the goals of education for international understanding, conversant with methods and resources for such programs, and able to help create world-minded children and youth;

Buttressed by a dynamic faith or philosophy of life whose basic tenets can be universalized.

Conclusion: Changing the Curriculum

No matter where a teacher teaches or what the course of study may be, there are opportunities to develop world-mindedness in children, directly or indirectly.

Teachers who have won their reputation for competence and who have good relations with their supervisors are usually able to carry on experimentation even where the curriculum may be archaic.

Where there is a desire for bringing the curriculum up to date the entire teaching staff in a school may want to study over a period of months the implications of the world scene upon school work. Or a small study group may pursue this subject, reporting its findings to the entire group.

A recommended method of curriculum change is to hold a workshop for a school system or to have a nucleus group go as a body to a summer workshop in a nearby college, where they can work out changes to suggest to their school later on.

Curriculum change of a less ambitious nature may be carried on by the improvement of instructional resources. New books for the library or new films or filmstrips may help measurably to improve instruction about the world. Making available to teachers the names of persons who know something about life in other lands may also improve teaching.

A series of films on the world at meetings held at regular intervals or a small shelf in the teacher's room containing books which can be borrowed, can sometimes help to spark changes in a classroom or school.

Trips to nearby schools which are accenting programs in world-mindedness often serve as stimulants. The appeal to pride to do as good a job as another school does is not the best motivation but it is sometimes a starting point.

Probably the best form of curriculum change is the involvement of an entire school system in a study of its current program. Such a study should be a cooperative one, involving teachers, parents, administrators, and pupils. If conducted properly, this study should lead to greatly improved instruction in introducing boys and girls to the world.

International understanding can be promoted naturally in its manifold settings. New subjects need not be added to the curriculum. What is urgent is that the subjects already available are properly utilized. The addition of new subjects rather than the adoption of a new emphasis means specialist teachers, departmentalization, and specialization, which lead inevitably to thinking in compartments. Like spiritual values, the values of peace, international understanding, and international cooperation cannot be taught in separate lessons.

—I. L. KANDEL, in *Education Forum*

Any instruction which makes individuals more sensitive in human relations, more mature in outlook, more skilled in the procedures of thinking thereby contributes at least indirectly toward better handling of international relations.

—HOWARD E. WILSON, *Universities and World Affairs*

The expansion of world horizons is achieved by means of a great diversity of experiences. Joining in the folk songs of other nations, taking part in plays and pageants depicting them, meeting people of various national background, reading stories, poems, and plays about life in other countries, observing their customs, costumes, homes, festivals, rituals, foods, play, work, and language through literature, audio-visual aids, and, where possible, direct visits—these are some of the methods employed in modern schools. The purpose is to reach emotional as well as ideational levels of learning, in order that basic attitudes of good will may be formed.

—JOHN DEBOER, *Design for Elementary Education*

To extend their lives to all parts of the earth men do not need to multiply their places of residence. They can remain where they are and multiply and lengthen their lines of intercourse. The area of the surface of the earth which a man occupies is proportional to the number and range of his relationships, and not merely to the extent of his travels or the variety of his habitations.

—RALPH BARTON PERRY, *One World in the Making*

The great secret of the coming age of the world is that civilization rests not on Reason but on Emotion.

—BENJAMIN KIDD, *The Science of Power*

Chapter *3*

Appropriate Experiences and Resources

Start a group of children on a treasure hunt and they will use a wide variety of methods to find the coveted prize and have fun in the process. Eventually they may all arrive at the final goal even though they have traveled different routes.

So it is with the discovery of the world by children. The methods may vary from individual to individual and from group to group. It is not the methods that matter most, providing they are consistent with the end to be achieved; it is the goal of world-mindedness that counts.

There are scores of experiences for children which can be helpful in introducing them to the world. Consequently, teachers need to use wise judgment in selecting the best, providing those which are tailored to meet the needs of their young charges. Many factors need to be taken into consideration. The age of children, their aptitude and maturity, the needs of society, the interests of boys and girls, the resources available, and the abilities and interests of teachers are some of the factors which need to be considered.

27

Likewise the need for variety must be taken into account. Playing on one string is just as monotonous in school situations as in music. A variety of methods is likely to reinforce learning.

In this chapter we shall look at some of the most appropriate experiences for pupils and a few of the resources for such activities.

Through Living and Travel Abroad

Carefully guided, living and travel abroad can be a rich experience for boys and girls. Parents stationed in foreign parts can make living abroad a tremendous education if they help their offspring to understand and respect the people they meet and the sights they see, no matter how different these may be from what they are accustomed to at home.

Most educators today feel that family travel can be encouraged even with young children, but none of the leading organizations interested in foreign experience recommends travel alone even for junior high school pupils.

In schools near the borders of Canada and Mexico, short trips can be made by school children or exchanges arranged for small groups. A one-day trip to Montreal by the fourth grade of the Laboratory School at the Plattsburg (New York) State Teachers College and a three-day trip to Cuba by children in the North Beach Elementary School in Miami, Florida, are examples of carefully planned experiences of this kind.

Occasionally there are children in a class who have just returned from a period of living abroad or who are planning to go with their families to other parts of the world. Such situations can serve as excellent motivation for a study of the countries they have visited or plan to visit, providing that the children who do not have these experiences do not feel left out.

Sometimes children can travel vicariously with older persons. Nine classes in the Edgewood School in Scarsdale, New York, recently spent considerable time studying the nations their principal had visited the previous year, in a school-wide project known as "Around the World with Mrs. Robinson." In addition to the principal, several other persons from abroad were utilized as resource persons and the culminating activity was a tour of the world by the parents, with each room decorated with the materials on a given country which the children had prepared.

Schools in Norway and the Union of South Africa sometimes ask the officers and crews of boats to send back all the materials they can collect from foreign countries and the children follow their travels with keen interest.

Through People

The best way to introduce children to the world is through people. Margaret Mead has gone so far as to say, "You can promote knowledge about, but not real understanding of other people, without persons from those countries."

Child psychologists like Dr. Arthur Jersild point out that "children at all age levels are much preoccupied with people and personal relations, so that stress on people in studies of other lands is an approach that will almost always appeal to children of various ages."

The greatest impact is usually made by one's peers. Opportunities for children to meet their opposite numbers from other parts of the world are rare, but they do exist. An outstanding example of this is the Children's International Summer Village, a project developed in 1951 in Cincinnati. In this camp children between the ages of ten and twelve from nine nations were brought together in a carefully controlled experiment under the direction of Dr. Doris Twitchell Allen, a psychologist long interested in intergroup relations and world affairs.

Where children from other countries are in a school, their experiences should be shared, but care should be taken not to exploit them or to keep them from being singled out as different by undue concentration on their background.

Schools and school systems would do well to keep a card index of adults from abroad or with foreign experience who can be helpful as resource persons in the school. Such persons should of course really know the lands they discuss, be interested in children, and be able to communicate with them.

Much more advantage should be taken of the presence of 35,000 students from abroad studying in American colleges and universities.

Pioneer work in setting up standards for the use of such persons is now being carried on by the International Teaching Service Bureau at Teachers College, Columbia University, under the direction of Dr. Donald Tewksbury. This Bureau, for example, is most anxious that visitors to schools be invited into the classrooms and take part in the ongoing activities of children rather than performing merely as platform speakers in school assemblies.

Families can also be encouraged to have students or other adults from abroad in their homes, giving these visitors opportunities to share in family life and to contribute to its enrichment. The most vivid such experience the writer has seen occurred during a weekend in the home of a Danish couple in France with two young tow-headed children. Their special guest was a dark Haitian who had a remarkable understanding of children. Playing with him, eating with him, climbing all over him, and even examining the palms of his hands and his tongue to see if they were also black was a tremendous experience in international understanding, made possible in the intimate atmosphere of a home by understanding parents and an outstanding and understanding visitor.

In addition to students from abroad there are many other persons who can become valuable resources for schools. The large number of teachers in this country on fellowships of various kinds, speakers who visit such groups as local Rotary, Kiwanis, and Lions clubs, returned service men, and teachers who have been abroad on exchanges or fellowships can all be helpful. The Seattle, Washington, schools are making use of consular officials as another group who can contribute to international understanding. High school students in the United States under the American Field Service or the School Affiliation Service of the American Friends Service Committee are usually busy with their own high school work but can occasionally be invited to other schools and see new situations in the process of their visits.

Teachers and parents would do well to bear in mind that not all newly arrived immigrants want to be used in this connection. Sometimes they are trying hard to lose their "foreign" identity and often they are too much taken up with adjustments to their new land to be available for schools.

Through Television and Radio

Television can become one of the most potent means of introducing children to the world community. True, it has not yet developed far in this direction, but there are already a few programs which can help children of various ages to understand the world scene. Among such programs at the present writing are *Disneyland*, *Wide Wide World*, *You Are There*, *See It Now*, *Conversations—Distinguished People*, and *Meet the Press*.

Since children are likely to see programs which the family is viewing, parents and teachers should be aware of the background which they will need to watch telecasts intelligently and help them obtain such background.

In a less dramatic way, radio can also help. Such programs as *United Nations Report*, *America's Town Meeting*, and *American Forum of the Air* can be used effectively with older or intellectually brighter children.

Through Films, Filmstrips, and Slides

Films, filmstrips, and slides can also be forces in any world education program. Films usually carry a stronger emotional impact than books and still pictures. On the other hand, filmstrips and slides are less expensive, much easier to project, and they can be used much more flexibly than films.

The most up-to-date catalogue of films available is a booklet entitled *Selected Films for World Understanding* compiled by Wendell W. Williams of the Audio-Visual Center at Indiana University. Teachers should also make use of the *Educational Film Guide* and the *Filmstrip Guide* published by the H. W. Wilson Company, with frequent supplements.

Schools need to build up strong collections of films and filmstrips and also Kodachrome slides which can be arranged and re-arranged according to the topics being studied in schools. Often such slides can be borrowed from adults in the community or duplicates made from pictures they have taken on trips. Occasionally glass slides made by classes can be saved and used in other classes in future years.

Many of the state universities are now performing a fine service to schools through the loan of audio-visual materials.

Through Pictures, Charts, Exhibits, and Other Visual Materials

A whole volume could be devoted usefully to the many other types of visual materials for making the world real to children. Among these are pictures, charts and posters, exhibits, bulletin boards, models and mock-ups, and time lines. Well used, these can be vital learning experiences for children.

The proverb that one picture is worth ten thousand words is often true; it depends upon the picture. Teachers would do well to choose pictures carefully for they can make indelible impressions. Pictures, for example, which are chosen to represent the bizarre and picturesque phases of a nation's life, rather than to give a representative view, should be used carefully or not at all.

Children and parents can work together to collect old copies of such magazines as the *National Geographic, Holiday,* and *Travel,* cutting out those pictures which seem appropriate, and mounting them on cardboard for the school library and for use in classes. Pictures from current newspapers and current events magazines are also useful.

Teachers may also want to use mounted pictures from local libraries or copies of the picture sets published by the Informative Classroom Pictures Company, the *Instructor* Magazine Illustrated Units of Work, or similar sets from Compton's. Many persons will find the booklet on *Sources of Free and Inexpensive Pictures,* compiled by Bruce Miller of Ontario, California, useful. Drawings made by children can be obtained from the Junior Red Cross, from the Art for World Friendship project of the Women's International League, and from the American Friends Service Committee.

Charts and posters can also be collected or made by children. Travel companies, airplane companies, the various agencies of the United Nations, and many embassies have charts and posters for distribution. Mounted on cardboard or linen, they can be useful over a period of years.

Eventually some organization should develop a series of large charts on a variety of subjects about the world, suitable for hanging in classrooms. UNESCO might well provide an exchange for enlarged pictures about its member-states, thereby helping children all over the world to understand life around the globe.

Art departments, manual training shops, and printing departments in schools can often help make such materials, with benefit to all concerned.

Through Maps and Globes

Even with young children there is value in having a suspended globe or cradle globe in the classroom in order to give them an idea of the "round ball" on which they live. Little use will be made of such a globe but it should be available for reference. Placing a piece of clay on the spot where the class lives is a useful identification, and letting children handle and feel the globe is recommended in these early years at school.

In the primary grades children should make maps of their classroom, of their routes to school, of their school, and of their neighborhood. Such maps will help them to know these familiar places better and start them on their way to understanding the symbolism of maps.

Early in their experiences in school children should be introduced to air-age maps or polar projections, since these are the maps they will increasingly use in our age. Some of these ought to show other nations than the United States in the center so that children will learn that the world does not always revolve around their nation.

Many types of maps can be used effectively with children, including jig-saw maps, clay maps, papier-maché maps, salt and flour maps, electric battery maps, and others.

Teachers will find the maps in the Sunday New York Times and U.S. News and World Report especially helpful. In addition to the well-known map companies such as Denoyer-Geppert, Hammond, Nystrom, and Weber-Costello, there are current events maps available from Scholastic, News Week, and the World News of the Week Map Company. These are particularly good for bulletin board displays. The Friendship Press has two series of maps for children which are highly recommended. One is the Picture Maps series in black and white with cutouts for children to color and mount. These are available on Africa, Alaska, China, India, Japan, Mexico, South America, Southeast Asia, and the Southwest Pacific, the United States, and the world. The other is the Friendship Map series, in color, with symbols of important people, places, and customs. These are available on Africa, China, and India.

Children can learn much by making their own maps in various media, especially if the emphasis is upon relationships more than upon location.

A few companies are beginning to make simplified world maps and globes such as Rand McNally's World Polar Projection Simplified.

Through Textbooks

Most teachers rely upon textbooks for basic materials, even if they also use supplementary sources. The importance of textbooks, therefore, cannot be overestimated, and the care with which they are selected should be stressed. Fortunately they are increasingly well written and well illustrated and the concepts they emphasize are more and more useful to teachers who wish to develop world-mindedness in children.

Space does not permit a long account of how such textbooks should be used. Perhaps teachers need only to be reminded that children should be taught to use them as references, learning how to use indexes, to read maps, to examine pictures, to compare them with other books on the same topic, and wherever possible to check facts for current accuracy either in other books or with persons who know the countries or topics which the writers are describing.

The Teacher's Guides which accompany many of these books are valuable aids to busy teachers.

Through a Variety of Reading Materials

There are a host of other reading materials for use in schools and in homes. These include novels, plays, biographies, factual accounts, folk and fairy tales, and poetry.

As Sir Richard Livingstone has pointed out in *The Future of Education*, "Literature is a railroad ticket, costing very little, that takes men to every country in the world, a pass that admits to the greatest waxwork exhibitions, where every waxwork is made of flesh and blood."

Where books are not available locally, state libraries usually have extension divisions which can be used. Teachers are reminded that they will receive far better service if they are as specific as possible in their requests.

In addition to the usual reference books commonly used by librarians, there are several special lists of books which focus on literature about the world. These include *Books Are Bridges*, compiled by the American Friends Service Committee; Eva Dratz's *Aids to World Understanding for Elementary School Children*; a special bibliography in the April 1, 1953, issue of *The Education Leader* published by the State Teachers College in Pittsburg, Kansas; and Ruth Tooze and Beatrice Krone's volume on *Literature and Music as Resources for Social Studies*.

A novel approach is through the use of children's books from other lands. These are now available from The Package Library of Foreign Children's Books, 69–41 Groton Street, Forest Hills, Long Island, New York City 75. Sets may be obtained for $10 and up, depending upon the number of books desired.

Through Dramatizations

Often children begin to develop empathy by simple dramatizations based on what they have seen, heard, or read. These may be spontaneous and with almost no properties and costumes, or they can be more elaborately staged.

The American Association for the United Nations has compiled a handy *Bibliography of Dramatic Literature* which is available free of charge, consisting largely of plays on the United Nations system, but containing some other materials. Another handy reference is the magazine *Plays*, published by Plays, Inc., 8 Arlington Street, in Boston.

Carefully guided, the sociodrama can also be helpful. Situations can be discussed and small groups of children encouraged to act them out. It is often good to discuss how well the actors were able to put themselves into the shoes of other people and after such a discussion to re-enact the scene, either with the same pupils or with a new group.

Shadow plays and puppets are other activities which children enjoy and from which they can profit.

Through Music

Starting with young children, music of the world can be played and heard throughout the school years and will lead in many instances to further interest when children have grown into adults.

Some of the music should be songs which the children can sing. Good recordings should also be used and radio and television programs listened to or seen.

Through such experiences children can learn to respect and appreciate the people of other parts of the globe and to feel that they have shared in their lives. Music can also fortify learning through the emotional impact it so often carries.

An exceptionally useful reference for teachers on music is the volume, already referred to, by Ruth Tooze and Beatrice Krone on *Literature and Music as Resources for Social Studies*. Margaret Boni's *Fireside Book of Folk Songs* is a wonderful reference and the small and inexpensive songbooks of the Cooperative Recreation Service in Delaware, Ohio, are highly recommended. More specialized books include: Gertrude Jacobs' *Chinese-American Song and Game Book* and Marion Bergman's *Russian-American Song and Dance Book*. *Songs Children Like* contains songs compiled by the Association for Childhood Education and the National Council of Churches.

Many school and town libraries are now buying and loaning records as they do books. Teachers would do well to consult their local libraries and to encourage them to purchase records which can be used in schools or in the homes of children. The special records produced by the Folkways Record and Service Corporation should be kept in mind.

Many schools will want to take part in The International School Music Project of the American Red Cross, conducted in conjunction with the Music Educators National Conference, a department of the National Education Association. This project encourages the recording of school music for shipment to schools abroad and is a commendable method of communication among the children of the world.

Through Games and Dances

Children often like to play the games they know, but they can be interested in learning new games from time to time. Teachers will find scores of games from all parts of the world described in Nina Millen's *Children's Games from Many Lands,* in Frank Henius' *Songs and Games of the Americas,* or in the Fun and Festival series of the Friendship Press. More specialized games can be found in the Jacobs and Bergman volumes cited in the foregoing section on music.

Dances for young children should be simple and easily learned. They can of course become increasingly complicated as children grow older, but the main aim should be the enjoyment of dances from other lands rather than the learning of complicated steps. In some cases children will want to do the dances without much talk about the country from which they came; in other instances the dances can be used as a springboard for discussion about their meaning and the life of the people who do them.

Through Action Projects

As was pointed out in the previous chapter, boys and girls need to be involved in some projects in which they can act rather than merely talk about their world neighbors. The range of possibilities for such projects is great. Rural children may want to raise animals for sending abroad through CROP (the Christian Rural Overseas Program) or the Heifers for Relief project. City and rural children may want to participate in the many programs of the Junior Red Cross or raise money for CARE, UNICEF, or the UNESCO Book Coupon Scheme. They may want to raise money for the Meals for Millions project or sponsor a child through the Save the Children Federation. Or they may want to make toys or mittens for the Brethren or American Friends Service Committees.

In all of these projects it is important for the parent, teacher, or other adult in charge of a program to communicate with the organization before the project is under way and to follow instructions carefully once the program is launched. Otherwise children may waste a good deal of time, money, and effort on projects which are no longer being carried on, or cause trouble for the sponsoring agency because they have not met the agency's regulations.

Older children may want to prepare panel discussions for church and civic groups, take part in drives in the city, or participate in plays and pageants.

Teachers will find a wealth of practical suggestions in a booklet entitled *Sharing is Fun: Projects Booklet for Children*, published by the Koinonia Foundation, Pikesville Box 336, Baltimore 8, Maryland. They will also find a wealth of suggestions in Harold Snyder's book *When Peoples Speak to Peoples*.

Through Celebrations and Symbols

Celebrations have an emotional overtone which is helpful to learning and they can include children of all ages, or even adults. Much use should be made of pageants, plays, assembly programs, and celebrations of various kinds in any program in international understanding.

Symbols, too, can play a part in developing attitudes toward other people, countries, and world organizations. As Harold Lasswell has pointed out, "A person is positively identified with mankind as a whole to the degree that he includes within the structure of the self a symbol of humanity toward which positive effects are directed."

Helping children to find or make such symbols and to identify with them is one job of a school. The U.N. flag may be used, a Hall of Flags of various countries may be established in a school corridor, or a citizen of the world may be selected each year by the student body as a culminating activity for a study of biography, with appropriate exercises in conjunction with the hanging of the picture of the person selected.

Through Museums, Libraries, and Other Community Resources

Parents and teachers should be aware of the many services of museums, libraries, art galleries, and other community institutions, and encourage children to make use of them. In some instances trips by classes can be made; in other cases individuals or groups can be encouraged to visit these places.

Illustrative of the work of museums are some of the activities carried on in The Newark Museum in recent months. In the spring of 1955 Africa was the theme of a special four-day festival during the spring vacation, when children took part in Adventures in Africa. They learned about navigation for their trip from the planetarium lectures, about Art in Life in Africa from an exhibition by that title, and about African animals in the science and nature workshops. Another unusual feature of that museum's work was an exchange of children's work with the Glasgow Museum and Art Galleries. Use has been made of their especially fine collection on Tibet and of various other materials on other lands and peoples.

Schools should avail themselves of such rich offerings in museums and occasionally make suggestions as to ways in which these institutions can supplement class work.

Through Hobbies

In the intermediate and upper grades boys and girls are interested in a wide range of hobbies. Stamps may be saved, coins assembled, dolls collected, or postcards hoarded. These and other pastimes can be encouraged by having children bring their collections to class or by having them exhibited at hobby fairs or in the school library.

A question from the teacher or a reference from her may help the collectors delve deeper into the background material on their hobbies, giving them new insights into the people of the world as well as new pride in their pastimes. Teachers can also encourage pupils to begin collections which will provide fun and knowledge for years to come.

Teachers should bear in mind the volumes on hobbies, such as Julienne Hallen's How to Make Foreign Dolls and Their Costumes, the many books on cooking in different parts of the world, and the publications on stamp collecting, such as the booklet issued by the Pan-American Union on this topic.

Through Art

No listing of the ways in which children can be introduced to the world would be complete without reference to art. Perhaps the most dramatic use of art has been the International Art Exhibit started by the Indian cartoon magazine Shankar's Weekly as an experimental feature in 1949. In 1954 Prime Minister Nehru and other high officials in India attended the opening of this exhibit and the magazine devoted a special issue of 160 pages to children's art around the world. In our own country the Museum of Modern Art in New York City has frequently hung a collection of children's drawings from different parts of the world. Other museums have had similar exhibitions.

The greatest value, however, is in the act of preparing drawings. Learning to observe people and objects, reading about the background needed for a drawing, and the creative act itself are all valuable activities for children. Where these experiences are tied in with aspects of the world community, art can be a dynamic force in developing world understanding. Children can learn how world-wide art really is, how people express themselves in many different ways all over the world, and how we are debtors to people everywhere for their artistic creations.

Trips to museums, the use of colored lantern slides, the reproductions of famous paintings, handling and wearing costumes, examining the pottery and handicrafts of various countries, and exchanging drawings with children in other parts of the globe are among the activities which can help.

Two of the books which reproduce the drawings of children of other nations are Norma Cohn's *Little People in a Big Country*, which includes pictures by Russian children of trains, planes, and other interesting objects; and Marion Cothren's *Pictures of France by Her Children*, a volume with thirteen drawings in color of scenes from France, including a few war scenes which need to be interpreted by teachers.

Through Current Events

Wide use should be made by teachers and parents of current news broadcasts, current events magazines, and daily newspapers in order to help children understand what is going on in the world and to increase their interest.

Teachers will want to guard against placing the broad, heavy problems of adults on the narrow shoulders of children, but at the same time children need to know what is going on around them.

Some schools would do well to follow the example of Westtown School, near Philadelphia, where a large map of the world hangs in the assembly hall and once a week one of the members of the faculty uses this as the focus for a current events background talk. Other schools will want to involve gifted children in presenting such school-wide background assemblies.

Mock broadcasts in the classroom, reading aloud as a group from current events papers, learning to read newspapers, panel discussions, and bulletin boards are some of the activities which should be carried on. It is doubtful if debates are helpful even though much enjoyed by children, since they tend to make issues too clear-cut when in reality there are always a variety of positions on any one world event.

Teachers need to bear in mind some of the dangers of current events instruction as it relates to the world scene. One danger is the quick perusal of many issues in the news, without stopping occasionally for "depth" studies of one specific world problem. Another is the tendency to form judgments with insufficient evidence. A third is the pupils' lack of necessary background on many events, which teachers must often supply.

Among the many ways of handling world current events are the references which teachers bring out in regular lessons, listening to broadcasts, devoting a few minutes each day to current news, keeping bulletin boards with sections on various parts of the world or one section for world news, keeping scrapbooks on special topics, devoting an occasional period of fifteen to thirty minutes to background on a current event theme, a unit on propaganda, the use of current events papers and newspapers, special assemblies, and the development of specialists on topics or areas of the world by having certain children follow one theme or one area for a period of several weeks.

In teaching controversial issues teachers should show that there are generally many points of view rather than merely two. They will often find that a continuum or long line on the board with different points ranging from right to left is a helpful device for older boys and girls. Teachers will also want to help pupils to differentiate between facts and opinions. Listing "facts" and "opinions" on the board on any given issue is often a helpful device. Teachers should also help pupils to see how other nations feel on a given issue, no matter whether we agree with them or not. Having children play the roles of people in other parts of the world and talk as they might talk is often an excellent way of approaching this goal.

Teachers should develop some "ground rules" for the discussion of controversial issues. These might well include the citing of sources for facts, the prohibition of name calling or propaganda devices, and the use of such phrases as "I think" or "It seems to me" rather than the dogmatic statement of opinions.

In handling controversial issues teachers need to be aware of their own prejudices and try to keep them in the background. They should build the kind of rapport with their class and with the community that enables them to handle controversial topics; they should develop as wide a background on world events as possible; and they should learn how to conduct group discussions, channeling them often rather than letting them spread all over a given field. Many teachers will find the free booklets of the Junior Town Meeting League and the leaflets distributed to teachers by current events magazine publishers useful on this latter point.

Conclusion

Many methods have now been suggested by which children may be helped to discover their world. Some of them will be amplified in other parts of this volume. No one of these methods carries with it a guarantee of right attitudes or relationships. Each of them has to be used wisely under competent guidance to attain the best results. A variety of them is needed for a well-rounded approach in order that the interests and needs of all the children are met. Taken together they can provide rich, meaningful experiences for teachers and pupils in learning about the world in which they live today and will live tomorrow.

Columbus, more than the atomic scientists, made this one geographic world. Woodrow Wilson saw that we all live in one world in a political sense, and Wendell Willkie popularized the concept for the man in the street. However, few of our leaders have begun to understand that we live in one world in an ecological—an environmental—sense.

—WILLIAM VOGT, *Road to Survival*

Geography has a role to play in peace which is as fundamentally important as the role it plays in wartime.

—PRESTON JAMES, in Clyde Kohn's *Geographic Approaches to Social Education*

The tide of the earth's population is rising, the reservoir of the earth's living resources is falling. Technologists may outdo themselves in the creation of artificial substitutes for natural subsistence, and new areas, such as those in tropical and subtropical regions, may be adapted to human use, but even such recourses or developments cannot be expected to offset the present terrific attack upon the natural life-giving elements of the earth. There is only one solution: Man must recognize the necessity of co-operating with nature. He must temper his demands and use and conserve the natural living resources of this earth in a manner that alone can provide for the continuation of his civilization.

—FAIRFIELD OSBORN, *Our Plundered Planet*

You must have a social philosophy of one shade or another or you must not teach geography. . . . If geography opens up controversial social-political questions, it in no way determines the stand you will take. But if you have a sense of justice and tolerance, it seems almost unavoidable that you should become more socially minded and that you should reconsider such matters as class domination or national domination. The study of geography should breed tolerance. One need not necessarily have love for Ukrainians, Portuguese or Annamese. But if you understand how people came to be, if you understand their history, environment and cultural contacts, you come inevitably to know that to a large measure people are as they are because they are conditioned to be so. Much of this conditioning comes from economic circumstances and a large measure of economic circumstance is the result of the regional character; that is, geography.

—RODERICK PEATTIE, *The Teaching of Geography: A Dynamic Approach*

Chapter 4

The Earth as the Home of Man

The story of the earth can be a thrilling one to children of all ages. There are so many chapters in it that are filled with mystery and adventure that almost every boy and girl should find it interesting.

There is the story of the formation of this planet and the history of the seemingly endless period in which the earth was the home of animals whose fossil skeletons we store in museums today. There is the mystery of the movement of the earth as it revolves around the sun and moves on its own axis to give us day and night. There are the colorful and tragic stories of the men who dared to declare the earth round, defying the so-called wise people of their day, and of those who ventured into the great unknown and discovered uncharted continents, oceans, mountains, and even groups of people with civilizations at least as advanced as theirs.

And still the quest goes on for more data about the world, with expeditions to the Arctic and Antarctic, with explorations through giant telescopes such as the 200-inch lens at the Mount Wilson Observatory in California, with diving into the depths of the oceans

45

to learn about nature there, and with scientific experimentation and speculation about flights to Mars or the moon.

Most important is the history of the earth as the home of man. This is a continuous account of man on the move, exploring new parts of the earth and colonizing them. It is likewise the story of how man has tamed the elements, domesticated animals, learned to plant on the surface of the globe, and to mine within it.

The earth has fed man and bled him. He has conquered it to some extent, learning how to ride across its waters, to tunnel through its mountains, to dig canals, to terrace the earth, and to bridge its streams and rivers.

Yet man has wasted the earth, too. Millions of acres of desert and denuded hillsides are the monuments to his pillage and destruction. Today he is paying a huge price for the folly of his ancestors and his own waste. Meanwhile he is trying to bring back to life vast wastelands, seeking new sources of food from the air, from the sea, and from the laboratory, and trying to double or triple the present production of food by new and better ways of growing crops.

This earth is man's workshop and his laboratory. And it is his playground, too. He rushes to the mountains or the seashore to escape the heat and the humidity. He dons skis to glide over its surfaces. He swims in its waters and plays on its land. There is pleasure on this giant ball as well as work.

In telescopic form, this is the world which we are permitted to help children to discover. Parents and teachers are their guides, but the excitement of discovery must be theirs. There is work involved in equipping these young explorers, but there is pleasure, too, for those who gladly teach.

Preschool and Primary Grades

A group of young children has been down to the seashore for the day. They have waded in the ocean, splashed water over each other, scooped sand with tiny shovels into bright pails, collected all shapes and sizes of shells and curious debris from the sea, built little canals to let the water trickle into its channels, and made giant castles with their hands—all too soon to be destroyed.

Another group has taken part of a beautiful autumn day to walk through the woods, to scuff through the fallen leaves, to pick up some of the brightest castaways from the trees, or to hide tiny bits of stone and wood in their pockets or purses. Perhaps they have stopped by a stream to hunt the fossils which the water has loosened from the limestone rock and have asked all kinds of questions about these little rock animals.

Still another group has taken a trip through a botanical garden or park and has enjoyed feeding the squirrels or looking at the flowers.

Or another group of children has visited the planetarium and marveled at the story of earth and sky.

In such ways children need to discover the earth—through water, sand, leaves, fossils, flowers, and stars. These are happy experiences for them, highly emotional in nature, shared with their peers, their friends, and their families.

It will be years before they understand the solar system, but they can learn early in life that they live on a large ball called the earth, and that it spins in the air like a top. They can learn that night and day have something to do with the spinning of the earth. They can see the earth and feel it and turn it in a cradle globe or a reproduction in the form of a balloon.

They can learn from the fossils or the rocks they bring to school that this earth is old and that the sand in their sandbox was once like the rocks. By rubbing stones together they can actually see how the sand was formed.

By direct experiences they can learn about the various bodies of water called oceans, rivers, lakes, or streams, depending upon where they live. They may even learn that the blue parts of the globe represent water and the green and brown parts usually refer to rich earth and rocky land.

By planting seeds in rich, black earth and in sandy, rocky soil they can discover that there are different kinds of soil and that most plants grow best in rich earth with plenty of sunshine and water. Even in crowded city schools, boys and girls can learn something about the sun, soil, and water from the seeds planted in milk cartons and carefully tended over a period of weeks.

Young children need to experience the earth by playing in sand, soil, and even mud. They need to feel it and enjoy it. Eventually they need to know that it is valuable as well as enjoyable and that people plant trees to save it from going down the streams and rivers to the sea.

Boys and girls can also learn something about the earth as a giant storehouse. A trip to a coal mine or a silver, lead, or zinc mine is a possibility for some. Where such trips are impossible, films, filmstrips, and pictures can provide vicarious experiences.

Boys and girls can bring to school samples of things which grow under the ground or above the earth's surface. Gradually the concept of the earth as a place full of valuable things can take on meaning. It will begin to mean the black rocks called coal which children obtain from the custodian or from home, the carrots and radishes they have dug from their own garden, or the tomatoes which Joan and Jerry shared with them at lunchtime.

The resources for carrying out such a program are ample. The great out-of-doors should be the science laboratory for children. In large cities the parks and zoos, the botanical gardens, plus occasional small plots of ground or window boxes must suffice. The planetarium can be visited by older primary grade children.

Young children should be introduced to the idea of the balance in nature by their own aquarium and terrarium as well as by stories about how the earth replenishes itself and how air, water, fish, animals, and other parts of the earth aid each other.

They should have a globe somewhere in the room and have some elementary instruction about maps, learning a few of the simple symbols which they will use all their lives. In this connection teachers will want to have a suspended globe or cradle globe and use the Atlasphere balloon globe produced by the Blaine Company in New York City.

Some day an enterprising school will provide a physical map of the world in concrete on its playground, so that primary school children can become acquainted with some of its major features through play on it, before they actually study it. This has been done in a school in the hills of Granada, Spain, as pictured a few years ago in an issue of *Life* magazine.

Young children should have pets at home or at school, cats or dogs or tropical fish. Where it is impossible to keep them at school over long periods, they can be brought in for a day. Where children cannot have pets at home permanently, they can have them for short periods of time. A promising practice is the lending library of pets from zoos, with two weeks as the best length of time for children to "borrow" them. In extreme cases children can at least observe and handle pets at zoos or in the few children's museums which keep live animals, such as the Brooklyn Children's Museum, which has pioneered in this work.

Gardens can give children more meaningful experiences about the sun, soil, and water than a host of audio-visual experiences. Where home and school gardens are out of the question, window boxes or small dishes of shallow water for sweet potatoes, lima beans, carrot tops, or avocado seeds can be used. Children can also observe cloud formations, examine water in its different forms, observe the sun and stars, and learn about the earth in other ways.

Trips should be made to the zoo, the circus, the park in a city, and to a wide variety of places in smaller towns and the country.

Of course there should be paints and brushes and clay for children to reproduce what they have seen. Whether their reproductions are scientifically accurate does not matter; they should paint what *they* have seen and give teachers and parents clues as to what to help them look for another time.

Through these and other experiences young children can learn about the world in which they live, how it affects them and other people, and how they can adjust to it and use it. Also, they can learn to regard it with awe and wonder, qualities too often neglected in our current curricula.

Among the general books which introduce children to the earth are Jeanne Bendick's *All Around You: A First Look at the World*, Josephine Pease's *This Is the World*, and Elsa Werner's *The Golden Geography: A Child's Introduction to the World*. In a clever story entitled *World Round*, Inez Hogan has introduced children to the idea of continents through a whale's trip around the world, meeting the animals of every part of the globe. Miriam Schlein has produced two small volumes for primary grade children on the earth, entitled *Go with the Sun* and *The Sun Looks Down*. The story of sunset time around the world is told by Herman and Nina Schneider in

Follow the Sunset and the story of the wind described by Alvin Tresselt in *Follow the Wind.*

One of the best books to introduce young children to the solar system is the Schneiders' simple account in *You Among the Stars.*

For children interested in plants Irma Webber has a series which includes *Anywhere in the World* (on plant adaptation), *Bits That Grow Big* (on plant reproduction), *Travelers All* (on seeds), and *Up Above and Down Below* (on how plants grow).

Among the Little Wonder Books for the primary grades on the earth are *Where Animals Live* and *Life in the Sea.*

On water one of the most delightful accounts is Alvin Tresselt's *Rain Drop Splash,* enhanced by large and colorful illustrations.

A few of the films and filmstrips listed in the section on the middle grades are suitable for boys and girls in the primary years. One film in particular is intended for this age, namely *We Visit the Seashore.*

Teachers will find useful suggestions on all the topics in this and later sections of this chapter in such volumes as Glenn Blough and Albert Huggett's *Elementary School Science and How to Teach It* and Gerald Craig's *Science for the Elementary School Teacher.*

The Middle Grades

Many of the topics just mentioned can be pursued farther and further in the middle grades. The earth can be explored as a part of the solar system, with a clearer idea of day and night and the seasons. Children can learn that most of the world is water and that men live only on a very small part of the land surface. Longitude and latitude need not be stressed, but they can be introduced as ways of helping people to locate places on the earth and as a part of the necessary knowledge of fliers.

Children in these grades can grasp the concepts of how the earth affects man and how man has changed and used the earth's surface. The stories of harbors, bridges, subways and tunnels, and airports can be told and read. Boys and girls can learn a little, too, about terracing and irrigation, and make reproductions of these methods of man to utilize the soil.

Maps are important at this stage of development. The concept of continents and such land and water forms as islands, peninsulas, bays, seas, lakes, and rivers can be studied. Children find it fascinating to explore some of the major rivers of the world, such as the Nile, the Tigris-Euphrates, the Yellow, the Congo, the Indus, the Volga, the Amazon, the Danube, and some of the rivers of the United States, learning how these have been the highways of man for centuries. The major mountains of the world can be studied in an elementary way and maps of various kinds made of them, helping children to discover how they have been barriers between peoples, whether they are studying the Himalayas or the Andes, to take two outstanding examples. Stories of the scaling of the highest peaks often prove fascinating to boys and girls of this age.

Finally, they can make a simple study of conservation and its importance in preserving the resources we have and in replenishing our supplies where that is possible.

Considerable attention should be given to the ways in which man has used the earth as well as how he has been affected by it.

The experiences by which these concepts are introduced can be many and varied. In order to understand the earth as a part of the solar system, children should construct their own miniature planetariums. This can be an experience in applied mathematics as well as science. They may want to study the shadows in the school yard or playground. They may be able to visit a nearby observatory or planetarium and to purchase their own small telescopes. The folk tales of the stars can be used effectively at this point as part of the language arts program of a school.

The construction of a large globe, made with wire and paper or canvas, can become a major center of interest. An elementary school in Shaker Heights, Cleveland, started such a project a few years ago, with each successive class adding some major geographical features to their globe. Carried on as a class or school project, this can be a memorable learning experience.

Where large reproductions of the world are available in the community, trips should be made to them, such as the globe in the Christian Science Monitor building in Boston or the Babson Institute in Wellesley, the Daily News building in New York City, or the airport in St. Louis.

The movements of man to the most suitable parts of the earth can be studied as a part of a unit on The Earth or as an integral part of any science and social studies program. Children will soon discover that the temperate zones have become the major abode of man. Some of them will be interested in the ways in which scientists are exploring the possibilities of making other parts of the globe habitable.

Almost any part of the earth can be used to illustrate how the earth has affected man and how he has used and changed it. Norway, for example, is a mountainous country where people have learned to live on the fringes of the fjords and to take their livestock into the mountains in the summer. But these Norwegians have also learned how to make electric power from their mountain streams and to put out to sea, from the days of the Vikings to the present.

In The Netherlands the people have made their homes of brick, using the clay and sandy soil which was available around them. They have also discovered that their sandy soil is good for vegetables, flowers, fruit trees, and grazing and they have built their economy around these products. Since there is wind most of the time, they have used it until fairly recently for making power through windmills. And since the surface of the country is flat and money not too plentiful, they have resorted to bicycles for transportation. Similarly, they have learned to drain the swamps and to build dikes to increase their land. One of the most thrilling engineering projects in recent times is the draining of the Zuider Zee and the establishment of model towns on the new land.

As pupils study different nations or find examples of these major concepts from various parts of the globe, they can learn about terracing in China or the Philippines and the turning of deserts into fertile land in Israel, India, and Pakistan. They can study canal building in Egypt and Panama, learn about the tunnels in Switzerland and Italy, or find out about bridges in many parts of the world.

Maps of many kinds can help children to learn about the continents, the major mountains, the various bodies of water, and the fertility of soil in different parts of the world. At this stage in their development boys and girls can also begin to learn where the major resources of the earth are located and how man has used them for many purposes.

Some children may find an elementary study of geology interesting at this point. A vivid description of such a study by a third grade in the Bronxville, New York, schools is outlined in considerable detail in Alvina Burrows' book on *Teaching Children in the Middle Grades*.

The importance of firsthand, concrete experiences and of experiments cannot be emphasized too much. Books, audio-visual resources, and trips to farms, research centers, weather stations, and similar places can also be rich experiences.

Fortunately there is considerable material for the middle-grade reader on the earth as the home of man and other living things.

Sophia Fahs' *Beginnings of Earth and Sky* can be read to primary grade children and be read by middle-grade boys and girls. Four recent volumes on the earth and the solar system are John Lewellen's *The True Book of Moon, Sun and Stars*, Marie Neurath's *I'll Show You How It Happens*, Anne Terry White's *All About the Stars*, and Herbert Zim's *What's Inside the Earth*. The Neurath volume has the colored pictographs for which the author is famous and the Zim account has sections for children to read and other parts for parents or teachers to read to them. In this same category is Zim's graphic account of *The Sun*.

For a general introduction to the earth some teachers will want to use Mabel Pyne's *A Little History of the Wide World*.

The First Book of Water by the Norlings is an excellent introduction to this broad subject and Ferdinand Lane's *All About the Sea* is a more specific volume on one aspect of the larger topic. Supplementing them is Eleanor Clymer's account in *Make Way for Water* of a reservoir which is built on the farm of Peter Venner's father, showing some of the uses of water for cities and how it is obtained. The story of the Dutch reclamation projects is described vividly in Edna Potter's *Land from the Sea*. In *The Big Wave* Pearl Buck has written a story of Kino, a Japanese boy, and his friend Jiya whose parents are killed in a typhoon. Vera Edelstadt has a beautiful prose poem on water in her *Oceans in the Sky*.

In three books on *Let's Go to the Brook*, *Let's Go to the Desert*, and *Let's Go to the Seashore* Harriet Huntington has written simply and clearly of water and deserts.

An unusual series of books which help children to get the "feel" of natural wonders are those of Holling C. Holling on *Minn of the Mississippi, Paddle to the Sea, Sea Bird Flying,* and *Tree in the Trail.* Although devoted to nature in the United States, they are included here because of their popularity with children.

Of the many volumes on the earth and rocks, Cormack's well-illustrated volume on *The First Book of Stones,* Maud and Misha Petersham's *Story Book of Earth's Treasures,* and Anne Terry White's *All About Our Changing Rocks* are singled out for special mention.

A popular account of weather is contained in Ivan Tannehill's *All About the Weather.* Another in the same series is Frederick Pough's *All About Volcanoes and Earthquakes.*

On dinosaurs there are two volumes worthy of mention, one by Roy Chapman Andrews, entitled *All About Dinosaurs,* and another by Herbert Zim with the brief title *Dinosaurs.*

In *Rocket Away,* Frances Frost takes children on an imaginary trip to the moon with David and Jane via a Hayden Planetarium show.

Mention should also be made of the many excellent science volumes now available for all grades in the elementary and junior high schools.

Films and filmstrips for this age group and for upper grade pupils exist in profusion; several are listed in Appendix B.

The Upper Grades

By the time boys and girls reach the upper grades they should be able to understand better many of the concepts already mentioned in this chapter and add a few more complicated ones.

The ways in which land and climate have affected human beings can be illustrated in a variety of parts of the world, with special reference to the river valleys of the Nile, Tigris-Euphrates, Indus, and Hwang-Ho, where it is believed that early civilizations began.

Mountains as the great barriers to contacts between people can receive fuller attention, especially as pupils study the history of South America, China, India, and Italy.

The effect of geography upon political life can also be introduced at this stage. The ways in which the geography of Switzerland has affected its policy of neutrality, the ways in which the location of the United States has influenced its political isolation until recent times, and the long effort of Russia to secure warm water ports are three striking examples of a concept which can be illustrated with many examples.

At this stage children can begin to learn how the struggle for raw materials around the world has led to imperialism and colonialism. Examples can be drawn easily from current events, whether it is Iran, Saudi Arabia, Indonesia, or Thailand which is in the news at the moment.

Boys and girls need to learn how dense the population of some parts of the world is and how that affects world affairs, from the two and a half million persons on the small island of Puerto Rico to the ninety million on the relatively poor island of Japan.

The story of how people today in many parts of the globe are building dams and irrigation projects should be a thrilling one, giving pupils a sense that the world is moving in the right direction to give people everywhere more to eat and higher standards of living.

Closely linked with this are the efforts to find new sources of food: by increasing the rice supply through better farming methods as devised by the Japanese, by supplying fertilizers to the farmers as is being done on a large scale in India, by salvaging the deserts as is being done in Israel and Pakistan, or by bringing submarginal lands into use. This can be tied in closely with developments in the United States, such as the planting of the tree belt a few years ago in the Middle West, the current use of contour plowing, and the development of hybrid corn.

The work of the Food and Agricultural Organization of the United Nations and the research projects of UNESCO in the use of arid lands will interest some pupils.

Because of the tremendous importance of atomic energy, a simple study of it can be made, with particular emphasis upon its peacetime uses.

Rose Wyler and Gerald Ames have produced three volumes on the earth which fit well into the proposals of this chapter. They are *Planet Earth, Restless Earth,* and *Life on the Earth.* With these books should be mentioned Maxwell Reed's long-popular account of *Earth for Sam.* A short and readable booklet in the Little Wonder Series is *The Earth,* written for the sixth-grade level.

Prehistoric times are vividly portrayed in another Little Wonder book on *Early Life on the Earth.*

The weather and water are the themes of Harold Coy's *Real Book About Rivers* and Ivan Tannehill's *All About the Weather.*

On the solar system recommended volumes include the Fentons' *Worlds in the Sky,* McNeil's *Between Earth and Sky,* Maxwell Reed's *Stars for Sam,* and Williams' *A Dipperful of Stars.*

Three familiar writers for this age group have produced books on minerals, any of which can be used with profit and pleasure. These are *Riches From the Earth* by the Fentons, *Rocks, Rivers, and the Changing Earth* by the Schneiders, and *Minerals: Their Identification, Uses and How to Collect Them* by Herbert Zim and Elizabeth Cooper. The brief accounts of commodities, produced by the Pan-American Union, are also valuable.

The history of water and its uses, together with experiments, is told by Sarah Riedman in *Water for People,* and two superior accounts exist on the sea in Reed and Bronson's *Sea for Sam* and Epstein and Williams' *The Real Book about the Sea.*

The best brief account of the effect of the earth on politics is contained in an Oxford Book Company booklet on *Geography and Human Affairs* by William S. Roeder, which some junior high school pupils can read with profit.

Typical of the several accounts of atomic energy are Margaret Hyde's *Atoms Today and Tomorrow* and John Lewellen's *You and Atomic Energy and Its Wonderful Uses.*

Among the pamphlet materials are Bertha Parker's beautifully illustrated and accurate booklets in the Row, Peterson Basic Science series on *The Earth's Changing Surface, The Earth a Great Storehouse,* and *Beyond the Solar System.*

Maps of various kinds need to be made and used, whether they are the battery type which junior high school boys so often like to make; soil maps, harbor maps, maps showing the fertility of parts of the earth, physiographic maps, or world resource maps.

Some of the publications of the U.S. Soil Conservation Department and of the Food and Agricultural Organization of the U.N. can be used by gifted pupils. Teachers will find particularly helpful the booklet *Food for All: A Sixth Grade Experience* or the *Food and People* series issued by UNESCO.

The topic of The Earth as the Home of Man is a large one, but it should be fascinating for all grade levels. A comprehensive and cumulative curriculum, based upon the needs and interests of children and society, can develop the major concepts mentioned in this chapter effectively, using the wide variety of resources and experiences now at hand for learning. In many ways children can learn about the earth as the stage on which everything we shall write about in the remaining chapters of this book takes place.

There are two billion of us, living and working and having fun. Some we will never know, some we know very well. We are all people, different from each other in many interesting and curious ways. Yet we are all alike because each of us is so important.

—EVA KNOX EVANS, *People Are Important*

This, perhaps, is the deepest of all our human needs; to be emphatic in imagination. When we can imaginatively move inside the lives of others, we add a powerful new dimension to our being.

—HARRY OVERSTREET, *The Great Enterprise:*
Relating Ourselves to the World

It seems to me very important that we should be able to feel, as well as to say, that we are all members of the tribe of man, because unless we have this feeling there can be no effective government of man.

—EDMOND TAYLOR, *Richer by Asia*

That person is most cultivated who is able to put himself in the place of the greatest number of persons. —JANE ADDAMS.

We cannot understand that other fellow, who makes up most of the world, unless we know not only how he thinks and feels, but why. And we must also know that, given his situation and history, it is inevitable that he thinks and feels as he does. This inability to connect cause and result in human affairs is the weakness in our total American education.

—PEARL BUCK, in a speech at George School

The difference between peoples has either been overemphasized and treated as innate racial characteristics, or underemphasized and treated as unessential, frequently by misinterpreting the democratic doctrine of equal rights of men. —KURT LEWIN, *Resolving Social Conflicts*

I see ranks, colors, barbarisms, civilizations.
I go among them, I mix indiscriminately.
And I salute all the inhabitants of the earth.

—WALT WHITMAN, *Leaves of Grass*

The democratic solution is that of orchestrated heterogeneity.

—CLYDE KLUCKHOHN, *Mirror for Man*

——————————————— Chapter 5

Two and a Half Billion Neighbors

Scattered over the surface of the earth are two and a half billion men, women, and children. They are the actors on the world stage described in the previous chapter. In today's world they are all neighbors, living close to one another; in tomorrow's world they will live even closer.

The most important task of parents and teachers and others who work with children is to introduce them to these world neighbors and to help boys and girls to accept their contemporaries with all their similarities and with all their differences. This is an enormous assignment, but it can be an exciting adventure for everyone concerned.

Basically this process begins soon after birth, for it is accepted now that people tend to treat others in much the same way as they have been treated. The child who has been accepted, who has been given a sense of belonging, who has been made to feel that he is loved, develops a sense of security. He does not need to mistrust others. He does not need to belittle others in order to feel more important himself. He does not have to hate. The secure child can accept others, despite differences.

In the early years children tend to be little mirrors, reflecting the attitudes and actions of their fathers and mothers and others in the family unit. Or, to change the figure of speech, they are small recording machines, picking up tonal inflections, as well as words. They do not need to be taught how the family feels; they catch its attitudes and mimic its behavior.

Any effective program of introducing children to the people of the world must therefore begin in the home. Children need to be nurtured in an atmosphere of love and affection. They need to be reared in an environment of cooperation, free from authoritarian attitudes and actions. They need to be exposed to parents who express positive feelings toward people of different races, religions, social and economic status, ideas, and nationalities. They need to feel that they are wanted, that they are contributing members of a cooperative unit, and that they are successful in tasks suitable to their age, aptitude, and ability.

There are several things a family can do even before children start to school in introducing them to the people of the world. The most effective is to have individuals from abroad as guests in the home from time to time. Sometimes families can take trips together, ranging from the nearest airport or the nearest wharf to excursions across the border into Mexico, Canada, or Cuba. Young children will not remember the details of such trips, but they will associate these events with happy family experiences.

Parents can also set the stage for later learning by the stories they read to children and the picture books which are available in their homes.

They can help children to accept others by the comments they make on the religion, color, or beliefs of their neighbors, business associates, church or club members, and other acquaintances, or by their interest in current happenings and their attitudes toward them. Many of the comments of parents and older brothers and sisters will not be understood, but the interest or disinterest of members of the family and their general attitudes will be caught.

More indirectly, the extent to which children share in some family decisions, the ways in which they are disciplined, and the degrees to which they are accepted as children will condition their acceptance of the peoples of the world later in life.

Preschool and Primary Grades

When children enter school, they bring with them their prejudices and intolerances. Their first few years should give them many opportunities to learn to live with others. If there are children in the group who are of different backgrounds, the horizons of all can be widened and they can learn to live with boys and girls of many kinds.

Certainly no teachers are so important in the formation of attitudes, the acquisition of skills, and the development of behavior in world-mindedness as those of the nursery school, kindergarten, and primary grades. As "substitute" or "supplementary" parents, these teachers can have an enormous influence.

In these early school experiences children should learn to accept boys and girls of different physical characteristics, of different home and community backgrounds, of different religions, and of different races. Teachers can err in overprotecting minority group children or children from abroad, or they can err in assuming that boys and girls should not have preferences among their peers. Teachers are much more likely to err in projecting their own prejudices upon children. Because of this danger, teachers need to probe deeply into their own dislikes and correct them so far as that is possible.

Even small children can be introduced to the idea that there are many, many people on the earth and that these people have much in common. They all eat, sleep, play, work, and have families. Most of them worship in some way. They all have ideas of what is right and wrong.

Children need to learn that each of these people is important and that all of them need each other to have happy times and to get the world's work done. They also need to learn that many of these people can be their friends even though they live far away.

Children should learn that people in various parts of the world are different. They are different in color, in the texture and color of their hair, and in their height. They eat in different ways. They sleep in different kinds of beds. They play different games, do different kinds of work, live in different kinds of houses, and go to different places of worship. Their ideas of what is right and what is wrong are often different.

Probably the largest concept, encompassing all these mentioned above, is the idea that the world is a large family or a big neighborhood with people in it who are both alike and different. This should be a recurrent theme throughout the early years at school.

The best experiences for children in learning about the world's people are contacts with their peers who have come from other parts of the world or with older boys and girls and adults from abroad who like children, understand them, and can communicate with them. Whether these contacts are in the school, in the home, or elsewhere, matters little. What is important is the quality of these experiences.

In some cases there will be such children from outside the United States, especially from Puerto Rico or Mexico. In a few cases exchange students in senior high schools can be invited into preschool and primary grades as friends rather than as VIP's on the school assembly platform. Sometimes parents or grandparents born abroad can come to school and children can learn to know them in a friendly environment.

In some localities teachers from abroad who are studying in nearby colleges and universities can be invited to visit, sharing activities with children of this age rather than appearing as "speakers." Or they can teach children simple songs and games from their countries, show them objects from abroad, and speak briefly in their own language— an experience which is fascinating to young children.

Teachers will always need to be on the alert to utilize these experiences to the full. Some of the strangeness of these so-called "foreigners" will be intriguing to children, but some of their differences will need to be explained just as teachers explain the different ways in which young children do things.

Films, filmstrips, large pictures and other audio-visual methods can be used to help children learn about the people who live in other parts of the globe. Dolls of different colors dressed according to the countries they represent can be played with and talked about, toys from other lands can be used and mentioned as coming from far away. Carts, hats, belts, and other objects can be handled and discussed in simple, everyday language. Of all the things which the writer has used with young children, the most interesting have been a small piece of lava from Guatemala which will float in the water, and a collection of hats from India and Pakistan.

Young children can carry on correspondence with their peers abroad under the careful guidance of adults. Recently, for example, the first grade of the Oak Lane School in Philadelphia received little crepe-paper dolls from their partner school in France, La Maison D'Enfants. Each doll bore the message, "Will you be my American friend?" signed by a French child. Simple replies were composed, with the help of the teacher. These were taken by the group to the post office to be mailed, together with packages from other classes. Other children in the School Affiliation Service have sent drawings and photographs of themselves, copies of their favorite Golden Books, candy and cookies, and other cherished possessions. The faster these can be sent and the quicker children can receive replies, the better for this age group.

Dressing in the clothes of people from other parts of the world is another exciting experience which a few museums are glad to arrange, having the children listen to stories about the people whose dress they are wearing. This has been a popular feature, for example, at the Brooklyn Museum.

Fortunately there are many story and picture books for the preschool and primary-grade child. Well used, they can promote excellent learning and serve as a "readiness program" in international understanding. Where stories can be acted out, children will remember them better and become identified with their story-book friends. With some children in the primary grades, teachers can begin to use the globe, pointing out where these fictional children and their families live, without introducing difficult geographical concepts.

Isabel McMeekin's *A First Book About Babies: All Around the World* can be used early in schools, showing how much babies are alike in many places on the globe. *Patchwork Kilt* by Mabel Watts is the story of a Scottish lass who loses her kilt just before the fair, but whose relatives come to her rescue and make her another one—just in time.

Ludwig Bemelmans has told the story of an individualistic little girl having a wonderful time in Paris in *Madeline*, and he has recently continued her story in *Madeline's Rescue*. *Lucky Pierre* is the account of a Breton boy who loved to fill his pockets with odds and ends as children everywhere like to do, and who finds good use for his knickknacks in a crisis at sea, as told by the Beims. Mabel O'Donnell and Margaret Bloss have done a more general booklet on *French Children* in the Row, Peterson series to which reference will be made frequently.

Among the several books on Scandinavia, or on Scandinavians in the United States, those by the D'Aulaires are especially delightful, with colorful illustrations adding much to the text. They include *Nils*, *Ola*, and *Children of the Northlights*.

On Italian children there is another volume by Mabel O'Donnell and Margaret Bloss, and Leo Politi's *Little Leo*, which tells the story of a little boy from California who goes to Italy and teaches his playmates to play Indian.

On boys and girls in Switzerland there is Mabel O'Donnell and Margaret Bloss' *Swiss Children*.

Lee Kingman's *Ilenka* and Lorraine and Jerrold Beim's *Sasha and the Samovar* can help boys and girls to get acquainted with their peers in Russia.

African children are portrayed in such volumes as Allena Best's *Penny Whistle*, a story of a little boy who learned songs from the jungle dwellers and played them on his whistle; Joseph's *Sondo: A Liberian Boy*; Norman Davis' *Picken's Great Adventure*, an account of a boy's adventures in the jungle with a companionable monkey; and Robert Davis' *Pepperfoot of Thursday Market*, the story of three Berber boys and a donkey on the plateaus of North Africa.

Nina Millen has written *A Sari for Sita* and Raymond Creekmore *Ali's Elephant*, both of which give a little of the flavor of Indian life, although they are primarily stories of Indian children.

There are even more stories about Chinese children. One of the most recent and best is Yen Liang's *Tommy and Dee-Dee*, with the activities of the Chinese boy given on one page and those of his American counterpart on the facing page, showing their similarities and differences. Others include Eleanor Lattimore's *Peachblossom*,

Evelyn Young's *The Tale of Tai* and *Wu and Lu and Li*, Raymond Creekmore's *Little Fu*, and William Carmichael's *Lee Fong and His Toy Junk*.

Creekmore has done a story of Japan in *Fujio*, a tale of a boy who lives at the foot of Fujiyama, his everyday life, and his trip up the mountain. Halladay's *Toshio and Tama: Children of the New Japan*, and Yashima's *The Village Tree* are other accounts of this island nation for primary-grade children.

Mexico is another country on which there are numerous stories for children. Boys and girls can easily identify with *Angelo, The Naughty One* by Helen Garrett, because he, too, dislikes taking baths. Or they can enjoy the story of Mexican children in *The Painted Pig* by E. R. C. Morrow; the adventures of Chucko and his burro in the Beims' *The Burro That Had a Name*; and of the Crists' *Chico*, who worried about the drought.

Manuelito of Costa Rica, by Zhenya Crespi, portrays warm family relationships in a locale not far from the capital city of San José. A bit of Ecuador is told in Ann Clark's *Looking-for-Something*. Pura Belpre's *Perez and Martina* and Jeanette Brown's *Rosita: A Little Girl of Puerto Rico* should help children to appreciate their near neighbors and fellow Americans from that island commonwealth.

A few children in the second grade can read with pleasure the volumes in the Row, Peterson series on *Chinese Children, English Children, French Children, Italian Children,* and *Swiss Children,* while others may have these booklets read aloud to them.

Occasionally there are stories in such children's magazines as *Child Life, Jack and Jill,* and *Story Parade*, and in the weekly current events magazines for primary grades. These should be clipped and saved for future use.

There are practically no films specifically prepared for the primary grades. Eye Gate House has produced a series of filmstrips, however, for these early grades, including stories about "Sahmed of Egypt," "Wambo and Tawa of the Hot Lands" (Africa), "Ahmed and Adah of the Desert Lands" (Egypt), "Ling-wu and Che-tsoo of China," and "Toyo and Yuki of Japan." "Chang" is the story of the daily life of a Malay boy, and "Snipp, Snapp, Snurr" and "Flicka, Dicka, Ricka" of Swedish children in filmstrips.

The Middle Grades

By the time children have reached the third grade, most of them can begin to learn where the people of the world live and how they have been affected by the land or have changed it.

In these middle grades they can also learn a little about the major groups of people around the world which are usually referred to as races, without becoming involved in any detailed study of race theories.

They can also be introduced to the idea of the emigrations of people and to the fact that there are many refugees in the world today.

Children in grades three, four, and five can also learn that people differ within countries, so that they will not carry away with them stereotypes of one type of person in a given nation.

In this period of their school experience children should begin to use and construct maps much more often. In this way they can learn the effect of geography upon settlement, gaining an understanding, for example, of the fact that most of the people of the earth live in four large parts of the globe—eastern Asia, India and Ceylon, Western Europe, and the eastern part of North America. Reference may be made to some of the smaller areas of the world which are densely populated, such as Formosa, Java, Malaya, Puerto Rico, and West Africa, without dwelling on these places.

Simple charts and graphs can be introduced to help children gain an understanding of these concentrations of people. One of the most effective of these is to think in terms of a hundred typical representatives of our world neighbors, with approximately 53 of them coming from Asia, 16 from Europe, 8 from Africa, 8 from the U.S.S.R., 7 from North America, 7 from Latin America, and one from Australia, New Zealand, and the islands of the Pacific.

A simple reproduction of the human family, such as the one Irmengarde Eberle has included in her book *Big Family of Peoples*, will also be helpful, even though it is overly simplified from a scientific point of view.

Simple science work can help children to understand that there are differences in blood types, but not between the blood of people of different races.

Boys and girls in the intermediate grades should continue to meet people from abroad, but they can begin to use local museums to see reproductions of persons whom they will not meet in face-to-face relationships. Since many museums concentrate on "primitive" peoples and on family groups from the past, it is important for teachers to supplement any museum trips with up-to-date films, filmstrips, and pictures showing contemporary people around the world.

Stories in such magazines as *The Junior Red Cross Journal*, *The Children's Digest*, and current events magazines can be helpful.

Picture files in the local library, school library, or classroom can provide important visualizations. In many instances children can collect magazines and help in the mounting of pictures for use by their own class and future classes.

There are many books for the middle-grade reader on children and their families in many parts of the world. Slow readers will still enjoy many of the titles mentioned in the previous section and better readers will revel in some of the volumes listed under the upper grades part of this chapter.

Among the volumes which merit special attention are Ruth Benedict and Gene Weltfish's *In Henry's Backyard: The Races of Mankind*, a simplified version of their adult booklet, and Eva Knox Evans' *All About Us*. Although both of these accounts are slanted toward the people of the United States, they are excellent introductions to the people of the world. Eva Knox Evans' *People Are Important* can also be used with some children in this age range, although probably more suited to upper-grade pupils.

So far as the writer has been able to determine, there is no reliable, interesting, up-to-date series of books on the children of various countries written specifically for the middle grades. There are at least two sets of books in this field, but both of them tend to distort the lives of children around the world, to develop stereotypes, and to picture them as they were years ago rather than as they are today. Even some of the volumes in the *Encyclopedia Britannica* series, so widely used, are out of date. This is especially true of the volumes on Japan, The Netherlands, and Switzerland. Nevertheless this series can be used, either individually or in the single volume *We Learn About Other Children*, which brings them together in a single book.

An intriguing story of France is Claire Bishop's *Pancakes Paris* in which ten-year-old Charles receives a box of pancake flour from the United States and goes to the Embassy to get the recipe translated directly. On Switzerland there is Peter Buckley's *Michel of Switzerland* and May Buff's *The Apple and the Arrow;* on Denmark Hedvig Collin's *Wind Island;* and on northern Norway the D'Aulaire volume on *Children of the Northlights,* already referred to. *Nino* is a true to life story of a small Italian boy in Tuscany, told by Valenti Angelo, and Claire Atwater's *Manoel* describes life in a small fishing village in Portugal and in Lisbon through the eyes of a young Portuguese lad.

Louise Steintorf has written two accounts of African boys and girls, one on the *Children of North Africa* and another on the *Children of South Africa* based on years in that continent. *Thirty-One Brothers and Sisters,* by Reba Mirsky, is the exciting story of Nomusa, the daughter of a Zulu chief, and her many brothers and sisters.

On the Middle East there are few satisfactory volumes. A recent one on Turkey is Marjorie Darling's *Journey to Ankara,* the story of young Ohran's trip to the capital. Youel Mirza's *Children of the Housetops,* on Iran, was written several years ago but still gives a good picture of boys and girls in that land. A shepherd boy who recovers some stolen camels is the theme of Ruth and Helen Hoffman's *Little Arab Ali,* laid in Iraq.

Three good volumes on India for this age group are Jean Bothwell's *Sword of a Warrior,* her *Little Flute Player,* and her *Little Boat Boy: A Story of Kashmir.* Kashmir, now in dispute between India and Pakistan, is also the scene of Heluiz Washburne's *Rhamon: A Boy of Kashmir.*

As usual, China stands out as a place about which many authors have written. The best known of these are Pearl Buck and Eleanor Lattimore. From the pen of the first comes *The Water-Buffalo Children* and *Yu Lau, Flying Boy of China,* and from the pen of the latter, *Little Pear, Little Pear and His Friends, Three Little Chinese Girls, The Questions of Lifu,* and *The Story of Lee Ling.* In addition there is Beatrice Liu's *Little Wu and the Watermelons.*

It is good to have a book on Tibet, for accounts of that land are rare. *Yinka-tu the Yak* is the story of a boy and his yak as told by Alice Lide.

The Philippines are presented by the Schwaljes' *Cezar and the Music-Maker* and by Lysle Carveth's *Jungle Boy*.

Among the several volumes on Latin America, only a few can be cited here. They include Alan Crane's *Nick and Nan in Yucatan* (on Mexico), Crespi's *Manuelito of Costa Rica*, Pearl Wimberley's *Child of Colombia*, and Von Hagen's *Chico of the Andes*, the story of an Indian boy who lives in the mountains.

An exciting and accurate adventure story of Eskimo children has been co-authored by Heluiz Washburne and Anauta, an Eskimo, and is titled *Children of the Blizzard*.

The Encyclopedia Britannica Company has many volumes on the children of other lands, some of which are dated, but most of which are still good. Some of these are grouped in Appendix B under their film series: Neighbors of Europe, North American Neighbors, South American Neighbors, Neighbors of Asia and Africa, and Island Neighbors.

Fourteen of these Encyclopedia Britannica films are also available in filmstrips from the Encyclopedia Films. Young America has two sets of filmstrips on the children of Latin America and the children of the Orient. A number of filmstrips are also available from Popular Science on the children of Sweden.

Middle-grade children are fond of dramatics and this interest can be put to good use in plays which they write themselves and act out or in plays and dramatizations of the books mentioned written for them by adults. A fine example of the former is a play entitled *The World Meeting*, based on Eva Knox Evans' book *People Are Important*, and written by the fifth-grade children of the Logan School in Philadelphia under the direction of Anne Waldow. This play was published in the 1954 issue of *Social Education* magazine.

The Upper Grades

As teachers know, concepts which they have tried to develop in the primary and intermediate grades are not grasped by all chilldren. The ideas presented in the foregoing pages need to be reiterated and reinforced in the upper grades, with new experiences and new materials.

In these later years other concepts need to be stressed, too. By this time children should be able to appreciate some of the internal and personal differences as well as the external and obvious characteristics of people around the globe. They can better realize that opinions, beliefs, values, and sensitivities are fully as important as language, color, customs, and dress—in most cases far more important.

The similarities between people should not be ignored at this stage in the development of boys and girls, but differences can be handled better here than in the primary or even the intermediate grades.

At all these levels, of course, there should be an attempt to help children to understand and respect the variety of people around the world and to appreciate why they live and think and act as they do.

If teachers stress that people in different parts of the world can be like us, they must also stress that we can be like them. Each group has characteristics that are laudable; no country or group has a monopoly on the qualities to be emulated.

This older group of boys and girls can also examine with much more thoroughness the concept of race and its ill effects on the world. The story of Nazi Germany and its distortion of the truth may be the most effective illustration of this point, although there are many other parts of the world, including the United States, where prejudice exists. Prejudice takes different forms in various parts of the world but it exists to some degree among all peoples.

At the same time boys and girls need to know that there are parts of the world in which races have mingled happily, as in Brazil and Hawaii. The tremendous strides made in this field in the United States in recent years need to be brought out, with some emphasis upon the problem and values of integration.

Either as a part of a unit on The People of the World or as a part of the study of nations or the United Nations, there should be some study of the problems of refugees and displaced persons. This should include the refugees in the Middle East, the mass migrations at the time of the partition of India and Pakistan, the exodus of millions of persons from East to West Germany, the flight of many

Koreans to the southern tip of that country and of many Vietnamese to the southern part of their land, and of millions of Chinese to Formosa, as well as smaller movements of population elsewhere. The responsibility of the United States in maintaining its place in the world as a home for oppressed peoples also needs to be a part of any such study.

As boys and girls make fairly intensive studies of different countries, there will be ample opportunities for showing the diversity *within* nations as well as between countries.

The rising tide of feeling against the white people of the world for their domination of other parts of the world is not an easy topic to handle, but it cannot be ignored in any realistic study.

The methods used in these grades will not vary greatly from those employed in other levels. There should be much more reading and individual and group research in class, in the school library, and in the local library. Encyclopedias are helpful, but it should be remembered that they are only one research aid.

The science and biography interests of this age group can be effectively used. Mock radio and television panels and programs can be stimulating. At this point community resources can be explored better than with younger children.

The gang feeling of these years can be channeled into effective committee work and into dramatics. In the junior high school years there is usually a great deal of interest in letter writing, especially among girls. Some of this interest can be capitalized upon in encouraging international correspondence or pen pals. A list of places from which names can be obtained will be found in Appendix C.

There is an encouraging development in the appearance of books on the people of the world for this age group. May Edel, an anthropologist, has presented the story of Franz Boas and of several groups of people in various parts of the world in a superior volume called *The Story of People: Anthropology for Young People*. Eva Knox Evans has turned her gifted pen into the world field in *People Are Important*, an outstanding volume written with a light and humorous touch. Irmengarde Eberle's *Big Family of Peoples*, with separate chapters on such groups as the French, the Germans and Scandinavians, the English, and others, is another valuable volume.

To these should be added Minocheher Masani's *The Growing Human Family*, a simple historical survey written by an Indian.

For those who cannot see the exhibit in person, *The Family of Man* book based on that exhibit will be of great interest. Since that outstanding photographic exhibit is on tour throughout the United States, it is hoped that many upper-grade classes will be able to see it.

The diary of an eleven-year-old Norwegian girl who attended the Children's International Summer Village in Cincinnati in 1951 has recently been published under the title *Ingvild's Diary*. Although the format is not too attractive, the contents are excellent, describing her feelings as she met and lived with children from many countries for a few weeks.

On the general topic of race, many upper-grade pupils can utilize Ethel Alpenfels' *Sense and Nonsense About Race* or the more difficult booklet by Ruth Benedict and Gene Weltfish on *The Races of Mankind*. A UNESCO publication *What Is Race?* has several excellent simple charts in two colors which should be used; or the pictures in *Life* magazine on "How the Races of Man Developed," taken from this booklet, can be substituted.

On the boys and girls of various parts of the world there are a number of books suitable for this age group. On Canada, Stephen Meader has told the story of two Canadian boys in Northern Ontario and their work on the trap lines of their father, in a book called *Trap Lines North*.

On France there is Claire Bishop's *Twenty and Ten*, a story of how twenty French children saved ten Jewish children hunted by the Nazis. An old favorite on Switzerland is Johanna Spyri's *Heidi* and a new volume is Peter Buckley's *Michel of Switzerland*.

Two quite recent volumes by Buckley tell the story of *Luis of Spain* and *Cesare of Italy* and their everyday lives. Both are well illustrated with black and white photographs by the author.

For some reason there are more books on Sweden than on most nations. Three of the best are Signe Lindegren's *Ingrid's Holiday*, an account of the summer work of a sixteen-year-old girl in a Swedish textile factory; Laura Fitinghoff's *Children of the Moor*, in which the battles of children against the hardships of nature are vividly portrayed; and Annette Turngren's *Flaxen Braids*, the story of a girl whose family was involved in financial reverses.

Attilio Gatti's *Kamanda, An African Boy*, is the story of an eleven-year-old from the Belgian Congo who joined one of the famous Gatti expeditions. *Pepperfoot of Thursday Market* is the story of three Berber boys and their donkey, described by Robert Davis.

On Asia there are Elizabeth Lewis' *Ho-Ming: Girl of New China* and her volume on *Young Fu of the Upper Yangtze*, both long-time favorites of boys and girls. Alongside these should be placed Margueritte Bro's *Su-Mei's Golden Year*, which shows the clash of ancient and modern ways and how one girl helped to persuade a village to adopt new agricultural methods. On Korea there is Lucy Crocket's *Pong Choolie, You Rascal* and on Japan her story of *Teru, A Tale of Yokohama*. She also has an account of the Philippines in *That Mario*. One of the few books about Thailand is Phyllis Sower's *Elephant Boy of the Teak Forest*, which tells of life on a canal in a teak forest and of the visit of the king's brother to the United Nations.

On Latin America Delia Goetz has written a number of books, the most comprehensive of which is *Other Young Americans*, in which the daily lives of boys and girls is portrayed. She also has a story of *Pandita: A Little Girl of Guatemala*.

Girls will particularly enjoy Esther Hall's *The Gaucho's Daughter*, a story laid in Argentina with many pictures of life in modern Buenos Aires. Boys will like Clark's *Secret of the Andes*, the tale of Cusi, an Indian boy, and his friend the Incan llama herder. *Two Children of Brazil* by Rose Brown is another volume which has been enjoyed by hundreds of junior high school pupils.

Santiago by Ann Nolan Clark is a moving story of a boy growing up as the adopted son of a Spanish woman in Guatemala and then returning to his own Indian tribe. It is magnificently illustrated with brilliant colors.

In addition to the films already mentioned in this chapter, many can view with profit such films as *Brotherhood of Man*, *Boundary Lines*, and *Family of Man*. Outstanding among the many films on the people of the world is *Nomads of the Jungle*, in which a group of boys in the Malay Peninsula are shown as they travel in the dense forest regions, build a bridge over a river, cook their own food, and display great ingenuity and skill in their life in an environment very different from the one to which American boys and girls are accustomed. *Giant People* is the story of the tall people of the Watusi tribe in East Africa.

Among the many filmstrips special attention should be called to "We Are All Brothers," based on the Benedict and Weltfish book mentioned earlier in this chapter.

There are many concepts to develop about the people of the world and a wealth of materials with which to develop these key ideas. The job is more one of selection and emphasis than of finding important and interesting things to do.

That ignorance of each other's ways and lives has been a common cause throughout the history of mankind, of that suspicion and mistrust between the peoples of the world through which their differences have all too often broken into war.

—Preamble to the Constitution of UNESCO

. . . it is the great diversity of the world that makes it an exciting place to live in and enriches human civilization.

—VERA DEAN, *On the Threshold of World Order*

Human life should remain as a home of many rooms.

—CLYDE KLUCKHOHN, *Mirror for Man*

The truth of the matter is . . . that the possible human institutions and motives are legion on every plane of cultural simplicity or complexity, and that wisdom consists in a greatly increased tolerance toward their divergencies. No man can thoroughly participate in any culture unless he had been brought up and had lived according to its forms, but he can grant to other cultures the same significance to their participants which he recognizes in his own.

—RUTH BENEDICT, *Patterns of Culture*

The occupation with living cultures has created a stronger interest in the totality of each culture. It is felt more and more that hardly any trait of culture can be understood when taken out of its general setting.

—FRANZ BOAS, in Ruth Benedict's *Patterns of Culture*

Men live in a community in virtue of the things they have in common; and communication is the way in which they come to possess things in common.　　—JOHN DEWEY, *Democracy in Education*

The struggle for an unprejudiced attitude towards the simple and yet so often misunderstood facts of human existence must start at the still inflexible mind of the child.

—ALBERT EINSTEIN, in Eva Knox Evans' *All About Us*

That program is most desirable which leads to an understanding on the part of children of the reasons why different people live as they do.

—CELIA STENDLER and WILLIAM MARTIN, *Intergroup Education in Kindergarten–Primary Grades*

Chapter 6

Ways of Living Around the World

What an amazing variety of ways of living there are around the world today. People eat everything from walrus blubber to crepe suzettes, live in everything from caves to skyscrapers, and wear everything from simple dhotis or loincloths to luxurious saris and Paris gowns. They travel by snowshoe, foot, cart, train, and airplane. They communicate in an infinite variety of ways, from drums to radio and television. Their occupations can be numbered by the hundreds, ranging from the farmers who use sticks to plow their fields to the people who watch over the robot machines in ultramodern factories.

What more fascinating field is there for children than the discovery of these variations in ways of living around the world?

No matter what part of the globe children may be visiting by the magic carpets of books, films, and other materials, they need to learn that people carry on the same general types of activities in many different ways.

But that is not enough. They need to discover why people live as they do. Among the many factors which teachers should bear in

77

mind in finding answers to this question are the climate and terrain, the location of a given group, the resources at hand, the influence of religions and value systems, the economic status, and the physical energy of people.

In studying the large underdeveloped areas of the world, it is especially important to stress the significance of isolation, the effect of a lack of education and communication, and the results of colonial status. Children need to know that the farmer who uses a stick does not do so because he is stupid, but because he has not known of other possibilities. In most cases he has had little or no education and little or no contact with other parts of his own country or other parts of the world. His isolation may have been caused by the colonial status of his country or it may have been self-imposed. Whatever the reason, the fact of isolation has been important.

At the same time boys and girls need to learn that few parts of the world are isolated any longer, and that ways of living are changing in most parts of our globe.

As they discover the various methods of living, children should learn that these ways may be different without necessarily being inferior. In some cases the methods of other people are superior to ours. In other instances they are appropriate for the people who use them, without being methods which we should copy.

Boys and girls should also be helped to understand that many different ways of living may be found within a single country, sometimes side by side in a small area.

As children look at the people of various parts of the world they should be trained to ask questions about the attitudes these people have toward their families, toward other people, toward work, property, money, and other aspects of day-to-day living. And they should be educated to inquire about the institutions which have been developed as an expression of these attitudes.

There are many ways in which these basic ideas can be developed. Particularly in the early years there should be a great deal of teaching from objects. Chinese chopsticks, Austrian dolls, Japanese fans, and German toys should lead children to ask questions about the people who use or make these objects and why they use or make them.

Occasionally such objects can merely be enjoyed without any discussion or "lesson" attached.

As in all the themes treated here, the best introductions to ways of living around the world are made through people and through meaningful activities. The visitor from abroad who brings some objects for children to examine can teach far more than the one who merely tells with words about life in his home, village, or country. Moreover, children can learn a great deal more from making things than merely reading about them. The construction of a model of a round, beehive house such as is found in Africa can help children to understand this type of building far better than words or even pictures can. The same is true of hundreds of objects from all parts of the globe.

Along with exposure to persons from abroad and creative activities there should be a variety of other methods to supplement and augment these basic experiences. Pictures need to be used, books need to be read, ways of living need to be acted out, discussions should certainly take place, and films and filmstrips shown frequently.

As children grow older, they will rely more and more on reading. But they will need auditory and visual methods, too. Acting out scenes from the daily lives of people, constructing dioramas, painting murals, and preparing exhibits should help them to understand the how and why of ways of living around the world.

Many of the topics suggested by this major theme should be incorporated into existing units on such topics as transportation, communication, food, homes, and work. In the intermediate grades teachers may want to develop special units on such themes as Transportation Around the World, Food Around the World, and Homes Around the World, delving into the different ways of doing things in representative parts of the globe. In the upper grades the theme of ways of living around the world may be treated as a part of the study of countries.

We shall here approach this broad theme by looking at some of the topics which it includes, outlining suggestions as to aims, experiences, and resources on each of the topics according to grade levels.

Food

What is more important or fascinating to children than food? Here is a natural interest through which much learning about the world can take place.

Early in their lives children can learn that food comes from many places, some of them close at hand and others far away. Some foods grow in the earth, some above the ground, and some from bodies of water. Young children can also learn something about the variety of eating habits, about the utensils used, and about the customs of eating in other parts of the world. In all these phases of study, the basic concepts to bear in mind are the similarities and the differences, without trying to decide which ways are "best."

As children grow older they can learn about the conditions under which various foods grow best. They can begin to understand some of the problems of transporting foods long distances. They can discover why there are different customs, whether it is the way in which the Japanese eat at low tables while sitting on the floor or on pillows, the way in which the Moslems wash their hands in a special rite just before eating, or the way in which the Dutch children thank their mothers at the end of a meal for her part in preparing and serving the food.

Eventually the interdependence of the world in food can be pointed out, and some of the problems of food and population explored. Considerable respect for other peoples can be built through studies of how the Chinese and others have learned to terrace their land, how the Indians and others have learned to irrigate their arid regions, and how the Japanese have learned new methods of rice production as a means of helping increase production for a nation with nearly 90 million persons to feed each day.

Some attention should be given in the study of food to the work of the Food and Agricultural Organization of the U.N. and to UNICEF, as well as to the work of nongovernmental organizations.

Such studies of food around the world can be handled in many ways. Young children may experience differences in foods and in eating customs through visits in the homes of their friends and relatives, and the differences observed can be discussed in class or at home. Mothers may prepare different dishes for school or parties.

Holidays or holy days may be used to help children to learn about foods and customs. Stories of children may bring out similarities and differences. Pictures are, of course, useful in this respect.

In the intermediate grades children may want to make an inventory of food from other lands which they eat or they may want to interview local grocery-store or fruit-store managers about the food they obtain from other parts of the world. They may want to ask visitors about food in their homes or read about foods and customs in a variety of books.

Still older boys and girls should make a study of some of the problems connected with food around the globe and what is being done to improve conditions. They may want to take some action to help other people, sending a CARE package abroad or contributing to some relief agency which distributes food.

Other activities may be the writing of letters to food companies for materials to be used in class, visits to foreign restaurants, the intensive study of one food product from its source to their tables, and the preparation of world food maps marked with samples or symbols of various products.

Unfortunately there is a lack of materials for the primary grades in this field. Teachers will need to build their own picture collections and make note of stories which include references to foods. The Popular Science filmstrip on "Early Man and His Food" can be used, as can some of the inexpensive booklets of the National Dairy Council on *It's Always Breakfast Time Somewhere*, *Milk Around the World*, *Hello, Alaska*, *Hello from New Zealand*, and *Hello from South America*. The Petersham books on *The Story Book of Corn*, *The Story Book of Rice*, *The Story Book of Wheat*, and *The Story Book of Food* can be helpful here and with middle-grade children.

For the middle grades there are more materials. Frank Carpenter's *How the World Is Fed* is a volume which has long been a favorite with children. Other older volumes include Dorothy Giles' *Singing Valleys: The Story of Corn*, Clara Hollos' *The Story of Your Bread* (from ancient times to the present), Ethel Howard's *How We Get Our Food*, and Webster and Polkinghouse's *What the World Eats*. A recent volume by Frank Jupo on *Nothing to Eat But Food* treats this same topic with a touch of humor both in the text and in the illustrations.

Free and inexpensive materials are available from several companies, such as the Pan-American Coffee Bureau, the Hershey Chocolate Corporation, and the United Fruit Company.

Among the materials for the upper grades are two colorfully illustrated volumes by Jannette Lucas on *First the Flower, Then the Fruit* and *Where Did Your Garden Grow?*, Irmengarde Eberle's *Basketful: The Story of Our Foods*, Sarah Riedman's *Food for People*, and Ralph Hancock's *Foods from Latin America*. The Eberle volume is particularly useful, with separate chapters on milk, meat, bread, fruit, vegetables, nuts, poultry, and similar topics. A few pupils will be able to use an article in the August 1949 *National Geographic* on "Our Vegetable Travelers." A UNESCO publication on *The Puzzle of Food and People* was prepared especially for junior high school pupils and is well illustrated with black and white photographs.

Teachers will find an article in *Social Education* for January 1945 on "Foods for the World from the Americas" helpful, as well as a special booklet entitled *Food for All: A Sixth Grade Experience*, which describes a study of the Food and Agriculture Organization of the United Nations by a sixth-grade group in Baltimore. There is also good background material in brief form in the UNESCO series on Food and People.

There are a number of cookbooks with recipes from all over the world. The most simple and least expensive of these is a booklet on *The World's Favorite Recipes*, issued by the U.S. Committee for U.N. Day.

Films are plentiful on this topic. They include such productions as *Bananas, Yes, Grain That Built a Hemisphere* (a Walt Disney account of the story of corn in the Americas), *Canadian Wheat Story, Rice Farming in Japan*, and *Tea-Rice-Coconuts* (in Ceylon, Java, and India). Several films of the Food and Agriculture Organization of the U.N. are quite suitable for use with upper grade pupils, such as *Battle for Bread, 55,000 for Breakfast, The World Is Rich*, and *World of Plenty*.

Several filmstrips deal with the theme of food around the world.

These include such titles as "Rice in Monsoon Asia," "Early Man and His Food," "Bananas Grow Upside Down," and "For America's Sweet Tooth: How We Get Sugar." Several of the filmstrips of the F.A.O. can be used in the upper grades, too.

Clothing

Clothing, too, is of interest to children and can often be used as a starting point for discussions about ways of living around the world. Perhaps the most important ideas to stress are that people wear certain clothes because of climate, economic conditions, the resources at hand, religion, politics, and tradition or custom.

The rubber boots of Korea and the wooden shoes of The Netherlands (especially in times past) are two examples of the effect of land on clothing. The effect of climate is perhaps best illustrated by the lack of need for clothing in the tropical parts of Africa. In developing this idea teachers can help to combat the popular notion that the Africans are immoral because many of them do not wear much clothing.

Illustrative of the use of the resources at hand are the reindeer skin clothing and hats of the Laplanders and the fur-lined costumes of the Eskimos, the straw and bamboo hats of South Asia and Latin America, and the sandals of thatch or fiber used in so many parts of the globe.

The income of people vitally affects their choice of clothes, too. In large parts of the world fashions do not change because people cannot afford new clothes every year, black clothes are worn because they show dirt less clearly, and people go barefoot rather than using their hard-earned money for shoes, which are a luxury.

Religion, too, affects clothing. The wearing of small caps or hats in the mosques and synagogues is an example, as is the removal of shoes by the men before entering temples and mosques. Although it is not a direct part of their religion, many of the women of Moslem countries dress with hoods or veils when they appear in public as a protection against men.

Politics also plays a role in the clothing worn in certain parts of the world. In India the Gandhi hat, made by the Indians, was a protest against the use of cloth made in England and a symbol of self-sufficiency. In Pakistan the Jinnah cap has become a symbol of Pakistan's independence and in the Gold Coast the white, peaked hats worn by the leaders of the independence movement have been painted with the red letters, "P.R.," or prison graduate, and have become a special symbol.

Tradition also plays a part in the type of clothes worn. One of the most colorful spots in the world for clothing is Guatemala where the members of each tribe can be identified by their distinctive dress. Some children will be interested in the fact that in this Central American country as in other parts of the world, the clothing of men is often as colorful as that of women.

In addition to the usual ways of handling this topic, use can be made of colorful reproductions of clothing from magazines and travel posters or brochures, mounted on bulletin boards or used in opaque projectors. Some older girls may be interested in discovering how foreign fabrics and styles have influenced clothing in the United States.

On this theme many teachers will find Elsa Beskow's *Pelle's New Suit* a wonderful story for opening this subject with primary-grade children. In the series of books by the Petershams there are *The Story Book of Clothing*, *The Story Book of Cotton*, *The Story Book of Rayon*, *The Story Book of Silk*, and *The Story Book of Wool*. Frank Jupo has prepared an excellent new volume on *Nothing to Wear But Clothes*, which combines facts with the light style of writing and humorous illustrations mentioned before on his book on food.

For older children interested in specialized accounts there are Nina Jordan's *Homemade Dolls in Foreign Dress* and Angela Bradshaw's *World Costumes*. Several of the children's encyclopedias also have good material on this topic.

Two sets of pictures on The Clothing of Other Peoples are available from the Creative Educational Society and a set of eight large pictures on Clothing in Other Lands may be obtained from the Informative Classroom Picture Publishers.

"The Story of Clothing" is a filmstrip which traces the development of clothes from many materials and is suitable for the elementary school, while a similar filmstrip on "The History of Clothing," produced by the University Museum in Philadelphia, shows the various types of clothing worn in different cultures and is suitable for the middle and upper grades. A set of slides on "Clothes Around the World" may be borrowed from the American Friends Service Committee.

Many teachers will find the resource unit on "Hats Around the World," developed in 1953 by a group of teachers at a workshop in Pittsburg, Kansas, an exceedingly interesting venture for grades four to six. This unit appeared in *The Educational Leader* for January 1, 1954.

Houses and Home Life

Children need to be helped to realize that most of the world lives in one-room houses, ordinarily built of thatch or mud, since these are the least expensive materials readily available. Children will need to be helped, too, to understand that climate is an important factor in the construction of houses, with homes in desert and tropical regions simply built, partly because the people are out-of-doors so much of the time.

The idea that most people live in villages, rather than on the land as farmers do in the United States, needs to be brought out. In areas of the world where the family is a much larger unit than in our country, all members of a total family group live close together or even under one roof, another effect of the attitude toward family upon ways of living.

History may also affect the construction of homes as in Germany, Austria, and other parts of Central Europe where houses were built in former times inside the walls of cities for protection. As the population increased, it was necessary to build up rather than out, and houses of several stories came into being. The modern skyscraper apartment house, whether in Johannesburg, Mexico City, Rio de Janeiro, Stockholm, or New York is the modern counterpart of these many-storied houses.

The idea that houses are built from the materials nearest at hand also needs to be developed, whether one is studying Switzerland with its wooden chalets, The Netherlands with its brick houses, or parts of South Asia with their bamboo homes.

And what differences there are in the interiors of homes! In most houses around the world there are dirt floors, packed until they are almost as hard as concrete. The furniture in such buildings is simple, consisting of a bed or hammock, a chest of drawers, a shelf or two for pots and pans, and a tiny stove. Often there will be some heirloom—a pretty bed covering, brass or copper utensils, or a special piece of pottery or china, or some brightly colored mats. Children should realize that all people prize their homes and want to have a few special decorations in them even if they are not rich.

Children should know that houses can be beautiful, too, whether they are the tiny cottages scattered across the countryside of Scotland, Ireland, Wales, and England, with their small flower gardens; the simple but tastefully decorated houses of the Japanese with perhaps a single painting in an alcove, a low table or chest, colorful cushions, and a beautiful lamp or lantern casting its shadow through the thin paper panels or partitions; or the gayly colored tile-roofed houses of Latin America, with their patios in the center, and their iron gates and cement walls covered with flowers or vines.

The fact that large numbers of people around the world live on boats will be new and intriguing to many children, whether they are learning about the sampan families of China or the barge families of The Netherlands.

Eventually children need to know about the filth and poverty of rural and urban slums in many parts of the globe, not excepting our own nation.

The methods of handling this topic will resemble the suggestions previously outlined. Two examples may illustrate the type of activities which can be carried on. One was the fifth-grade study of Japan in the classroom of Mr. Shoemaker in the Edgewood School in Scarsdale, N.Y., where a Japanese house was being built to scale under the direction of a boy born in Japan. When the house was completed, the boy's mother came to school to teach flower arrangements to the pupils. Since it was the week of Mother's Day, each pupil made his own flower arrangement to take home as a special gift on Sunday.

The other illustration was a study of Indonesia in the Joan of Arc Junior High School in New York City. A question as to the size of

Indonesian houses arose and the books did not answer it. An enterprising boy in the class found pictures of such homes in old *National Geographic* magazines, estimated their size from the figures of men and women in the pictures, and drew models of these homes large enough for the entire class to see. Such creative activities are possible in classrooms when the imagination of pupils is freed.

Occasionally a pupil will become interested in modern architecture in various parts of the world and should be encouraged to pursue this special study.

Few materials have been developed specifically on this topic for primary grade children. The Friendship Press has a set of pictures on "Children and Their Homes" which can be used with discretion by teachers. Ordinarily they will have to depend upon pictures which they have collected or which are available from libraries and museums.

The Board of Missions of the Presbyterian Church U.S.A. has an interesting "Cut 'n' Fold Series" for children on India, Japan, Northern Alaska, the Philippines, Puerto Rico, Southern Alaska, Syria-Lebanon, and West Africa.

Young children can learn how people live in different ways around the world through a few books, such as Elly Jannes' *Elle Kari*, the story of a little Lapland girl, with nearly full page photos which add much to the story. Somewhat similar is Lorraine and Jerrold Beim's *The Little Igloo*, the story of Tipou and the snow house he built for his dog. Home life, skiing, and school in Finland is depicted by Marguerite Henry in *Auno and Tauno: A Story of Finland*. Life on a "station" in Australia and Sydney is told by Elizabeth MacIntyre in *Susan, Who Lives in Australia*. For Japan there is Taro Yashima's *The Village Tree*, a tale of Japanese children enjoying a wonderful tree on the river bank of a village, largely a picture book but with a simple text, and Jun Iwamastsu's *Plenty to Watch*, an account of what children see in Japan en route home from school. Jean Ketchum's *Stick-in-the-Mud: A Tale of a Village, A Custom and a Little Boy* tells the story of a small boy of long ago and how the custom of building houses on stilts started.

Four filmstrips in the Janet Visits Europe series include some pictures of home life in France, Italy, The Netherlands, and Scotland. Two on "Jiro and Hanako of Japan" and single strips on "Home,

School, and Church," and "Work and Play" can help children picture home life in Japan. "Ling-wu and Che-Tsoo of China" does the same thing for that part of the world.

A valuable book for the middle or upper grades is William Burns' *A World Full of Homes*. In it houses of all kinds throughout the ages are described and illustrated with appropriate black and white sketches. Another general volume is the Petersham *Story Book of Houses*. Several of the volumes in the Children of Every Land series of the Encyclopedia Britannica contain pictures of home life, as do many other books on individual countries.

On life in Europe there is Hedwig Collin's *Wind Island*, the adventures of Kristian, Peter, and Hanne on the island of Faroe in the North Sea; the Buffs' account of *Kobi, A Boy of Switzerland*, which describes his summer herding cows in the high pasture lands; and Libushka Bartusek's *Happy Times in Czechoslovakia*, which tells about the village life of three children. Polish life is described in Eloise Lownsberry's *Marta, the Doll*, which tells about home life on a Polish farm through the eyes of a doll which was obtained at the market. In *Little Girl from the City* Voronkova gives a picture of rural Russia through the story of a little girl whose family was killed in World War II and who was adopted by a family on a collective farm.

In *Sheker's Lucky Piece* by McDonald the young hero's experiences reveal the customs, needs, and ways of living in the country and city in Turkey. Ancient and modern life in that nation is portrayed in Nezahet Ege's *Turgut Lives in Turkey*.

Through *Home at Last*, a volume which is largely composed of photographs, Gloria Hoffman gives readers a look at modern Israel. Another look at the same country is possible through Evelyn Greenberg's *The Little Tractor Who Traveled to Israel*.

Turning to Asia, Irene Bose has written an appealing story of *Totaran: The Story of a Village Boy in India Today*. On China there is Kurt Wiese's *The Chinese Ink Stick*, a gay account of life with text and illustrations by the author, and Beatrice Liu's *Little Wu and the Watermelons*, a warm and appealing story of a boy in southwest China who saves his money to buy a present for his mother, only to find that she needs money more to buy a field, so he gives her his savings for that purpose.

Special attention is called to Phyllis Sower's *Elephant Boy of the Teak Forest* because of its intrinsic worth and because materials on life in Thailand are so rare.

Middle-grade boys and girls should get a good view of life in Japan through Pearl Buck's account of prewar activities in *One Bright Day*, through Creekmore's story of *Fujio* and his family, and through Helen Mears' *The First Book of Japan* or Lily Edelman's *Japan in Story and Pictures*.

Insight into life in the Philippines can be gained through Arsenio Acacio's *Work and Play in the Philippines*, through a novel on daily life there as told by Lucy Crockett in *Lucio and His Nuong: A Tale of the Philippine Islands*, and through Esther Woods' *Pedro's Coconut Skates*, a lively tale about an eight-year-old and his escapades in the rural parts of that island.

A fine introduction to life on a ranch in Australia can be found in Stephen Fennimore's *Bush Holiday*.

On Latin America there are many volumes, of which three will be cited as representative of life in various parts of Central and South America. Crespi's *Manuelito of Costa Rica* depicts warm family relationships in that small Central American state and Ann Nolan Clark's *Magic Money* gives a further view of life in Costa Rica. *Red Jungle Boy* by Elizabeth Stern tells of the ways in which a Peruvian Indian boy adapts himself to life in Lima.

Since most of the films and filmstrips apply equally well to the middle and upper grades, discussion of these will be postponed in this chapter to the section dealing with grades six through nine.

A series of volumes published in England on *How Did They Live?* covers life in China, Egypt, India, Java, Mexico, Peru, Rhodesia, and Sumer. It is an attractively illustrated series and suitable for upper-grade pupils or better readers in the middle grades. Copies of the series may be obtained through the British Book Center in New York City.

Over a period of several months *Scholastic* magazine ran a series of articles by young people on life in their countries, some of which have been reprinted in a booklet on *How People Live*. This, too, is recommended for upper-grade pupils.

Vignettes of life in Europe may be obtained from René Bazin's *Juniper Farm* on which four young children work; from Dola De Jong's *The Level Land* and *Return to Level Land*, accounts of a Dutch family during and after World War II; in Margot Benary-Isbert's *The Ark* and *Rowan Farm*, in which a family forced to migrate to West Germany starts life anew without bitterness; and in Ludwig Bemelmans' *The High Wind*, an account of the Amrainer family in the Austrian Tyrol.

In her volume *Here Is India* Jean Kennedy has an excellent chapter on "Typical Indian Towns" and in Reginald Singh's *Gift of the Forest* one can obtain a good view of rural life in India. More intimate pictures of family life can be enjoyed through Hilda Wernher's *My Indian Family*.

A general account of Chinese families and life can be found in Lin Yutang's *My Country and My People*. The life of an upper-class family is portrayed vividly in Nora Waln's *House of Exile*. Much simpler is Malcolm Reiss' *China Boat Boy*, written for readers in grades five to seven. Other accounts of Chinese life are easy to find.

Wu Han is a young orphan adopted by a North Korean Christian family and through Nevins' book *The Adventures of Wu Han of Korea* readers see many aspects of home life in that nation.

Two books on Japan for older readers are Mildred Comfort's *Temple Town to Tokyo* and Marguerite Stewart's *Boys and Girls of the Orient*. Of special value is the chapter "In a Japanese Farmhouse" in the latter volume.

Accounts of city life in Latin America are rare, so Katherine Pollock has performed a fine service in writing *The Gaucho's Daughter*, with its description of life in modern Buenos Aires. Quite different is R. C. Adams' *Sky High in Bolivia*, which tells of life in the highlands of South America.

Almost all of the books mentioned in Chapter IX on "Countries and Cultures" have some pages on life in those nations. Teachers interested in further references might well turn to the bibliography on that chapter.

A series of films on families in different parts of the world, produced by the International Film Foundation under the direction of Julien Bryan, is outstanding. Among the several titles are *Japanese Family, Sampan Family, Pacific Island, Peiping Family, Peoples of the Soviet Union,* and a series of short documentaries on *Life in Great Britain Today,* which include *Scottish Miner, English Farm Family,* and *British Mill Owner.*

United World has also produced a series on families, which includes *Montevideo Family, Lima Family,* and *Good Neighbor Family.*

Life in Other Lands is the title of a series from the Coronet film company with titles on the Congo, Egypt, France, The Netherlands, Norway, Spain, Sweden, Switzerland, and the nomadic peoples of the Near East.

Filmstrips, too, are plentiful. Among the various series are the "People Are People" filmstrips, showing the life of twelve families around the world as they farm, prepare food, shop, play, bathe, study, and carry on other activities. A Popular Science series in color depicts home life in several nations.

Transportation

The writer counted twelve different methods of transportation between his hotel in Karachi, Pakistan, and the airport. There were the airplane, the bus, the tram or streetcar, camels pulling rubber-tired wagons, motorcycles and motorcycle rickshaws or taxis, bicycles and cucycle rickshaws, automobiles of many makes and vintages and right- and left-hand drives, burros carrying loads on either side which almost hid them, and trucks and jeeps. In other parts of the city there were railroads and boats of all shapes, sizes, and descriptions.

This may give the reader a glimpse into the many means of getting around and transporting goods in the world today. Any inclusive list for the entire world would have to include many more, including skis, snowshoes and sleds; hundreds of types of boats; and such animals as the vicuña and llama in South America and the elephant and yak in parts of Asia. Children working on this topic of transportation might find it interesting to compile an extensive list of all the means of transportation in the world, plus material on where these means are used—and why.

In their studies of transportation, children should know that people in many parts of the world make a great point of visiting their families on holidays no matter how far they have to travel or what modes of transportation they have to use. They should know that lack of good transportation keeps people from raising additional crops, for they cannot transport the products to markets in order to sell them. They should begin to appreciate how lack of transportation cuts people off from one another and discourages national unity, or how as in the case of the United States and Canada, good transportation has promoted national and international unity. Some science can be introduced as children learn about the various animals that can work in desert areas or at high altitudes. Recent developments in transportation should also be accented, such as the building of the Pan-American Highway or the phenomenal growth of air transportation, which has helped some areas of the world to jump the railroad age. Finally, the work of the United Nations in improving and safeguarding water and air routes should be stressed.

Children can take trips to the zoo and learn about the animals there or make visits to the airport or wharves. Back in school they can reproduce what they have seen.

In the intermediate and upper grades boys and girls should learn that the means of transportation depend upon the animals available, upon the climate and terrain, upon the cost of transportation, the degree of industrialization in a country, and even upon religion.

Maps of many kinds can be made, biographies of inventors of new means of transportation read, the cost of imaginary trips calculated, and the instruments used in various methods of transportation examined. Studies can be made of how airplanes stay aloft and how rockets, jets, missiles, and other intriguing inventions actually work. Time lines of the many inventions connected with transportation can be made. Finally, the work of the United Nations in this important field can be explored.

Typical of the materials available for teachers are Harold Mehrens' *Adventures in Aviation Education* and Charles K. Arey's *Elementary Science for the Air Age.*

Local airplane companies can often arrange for trips to the airport and sometimes for films and filmstrips. Children can plan trips to various parts of the world, discovering how they can get there, how much it will cost, and how long it will take.

For young children there is very little on transportation around the world. Paul Jensen's *Golden Book of Airplanes* can be used, as well as Marie Smith's *Joe's Story of the Airport*, and the recent volume by John McCullough and Leonard Kessler *Farther and Faster*, which traces the story of transportation from the use of logs and wheels to the present. There are a few films, such as *An Airplane Trip* and *Airport Activities*, for these grades, and filmstrips on "What Do They Mean to Us?" and "Let's Visit an Ocean Liner."

For intermediate grade reading there are several accounts. On the general field there is the Petershams' *The Story Book of Transportation* and *The Story Book of Wheels*. An over-all picture of transportation by the use of animals occurs in Mina Simon's *Beasts of Burden*, in which oxen are pictured in Portugal, the caribou in the Philippines, the burros in Mexico, Eskimo dogs in Greenland, reindeer in Lapland, camels in Arabia, the llamas in Peru, the yaks in Tibet, and the elephants in India and Burma. This is a wonderful new book which schools should begin to use.

Transportation in Latin America is described in Ralph Hancock's *Travel in Latin America*, in *Transportation in the Other Americas* by Pietro Lazzari and in *The Pan American Highway* by Catherine Coblenz. The last two booklets are publications of the Pan-American Union.

A new book by Walter Buehr, entitled *Through the Locks: Canals Today and Yesterday* emphasizes the Erie and Panama canals, but includes many others. A convenient chart of the world's modern canals is also included.

A different approach is taken in Lloyd Trevar's *Sky Highways*, in which an airplane trip is taken from Washington to Chungking and back, with maps plotting the journey through twenty-one countries. Another novel account is Rosanov's *Adventures of Misha*, who was lost in the Moscow railroad station and learns about various means of transportation and communication.

Among the many books on newer developments in air transportation, Marie Neurath's *Rockets and Jets* and Dorothy Allison's *Helpful Helicopters* should be mentioned.

Quite an addition has been made to literature in this field by Random House with its volumes on *Famous Airports of the World*, *Famous Bridges of the World*, *Famous Harbors of the World*, *Famous Railroad Stations of the World*, and *Famous Subways and Tunnels of the World*. All of these are written for grades four to seven and contain illustrations.

The only account in book form of the Alaskan highway is Douglas Coe's *Road to Alaska*. Another interesting volume for the upper-grade reader is John Lewellen's *Birds and Planes: How They Fly*, with over a hundred pictures, and a text which is accurate but non-technical.

The market is becoming flooded with accounts of space ships and rockets and all manner of new developments and dreams. In this field two outstanding volumes are the Coggins and Pratt book on *Rockets, Jets, Guided Missiles, and Space Ships*, and John Lewellen's *You and Space Travel*.

Teachers may want to use the Informative Classroom Picture Publishers' set on "Transportation—India: Ancient and Modern."

Four typical films on this topic for the middle or upper grades are *International Airport*, a description of the opening day ceremonies at Idlewild in New York City, available free from the U.S. Rubber Company; *Airport Activities*; *Giants of the Jungle*, a description of elephants as beasts of burden in Assam, India; and *Anyway to Get There*, a description of unusual means of transportation throughout the world.

Popular Science, Eye Gate House, and Young America all have filmstrips on the general theme of transportation. An unusual color filmstrip from the McGraw-Hill Book Company is entitled "River Boats, Llamas, and Airplanes." Much more specialized is a filmstrip from the New Zealand Embassy on "Maori Canoes for Transportation."

Communication

The study of how people communicate with each other should include the variety of ways of communicating both in the past and in the present and the reasons for these variations. Another point to emphasize is the development of languages, both oral and written, and the wide variety of languages now being used in the world, with Chinese, English, Hindustani, Russia, Spanish, German, Japanese, French, Malay, Bengali, Portuguese, Italian, and Arabic used in that order of users.

Children should also learn how people communicate through dances, music, art, puppetry and plays, and in many other ways. The development of pen pals can be encouraged as a practical means of communication. Older pupils can begin to see some of the complications in many countries where there are several major languages, such as India with at least twelve leading tongues.

In connection with the topic of communication the subject of learning foreign languages always rises. There is much to be said for the introduction of a language other than English in the primary grades, especially because of the accuracy with which accents can be picked up at that point in a child's development. In some areas of the United States it is natural and highly desirable for Spanish or French to be started in those years. Whether there is enough real motivation, however, for most children at this stage of their development is open to question. And whether the advantage of starting early and gaining a proper accent outweighs other arguments against early language training is debatable.

Certainly a world-minded person needs to speak well at least one language other than his own, but the burden of proof still rests on those who claim that this is best done in the early years in school, especially in sections of the country where a second language is never heard or used.

One topic which older boys and girls find fascinating is the story of inventions, such as the telegraph, cable, radio, and television. As children learn about these new inventions, they should be helped to understand the effects of discoveries on the development of the world community. These more mature pupils can also discover how the problem of communication has arisen in the United Nations and how that organization has adopted five languages for official use—English, French, Chinese, Spanish, and Russian.

Books devoted solely or chiefly to communication around the world are surprisingly few. Warren Schloat's *Adventures of a Letter* is largely on the mail system of the United States, but can be used.

Another picture book for the primary grades of this type is Joseph McSpadden's *How They Carried the Mail*.

For slightly older boys and girls there is another of the fine Neurath books, *Around the World in a Flash*, as well as Kurt Wiese's *You Can Write Chinese*.

A visiting scholar explains to the boys who discovered the Lascaux caves in France how the paintings there and similar ones elsewhere told the story of life in the glacial period, in a book by Hans Bauman called *Caves of the Great Hunters*. Two histories of communication are Julie Batchelor's *Communication: From Cave Writing to Television* and John Floherty's *Men against Distance: The Story of Communication*.

The story of the alphabet and of the calendar are told in Ogg's *The 26 Letters* and in Brindze's *The Story of Our Calendar*, both for upper-grade readers. Two other volumes worthy of special mention are Orlando Stevenson's *Talking Wire: The Story of Alexander Graham Bell* and J. Walker McSpadden's *How They Sent the News*, from smoke "words" to television.

Films on this topic are also limited. *The Story of Communication* is a history of this field produced by the Instructor Films. *The History of Writing* and *Chinese Writing* are two other recommended films. A United Nations production called *Searchlight on the Nations*, on the international exchange of information by press, radio, film, and telephoto, is intended for junior high school and older pupils.

"Early Communication" is a filmstrip which can be used in the primary grades, dealing with arm motions, smoke signals, fires, human voices, drums, mirrors, whistles, bugles, and other forms of communication. Eye Gate House has a series of nine filmstrips under the general title of "The Story of Communication."

Occupations

The topic of occupations continues to crop up in almost every section of this book, but it can be mentioned here briefly.

In their studies of other lands and peoples, children should learn that a majority of the world's inhabitants are farmers. Eventually children need to realize that most of these farmers are either tenants or serfs on someone else's land or the owners of very small tracts from which they eke out a subsistence living. The land problem is not an easy one for children to explore in detail, but one cannot possibly comprehend the economic and political problems of the world without some understanding of it.

In addition to farming, there are thousands of other occupations in the world today. As children read stories about people in other parts of the globe, they will come across many of these jobs. Some are virtually the same for all parts of the world, but some vocations are limited to a few areas.

An example of how the study of occupations can be profitable is the work of a seventh-grade class in Japan, reported in a UNESCO study of its experimental schools program. This particular study began with a trip to the Kawasaki port where the pupils watched rice and iron ore being shipped and unloaded. Their observations formed the introduction to lessons on the life of the rice farmers of South and East Asia and the life of iron workers in the Philippines and the United States. These led in turn to a study of the similarities and differences in living standards, the interdependence of people, and the need for international cooperation.

There are sections on occupations in some books primarily about people and countries, but apparently no one volume which treats this theme on a world-wide basis.

Among the films available on this topic are *Farmers of India, Farmers of Japan,* and *Farmers in South China. High Sheep Station* is a filmstrip on life in New Zealand, available from the New Zealand Embassy. The American Friends Service Committee's set of slides on "Workers Around the World" can be used effectively, too.

Schools

Children need to learn that a large percentage of their opposite numbers around the globe even today do not have any schools and consequently live out their lives as illiterates. They should not be thought of as necessarily ignorant because they cannot read and write, since illiteracy and ignorance are not synonymous. They should be considered unfortunate, however, in a world where reading and writing are basic tools.

Teachers should bear in mind the fact that education goes on in all societies, even though there may not be formal schools for passing on the culture to the young. This is probably too complicated a concept for pupils, but should be part of the teachers' background from which they draw for interpretation.

Children will be interested in the varieties of schools and school buildings around the world and even in the materials used, such as the bamboo sticks or shells for learning simple arithmetic or the sand or wooden tablets used in place of slates or blackboards.

Older boys and girls can learn how national governments and UNESCO are helping people to obtain a basic or fundamental education, consisting in most places of improvements in agriculture, the fostering of better health and sanitation, the furtherance of recreation, the preservation of skills in the arts and crafts, and the acquisition of vocational skills, as well as the learning of such basic skills as reading, writing, and arithmetic. Two books which tell the story of such efforts to bring education to the village people of the world are Elizabeth K. Tarshis' *The Village that Learned to Read* and a chapter in Selma Ekrem's *Turkey: Old and New*. In the former the main character is a small Mexican boy who resisted all efforts to educate him until he discovered the value of learning to read, write, and do simple arithmetic.

In many of the books on children around the world or on various countries there are descriptions of schools. A chapter on "The School for Little Girls" in Eleanor Lattimore's *Peachblossom* and a chapter, "In Japanese Schools," in Lily Edelman's *Japan in Story and Pictures* are examples of such accounts. There are two books on the schools for children in the outlying districts of Canada—William Bunce's *Here Comes the School Train* and Helen Acker's *School Train*.

Typical accounts for older boys and girls include a chapter on "A Nation at School" in Margueritte Harmon Bro's *Indonesia, Land of Challenge*; a chapter on "Going to School" in Cornelia Spencer's *Let's Read About China*; a similar account in Mary Nourse and Delia Goetz's *China: Country of Contrasts*; and one on "Going to School in Russia" in Shapovalov and Walsh's *Let's Read About Russia*.

The film *School in the Mailbox* is the story of correspondence schools for children on Australian ranches. A few pupils can profit from seeing a United Nations film called *Indonesia Learns*, which describes that country's fundamental education program. A new filmstrip has just appeared on life in an elementary school in Japan entitled "Our School Life," available from the Teaching Aids Laboratory of Ohio State University. "Schoolbells in the Desert" is an interesting recording about the work of UNESCO in the refugee colonies of the Middle East.

Conclusion

Each of the topics suggested in the foregoing pages can enrich the lives of children and help them to understand the similarities and differences in ways of living around the globe. Other topics which might have been included are arts and crafts, fun and festivals, and religions. Each of these is considered, however, in another chapter.

The sense of the beautiful is God's best gift to the human soul.
—W. H. HUDSON, in Robert Ulich's *Conditions of Civilized Living*

The best and noblest gifts of humanity cannot be the monopoly of a particular race or country. . . .
—RABINDRANATH TAGORE, in Nehru's *Discovery of India*

. . . it is in the painting, sculpture, and architecture of any epoch that the distinctive character of the age is most clearly seen, revealed as it inevitably is, by its marked individual style.
—PITIRIM SOROKIN, *History, Civilization and Culture*

It is not by accident that Renaissance painters painted Madonnas, that modern painters produce still life, and that the Chinese developed the landscape scroll. It was not by accident that the design on early Chinese bronzes and on some American Indian pottery relate to clouds and rain, or that Mayan carvings so frequently repeat the motif of the plumed serpent and the jaguar.   —HELEN GARDNER, *Art Through the Ages*

[Santha Rama Rau's father's advice to her]: "It seems too elementary to tell you that standards in art, as in food, vary from country to country. The point at which you start to understand the Japanese will be the point at which you find the same things as they do beautiful. By which I do not mean simply *recognize* what they think beautiful but actually get the same esthetic pleasure from them, although . . . one has to select—an activity youth is congenitally incapable of. . . ."
—SANTHA RAMA RAU, *East of Home*

Any child who has made his own bowl out of clay has a far greater respect for the pottery of ancient Greece or present day Indian pottery than the child who has never discovered the difficulties of fashioning a bowl or vase. . . . A trip to a museum has a more personal meaning for the child who knows that minutely detailed and careful workmanship has gone into an artistic piece of work. He is a keener, more enlightened critic for having experienced the feel of clay himself.
—LAWRENCE K. FRANK, *How to Help Your Child in School*

_____ Chapter 7

A World of Fun and Beauty

Parents and teachers are often so concerned with the problems of
the world and so worried about conditions in various parts of the
globe that they tend to forget the fun and beauty in the world. Yet
this world of happiness and gaiety, of color and form, of humor and
kindness does exist and should be developed with boys and girls.

Some General Concepts to Stress

Through all kinds of experiences children should begin early to
learn that there is beauty of many kinds in all parts of the world.
They should be introduced to the fascinating variety of animals
which inhabit the globe, the beautiful clothes which people wear,
the trees and flowers and natural beauty of the earth, the arts and
crafts which people create, the games children play, the music people
sing and play, the dances they perform, the homes in which they
live, the holidays they celebrate with colorful ceremonies and parades,
and a host of other forms of beauty everywhere.

As children learn about their world community, they should discover that ideas of fun and beauty vary from place to place and from person to person. In Asia, for example, there is high regard for the art of calligraphy or writing, in the Middle East high merit is attached to rug making and to the mosaics in mosques and buildings, in Mexico the most renowned artists have developed mural painting to a high degree, and in Denmark people have become artists in the production of silverware.

In desert lands an oasis is the most beautiful sight a person can see and in some parts of the world a slight rainfall calls for great rejoicing, with men and boys sometimes taking off their clothes to revel in the rain. An African chieftan may be as proud of his headdress of shining white leopard teeth or of his colorful, flowing robe as we would be of a shiny, new automobile.

Eventually children can learn that many people lead hard lives and that their festivals and music and dances are their chief source of relaxation. They can also begin to understand that in most parts of the world fun and beauty are closely associated with religion.

Eventually children can learn that fun and beauty are also clues to understanding individuals and groups of people. Anthropologists view the artifacts of a group in somewhat the same way that a psychologist uses projective tests to discover what is going on inside the mind of an individual. Children will certainly not be trained to delve into the minds of their world neighbors in this way, but they can understand that one way to appreciate other people is to learn what they enjoy and what they create and why they do these things.

If such concepts could be developed, how much more understanding and appreciation there would be of our world neighbors. Boys and girls would then understand how the Moslem has taken seriously the admonition not to make any graven images and so has expressed himself largely in mosaics rather than in pictures. The Japanese would then be viewed not as barbaric and backward but as extremely adept in the use of unpainted and unvarnished wood, in the making of exquisitely arranged gardens, and in beautiful arrangements of flowers.

Children can also learn early that they can enjoy many forms of fun and beauty and create them themselves. In all types of media they can express their own personalities, begin to learn skills which they can enjoy throughout life, and at the same time begin to understand and appreciate the patience, skill, and originality which has gone into the creations of other people, as Lawrence Frank has pointed out in the quotation at the beginning of this chapter.

Similarly boys and girls can find in games, dances, and other forms of creativity a wealth of experiences which will help them to grow as social beings.

Through various exchanges with children abroad, they can learn to share their fun and beauty with their neighbors in other parts of the world.

Some Methods to Be Used

There is greater need to provide a variety of experiences in carrying out these concepts than in almost any of the major themes here developed. Experiments of the author in getting children to write about the most beautiful things they have seen or experienced bear out the fact that the idea of beauty varies greatly from individual to individual and depends quite as much upon the atmosphere in which events take place as upon the form of beauty.

Some children will find their greatest satisfactions through the medium of music, others through arts and crafts, and still others in contact with nature. Many young children, particularly, will be thrilled by animals. Older children are more likely to be intrigued by hobbies which reveal fun and beauty around the world, whether it is collecting picture post-cards, dolls, or sea-shells. Occasionally a boy or girl will be interested in buildings around the world or in different forms of humor in various lands. Most children will find enjoyment in the celebration of holidays.

Much use can be made of games and dances in introducing children to the world. Teachers do not need to belabor the point that these forms of fun came from other parts of the world, but mention can be made of this fact in the lower grades and more emphasis can be placed on their foreign origin in the upper classes.

Music is one of the first ways in which children can enjoy the creativity of people from all parts of the globe. One of the most interesting developments in the use of music from other lands is the production of small books by the Winston Publishing Company which include a plastic record of some of the country's songs. Typical of these are *The Day the Clouds Bumped Noses—Ireland in Story, Song and Pictures* and *Little Bettina Make Believe—Italy in Story, Song and Pictures*. Older children will enjoy some of the music in the Columbia World Library of Folk and Primitive Music, edited by Alan Lomax, an ambitious project which will eventually include music from all parts of the world.

To the writer's knowledge, no school has experimented with introducing children to the music of Asia, with its different tonal arrangements. Here is a field for some interesting and valuable experiments in making children really world-minded in music.

Borrowing records from local libraries and building school collections are activities which should not be neglected in any program of this kind.

Files of colored pictures from magazines like the *National Geographic*, *Travel*, and *Holiday* are certainly needed in every school, even though such pictures can be borrowed from libraries in larger cities. Posters from travel agencies should be collected and mounted even though they often over-accent the glamorous aspects of life in any part of the world.

Color and sound films are important in portraying fun and beauty around the world, a fact which should be borne in mind by those purchasing audio-visual equipment. Kodachrome slides are an even richer resource, since they can be re-arranged in a short time to illustrate any specific topic. Parents and older pupils can sometimes be helpful in taking such pictures on trips abroad and loaning them to schools or having copies made for their use.

Every school should have a set of small flags of the various nations and if possible a set of large flags for display on special occasions. Sometimes these can be made by older pupils in art or home economics classes.

Some museums have collections of musical instruments, puppets and marionettes, and toys from other lands which can be used in the museums or loaned to schools. Wherever possible, children should have opportunities to handle such objects. Often they can make copies of them in their school work or in museums. The

Children's Museum in Detroit recently had an exhibit of toys from various nations, a type of program which many museums could plan.

As schools pay more attention to the world community aspects of the curriculum, they will undoubtedly want to make small collections of such materials themselves.

There is little material on toys around the world, although children will enjoy John Lewellen's *The True Book of Toys at Work* and teachers will gain much knowledge from Leslie Daiken's *Children's Toys Throughout the Ages*. Other related materials will be mentioned in other parts of this chapter.

When visitors from abroad are invited to schools, they should be encouraged to bring as many objects with them as they can, whether these be clothes, handicrafts, musical instruments, or other materials which will help children learn about the beautiful creations of their world neighbors. Wherever possible, simple games and songs should be taught to the classes by the visitor.

Parties and celebrations of many kinds should also be kept in mind as ways of introducing children to a world of fun and beauty.

Schools would do well to compile lists of materials which can be borrowed. Teachers should also be aware of the stores and shops where they can purchase or see the products of other parts of the earth, whether they are interesting food and candies, clothes and dishes, or a host of other objects. Trips to stores specializing in materials from abroad should be taken wherever possible.

Nor should reading be forgotten in developing the concepts mentioned in this chapter. The illustrations in books often help children to grasp concepts which have been talked about while the textual materials should help them grasp ideas about their world neighbors. Special attention will be given later in this chapter to the reading of folk tales.

Many of the experiences mentioned here should be carried on as a part of the incidental teaching of any grade. Others should be included in studies of other countries in the middle and upper grades. There is also need for several enterprising groups of teachers to develop resource units on Fun and Beauty Around the World. Frances W. Keene's book on *Fun Around the World*, for ages nine to fourteen, is an initial venture into the type of materials needed.

Animals

Parents and teachers are well aware of the popularity of animals with children. This is a topic which can be introduced early as a means of acquainting children with fun and beauty around the world. From animals they can also learn something about different parts of the earth's surface and why certain animals live in particular places.

Studies of animals need not be developed in units, but there is value in such an approach. The children in Mrs. Rena Manning's third-grade class in Apex, North Carolina, developed such a unit a few months ago after hearing the story of Bambi and seeing a giraffe made from papier maché which one of the pupils brought to class. Animals were studied and reproduced from clay and pipe cleaners and then made with old newspapers and wallpaper paste. Background murals were made of paint or colored chalk, showing the habitat of these animals. In the process simple reference materials were used, newspapers and magazines scoured for pictures, some map study undertaken, and considerable knowledge of various parts of the world gained.

Many books include pictures of animals and a few deal primarily with this topic. For the primary grades these include Ingri and Edgar d'Aulaire's *Animals Everywhere;* Raymond L. Ditmars' *Twenty Little Pets from Everywhere;* Marjorie Flack's *The Story of Ping,* a duckling on the Yangtze river in China; Marie Neurath's *The Wonder World of Animals;* John Purcell's *True Book of African Animals;* Miriam Schlein's *Elephant Herd,* a story laid in Africa and told in rhythmic prose; and Toba Sojo's *The Animal Frolic,* reprinted from a twelfth-century Japanese scroll. Friendship Press has a set of pictures on "Children and Their Pets" and Curriculum Films has a set of six filmstrips on "Work Animals Around the World" which can be very useful.

For the middle grades there is William Bridges' *Zoo Babies,* on animals in general; Wilhelmine Frisch's *The Storks of Lillegard,* on home life in Denmark and the storks as unusual pets; Ellis Credle's *My Pet Peepelo,* a lively account of a Mexican boy and his turkey; Alice and Martin Provenson's *The Animal Fair;* again John Purcell's *True Book of African Animals,* with excellent illustrations; and

Victor Von Hagen's *South American Zoo,* on animals from that part of the world. The animals of Australia are described and shown in Sheila Hawkins' *Animals of Australia,* a Puffin Book from England. The Australian News and Information Bureau supplies free of charge a useful large chart of Australian animals. A unit of pictures on "Animals of Other Lands" is available from the Creative Educational Society in Mankato, Minnesota.

There are fewer materials for the upper grades. Among those available are Frances Flaherty's *Sabu, the Elephant Boy,* chapters in William and Dorothy Irwin's *Australia and New Zealand* on "The Wonderful Animals of Australia" and "Birds that Work and Play," and an article in the June 1938 *National Geographic Magazine* which reports on a nine-months expedition to collect animals, entitled "Around the World for Animals." Jean Slaughter's recent volume on *Horses Round the World* will fascinate many older boys and girls. Boys and girls of any age can enjoy the film on the magnificent sanctuary for animals in Rhodesia entitled *Kruger National Park.*

Games and Dances

As a part of the recreational program of any school or as an integral part of any unit on a foreign country, games and dances should be used. Children ought to learn that there are many forms of recreation which boys and girls all over the world enjoy, whether it be flying kites or playing with dolls, rolling hoops or playing marbles. At the same time they need to know that games vary from place to place and that we can all enjoy the games of other parts of the globe. The same might be said of dances, too, with stress on the fact that people in other parts of the world lay more emphasis upon the dance than we do in the United States and that dances are often an outgrowth of religious rites.

Two books which bring together games from all over the world are E. O. Harbin's *Games of Many Nations* and Nina Millen's *Children's Games from Many Lands.* An inexpensive booklet on this topic is *Games of the United Nations Countries,* published by the United States Committee for United Nations Day. More specialized volumes are Marion Bergman's *The Russian-American Song* and *Dance Book,* Frank Henius' *Songs and Games of the Americas,* and Gertrude Jacobs' *The Chinese-American Song and Game Book.*

Upper-grade pupils interested in the ballet will find Gladys Malverne's *Dancing Star: The Story of Anna Pavlova* interesting reading, while boys will enjoy Bill Henry's *Approved History of the Olympic Games.*

The Cooperative Recreation Service in Delaware, Ohio, has produced a series of pocket-sized booklets on games and dances in various lands. Among their many titles are *All Time Games, Count and Capture: the World's Oldest Game, Fun with Folk Lore, Having Fun the Polish Way, Swing High: Korean Folk Recreation,* and *Puzzle Craft.*

The colored cards produced by UNICEF at Christmastime include paintings by many of the world's leading artists on games in their lands. Sports in other parts of the world are also included from time to time in articles in the *Sports Illustrated* magazine. An interesting article on "Games and Play for Children" appeared in *Childhood Education* for September 1953, with examples taken from several nations.

For upper-grade pupils there are a number of films in color on dances. Two on India which are available from the Indian Embassy are *Dances of India—Kathak* and *Dances of India—Bharatnatyam.*

A set of slides on "Games Around the World" may be borrowed from the American Friends Service Committee.

Holidays

Next to their own birthdays, holidays are the happiest days in the lives of most children. They are special days when the rigid routines are relaxed, when people are most friendly and happy, when children are often the center of attention, and when there is getting—and giving. Usually holidays are colorful, too. And there is plenty of food!

As symbols of the interdependence of people and of fun and beauty, attention should be given to at least a few of the many holidays which are celebrated in many parts of the world or even throughout the globe. Just which ones are highlighted will have to be determined by individual teachers and schools, for there are many from which to choose.

Regional or world days now include World Health Day on April 7, Pan-American Day on April 14, World Children's Day or World Peace Day on May 18, United Nations Day on October 24, and Human Rights Day on December 10.

In many parts of the world there is some kind of Festival of Lights. From Scandinavia to Italy it is the Lucia festival, held each year on December 13, with dramatic festivities in Italy, including the long procession of lights and the throwing of torches on a great pile of straw in the piazza in honor of the saint. In India the celebration is known as Diwali and comes at the close of the Dasera celebration of ten days in October, at the end of the monsoon period. Chirags or tiny clay dishes are filled with cotton wicks and placed on the edges of the roofs and in window ledges. The children are given special sweets—colored sugar "toys" in the shape of animals, and the special delicacy of puffed rice. Young girls make their wishes as the lights of Diwali are lit.

Among the special festivals for children are the Chinese Children's Day, the Doll Festival in Japan in March for girls and the Boys Festival in May there, and the Day of Swings in Korea.

Every country has its Independence Day and some nations share either this day or some other festive occasion. March 22 is the Arab League's day; April 19 is the Day of the American Indian, celebrated in many parts of Latin America; April 25 is Anzac Day in Australia and New Zealand; September 15 is Independence Day in Central America; September 11 is Teacher's Day in the nations of the Organization of American States, in memory of Domingo Sarmiento of Argentina; and December 14 is the special celebration in Bolivia, Colombia, Ecuador, Peru, and Venezuela of Bolivar's death.

Then there are the religious holidays, with January 17 as the birthday of Mohammed, the Jewish Passover in March or April, Easter in one of those two months, October 24 as the Moslem New Year, the Jewish Yom Kippur in October, Hannuukah in the late fall, and the Christian celebration of Christmas on December 25.

These are only a few of the many holidays around the world. Some schools might have an interesting year of assemblies based on this list. School papers might include a small box devoted to these special celebrations, with a brief explanation of their meaning and how they are observed. Occasionally schools will want to cooperate with community groups in some of these celebrations.

There is a wealth of materials on most of these holidays. Among the general volumes for teachers are Joseph Gaer's *Holidays Around the World*, an article in *Childhood Education* for November 1954 on "Special Days Around the World," and Dorothy Spicer's *Book of Festivals* and *Windows Open to the World*. On the religious holidays special note should be made of the series published by the Abelard-Schuman Press in their Great Religious Festivals series. These include such titles as *Chinese Festivals*, *Muhammedan Festivals*, *Purim and Hanukkah*, and *4000 Years of Christmas*, to mention but four. Nina Jordan's *Holiday Handicraft* has some material on toys and favors for holidays in other parts of the world, even though it is devoted chiefly to celebrations in the United States.

The Fun and Festival series of the Friendship Press has a wealth of materials on many national and regional celebrations.

Christmas around the world is a perennial favorite for schools, and the resources on it are many and varied. The National Education Association has a booklet on *Christmas Throughout the World* and the Pan-American Union has a program kit on "Christmas in Latin America." A filmstrip on *Christmas* from the Informative Classroom Picture Publishers includes scenes from France, Sweden, Persia, and Spain. The Society for Visual Education has a large number of filmstrips on this topic. Flat pictures on "Christmas in Many Lands" can be purchased in a set from the Informative Classroom Picture Publishers and a unit on "Christmas Customs" is available from The Instructor Company. A. S. Burack's *Christmas Plays for Young Actors* is one of several books for this occasion.

Among the many books of stories about Christmas are the Association for Childhood Education's *Told Under the Christmas Tree*, Alice Dalgliesh's *Christmas: A Book of Stories Old and New*, and Ernest G. Vetter's *Christmas All Year Round*. Two general books of carols are Karl Schulte's *Christmas Carols* and Marjorie Wyckoff's *Christmas Carols*, a Little Golden Book. Special mention should be made of Jessie Macarton Jones' *A Little Child*, a story in pageant form with illustrations of children of all races, and of Pachita Crespi's *Gift of the Earth*.

Typical of the many books for primary-grade children on holidays in various parts of the world are Alois Carigiet's *A Bell for Ursli* laid in Switzerland; Earle Goodenow's *Angelo Goes to the Carnival*, about an Italian boy who is captured by the fish and finds a prize-winning costume in a chest in the bottom of the sea; Thomas Handforth's *Mei Li*, in which a little Chinese girl and her brother go to the New Year's festival; and Yen Liang's *Dee Dee's Birthday*, about a young Chinese boy whose birthday includes the sword dance, fireworks, kites, and a parade with lanterns.

Children of the middle grades have a wealth of materials in Anna Broomell's *Friendly Story Caravan* and other similar volumes. On individual festivals there is Laura Bannon's *Manuela's Birthday*, about a small Mexican girl who received a doll from the United States on her first trip to Mexico City; Fairfax and Buie's *Ke Sooni*, the story of a Korean girl and the local festivals; Marjorie Flack's *Pedro*; an account of a fiesta day in Taxco, the silver center of Mexico; and Lindman's *Holiday Time*, a story laid in Sweden. To these should be added Elizabeth Morrow's *The Painted Pig*, the story of Pita and Pedro and the toy they bought at a Mexican fair; Virginia Olcutt's *Market Day and Holiday*, which describes festivals and children in several lands; and Elizabeth Solem's *Ushido and a Japanese Carnival*, in the Encyclopedia Britannica series on children in various parts of the world.

Upper-grade children will find Joseph McSpalden's *Book of Holidays* and Amy Lillie's *The Book of Three Festivals* helpful, as well as the several volumes in the Fun and Festival series already referred to. Especially interesting to them will be Jean Bothwell's chapter on "Feasts, Fairs, and Fun" in her book *The Story of India*.

Almost any school can borrow from a local branch of the Anti-Defamation League of B'nai B'rith a copy of the film *Your Neighbor Celebrates the Jewish Holidays*. Among the numerous filmstrips on holidays are those on Christmas from Popular Science, the Society for Visual Education, and the Informative Classroom Picture Publishers, listed in the Appendix. A set of slides on "Holidays Around the World" may be borrowed from the American Friends Service Committee.

Music

There are few better ways to introduce children to fun and beauty around the world than through music. In many ways it is a universal language. The instruments may differ, the music may be from different scales, the words may be in different languages, and the singers and players from different races, religions, and nationalities, but they all enjoy music and express themselves through it.

Throughout their elementary and junior high school years children should be exposed to much music from all parts of the world. They should listen to it, sing it, and wherever possible play it. Recordings, radio, television, and films can help them to see and feel it, but none can equal the feeling of active participation which comes from singing. Children can not only learn about music from other parts of the globe in this way, they can also develop group morale by singing together—sometimes softly, sometimes lustily.

In studying particular countries children may want to hear the national anthems as well as folk music and symphonies composed by persons from those nations. Singing or even listening to "Le Marseillaise" or "God Save the King" can often help children to realize how the people of those countries feel when such stirring music is sung or played.

Pupils should also be exposed to the variety of music around the world—the marimba bands of Latin America, the gamelan orchestras of Indonesia, the guitars and maracas of Mexico, the bagpipes of Scotland, the drums, horns, rattles, and five-string guitars of the Belgian Congo. Children enjoy making their own marimbas or xylophones from pieces of wood or their own drums from tightly stretched muslin and small wooden casks, and they can share vicariously in the fun of the people who use them, meanwhile gaining a little appreciation of their world neighbors.

In the early years most of the music heard and sung should tell some kind of story which children can easily comprehend, or else should be rhythmic enough so that they can follow it with genuine pleasure. Songs may sometimes include foreign words which the children can enjoy whether they always understand the meaning or not. More meaning will be attached to some pieces if the story is told before it is played or sung and the basic themes are easily identified.

In the process of learning about music in many lands, children can begin to "see" the countries from which the music comes and to "feel" as the people of those countries have felt. "The Song of the Volga Boatmen" can help children to feel as the peasants of Russia felt under the Czar, Sibelius' "Finlandia" can help them to picture the rivers and waterfalls of that northern nation, and Smetana's "Moldau" can give them a little of the flavor of Czechoslovakia. Saint-Saens' "The Carnival of Animals" and Debussy's "Golliwog's Cakewalk" are compositions of well-known French composers which are good music and easily enjoyed by boys and girls. They should know, too, as they grow older that all good music has not come from Europe. They should be introduced to the music of Carlos Chavez of Mexico and Carlos Gomez and Heitor Villa-Lobos of Brazil as contemporary composers from the new world.

Older children may want to record some of the best music of their glee clubs and send the records overseas for use in the schools of other countries, while individuals may want to exchange information about music in their nations with their pen pals.

Materials in this field are readily available to teachers and parents. Recordings are listed in the catalogues of leading music companies. Many of these are now available in special albums for children. Often local libraries loan recordings to schools as well as to individuals for use at home. This practice should certainly be encouraged through home and school or Parent-Teacher Associations. Special attention should be called to the recordings from other parts of the world produced by the Ethnic Folkways Corporation.

Certainly the most complete and up-to-date book on music in other nations is Ruth Tooze and Beatrice Krone's *Literature and Music as Resources for Social Studies*. Among the many books are Marion Bergman's *The Russian-American Song and Dance Book*, Margaret Boni's *Fireside Book of Folk Songs*, Gertrude Jacobs' *Chinese-American Song and Game Book*, and Edith Thomas' *The Whole World Singing*. The Cooperative Recreation Service has a fine collection of songs from many lands in a pocket-sized edition, entitled *Songs of Many Nations*. Inexpensive booklets on the *Folk*

Songs and Dances of the Americas are available from the Pan-American Union. One of the best music books for young children is Dorothy Commins' *Lullabies of Many Lands*. Many boys and girls will enjoy Satis Coleman's *The Marimba Book*.

Films on this subject include *Musical Instruments of China, Musical Instruments of India,* and *Melody of Hindustan.* Attention should be called again to the Columbia World Library of Folk and Primitive Music already referred to in the opening section of this chapter.

Folk Tales

Folk tales can be enjoyed by all ages, and through them boys and girls can learn much about a country, even though they will have to be reminded occasionally that these are stories and not true-to-life situations.

There is a tremendous volume of materials on this subject, from the widely known Grimm and Andersen stories to the lesser known tales from Africa and Asia.

Representative of books for young children are Bandeira-Duarte's *The Legend of the Palm Tree,* an Indian story of the gifts of this tree; and Lim's *Folk Tales from China.*

For the middle grades one can take a trip around the world, starting with Joseph Jacobs' *English Fairy Tales,* going on to Johan Hart's *Picture Tales from Holland,* Mary Hatch's *More Danish Folk Tales,* dropping down to Italy for Florence Botsford's *Picture Tales from the Italian,* heading east for Bartusek's *Happy Times in Czechoslovakia,* then traveling south to Africa for Ernest Kalibala and Mary Davis' *Wakaima and the Clay Man,* setting out for the Far East with Charles Meeker's *Folk Tales from the Far East,* Joseph Jacobs' *Indian Fairy Tales* and Berta Metzger's *Picture Tales from India.* From there one heads for China with Frances Carpenter's *Tales of a Chinese Grandmother,* stops off in Korea with her *Tales of a Korean Grandmother,* and flies across to Japan for Yoshiko Uchida's *The Dancing Kettle and Other Japanese Folk Tales* and his *The Magic Listening Cap.* South America is touched with Elsie Eells' *Fairy Tales from Brazil* and Mexico with Dan Storm's *Picture Tales from Mexico.*

Young America has a series of filmstrips in color on the folk tales of the world which teachers have found fascinating for children.

There are of course scores of other volumes which teachers know or can find in libraries.

The Beauty of Nature

There are hundreds and thousands of natural beauty spots around this old earth and boys and girls should be introduced to some of them in their years in school. The introductions can be made through a calendar on the teacher's desk, through colored pictures or posters on the walls, through Kodachrome slides, through old magazines in the library or classroom, or by textbooks and supplementary readers.

These beauty spots may include such mountains as Kilimanjaro in East Africa, Fujiyama in Japan, the Matterhorn and Jungfrau in Switzerland, or the Rockies and Andes in the western hemisphere. They may be magnificent waterfalls such as Victoria in Africa, two and a half times the height of Niagara, or Iguassu Falls in Brazil with its water falling over a crescent rim two and a half miles wide. Children can likewise be introduced to the horse chestnuts of Paris in the spring, looking like giant white candelabra, the May trees in England, the orchids of Central America, and the Japanese cherry blossoms or other colorful trees of that part of the world. They can see the beautiful leis of Hawaii and similar garlands used in the Middle East to welcome guests, be shown the formal gardens of France, and see the exquisitely arranged and well-kept gardens of the Japanese.

No one has collected such sights into a single volume but there are a few films, such as *Japan in Cherry Blossom Time*, and filmstrips, such as the "Scenic Wonders of North Island" in New Zealand.

Some Other Aspects of Fun and Beauty

Volumes could be written on all the themes mentioned in this chapter and on other topics not covered here. A few of these are suggested but not developed in the following paragraphs.

The arts and crafts of various countries should be known to children, with wide use made of the Made in . . . series of Knopf on Canada, China, India, Mexico, and Poland, and of such films as the *Handicrafts of India, Handicrafts of South India,* and the *Ancient Arts of Japan.*

Some children will be intrigued with the dolls of other lands. For such persons three books are suggested: Catherine Christopher's *The Complete Book of Doll Making and Collecting,* Julienne Hallen's *How to Make Foreign Dolls and Their Costumes,* and Nina Jordan's *Homemade Dolls in Foreign Dress.*

Children's drawings are another expression of beauty and should be made, exchanged, and exhibited. Three volumes of such drawings are Miller and Rutter's *Child Artists of the Australian Bush,* Norma Cohn's *Little People in a Big Country* (on Russia), and Marion Cothren's *Pictures of France by Her Children.* Children's drawings may be borrowed from the Junior Red Cross, the Art for World Friendship project of the Women's International League, and the American Friends Service Committee. The French Embassy loans two bulletin board exhibits, one on "Children's Paintings from North Africa" and the other on "Drawings by French School Children."

Some teachers may want to introduce children to a few of the world's masterpieces of art. This can be done in some cases in art galleries. For those who cannot do this, or as a supplement to trips to galleries, there are such books as Alice Chase's *Famous Paintings* and Katharine Gibson's *Pictures to Grow Up With* and *More Pictures to Grow Up With.*

Boys and girls are almost always intrigued with Chinese writing and also with the art of paper folding. Two volumes for middle-grade children on these subjects are highly recommended. One is Kurt Wiese's *You Can Write Chinese.* The other is Maying Soong's *The Art of Chinese Paper Folding for Young and Old.*

Imaginative parents and teachers will find many other ways of helping children to learn about their world as one of fun and beauty —everywhere. It is hoped that these suggestions will help them.

We are living in one world. Yet our thinking, our emotions and our actions are largely based upon the assumption of at least relative independence of individuals, groups, or religious, economic, political, racial or national societies. To our failure to realize that the well-being of any individual, group, or society in the world today is interdependent with the well-being of all individuals, groups, and societies is due the confusion and conflict in which we are living.

—CARLETON WASHBURNE, *The World's Good:*
Education for World-Mindedness

The self-interest of any individual increasingly transcends national boundaries. This objective assumes that man is first of all an individual with an individual life to lead in an individual sphere in the pursuit of individual happiness. Whether his conception of well-being be spiritually or materialistically motivated, the principle is equally true. If it is spiritually motivated and includes a moral duty to help his fellowmen, his self-interest goes beyond national lines. If his notion of well-being is purely materialistic, the facts of atomic warfare and economic interdependence require that his self-interest extend beyond the borders of his own country.

—Study Group, UNESCO Seminar, Paris, 1946

We are debtors to all the world. —JOHN WESLEY.

Our own descendants are not going to be just Western, like ourselves. They are going to be heirs of Confucius and Lao-Tse as well as Socrates, Plato and Plotinus; heirs of Gautama Buddha as well as Deutero-Isaiah and Jesus Christ; heirs of Zarathustra and Muhammed as well as Elijah and Elishah and Peter and Paul; heirs of Shankara and Ramanuja as well as Clement and Origen; heirs of Cappadocian Fathers of the Orthodox Church as well as our African Augustine and our Umbrian Benedict; heirs of Ibn Khaldun as well as Bossuet; and heirs (if still wallowing in the Serbonian Bog of politics) of Lenin and Gandhi and Sun Yat-sen as well as Cromwell and George Washington and Mazzini.

—ARNOLD TOYNBEE, *Civilization on Trial*

Chapter 8

An Interdependent World

Speaking before the annual conference of the National Council for the Social Studies recently, George Cressey said that "the first lesson of geography is interdependence."

Reduced to simple terms this concept means that we depend upon other people and they depend upon us for all the things which make for full living. We are interdependent in food, in raw materials, in finished products, in agriculture, in art and architecture, in medicine and science, in music, in education, in literature, in philosophy and religion, and in government. Life is not possible in our modern world without interdependence. The jobs which men and women hold depend upon other people around the world as well as upon people in our own country. Even our lives are dependent today upon the development of peaceful relations with other lands and peoples.

The increasing interdependence in the world today and tomorrow is due to a great many factors. Transportation has brought us close today and will undoubtedly bring us closer together as a world in the years ahead. The Atlantic and the Pacific oceans are no longer wide bodies of water; they are narrow channels bridged by fast ocean-going vessels and airplanes and jets. The telephone, the telegraph, the radio and television, and other means of communication have contracted the world until we now have instantaneous transmission of thoughts and actions around the globe. Travel has increased by leaps and bounds in recent years and will probably increase perceptibly in the near future. Man's search for new ideas and for solutions to old and new problems has taken him into every corner of the earth, and his interest and curiosity have led him to visit every known group of people on the face of the globe. Finally, man's humanitarianism has motivated his concern for the well-being of men, women, and children whether they are the victims of floods, earthquakes, racial discrimination, economic injustice, or political oppression.

Such interdependence has also caused problems of many kinds and often of great magnitude. As the world grows smaller, the problems of one area become the problems of every other part of the earth. There is less room for people to move without bumping into their world neighbors. Planning seems inevitable; the question is how much planning, in what fields, how and by whom, rather than whether there will be planning or not. The quest for raw materials and for markets grows more intense and adjustments on a world scale are necessary. In these and in scores of other ways interdependence has brought new problems and has intensified old ones.

At the same time interdependence has brought an increased possibility of the good life for people everywhere. The material riches of the earth are being increasingly developed so that men, women, and children can share in these resources and have more goods with which to lead fuller lives. Travel has brought us into contact with cultures from which we can learn while they are learning from us. The inventive genius of humanity is being released by trained scientists in many countries. The literature of many nations and cultures is being translated for the benefit and enjoyment of peoples everywhere. Life can be richer in every conceivable way because of the increasing interdependence of the world's peoples.

It is important to help boys and girls to see that they are involved in this growing interdependence and that they can share in the good things of life much more if they can contribute to the better use rather than the misuse or abuse of this growing interdependence.

Volumes could be written on each phase of this theme, but a quick look at representative aspects may help us to see how closely we are bound together.

Economics

The telephone in our home seems like a simple gadget, yet how many people realize that it is really a symbol of the world's interdependence. In it are forty-eight products from sixteen countries. From Australia come wool, lead, zinc, gold, and silver; from Asia, kauri gum, silk, tungsten, antimony, mica, hemp, chinawood oil, rubber, tin, shellac, cotton, teakwood, and leather; from Africa, copper, tungsten, silver, gold, chromium, cotton, platinum, and cobalt; from Europe, tin, lead, magnesium, flax, and magnetite; from South America, wool, carnauba wax, vanadium, asphalt, rubber, aluminum, tin, copper, mahogany, quartz, leather, and antimony; and from Canada, nickel, asbestos, silver, gold, and platinum.

The automobiles which are so important a part of our life use 300 products from fifty-six countries. Among them are lead from Mexican mines which is used in the battery; platinum for "points" in the distributor which comes from Canadian ore; aluminum from Canada which is used in the engine pistons; zinc from Canada and Mexico for the door handles, horn, and radiator; copper wire in the car's electrical system which is made from Chilean ore; wool upholstery and floor covering which came from sheep in Australia; burlap for "binding" for the upholstery from India and Pakistan; tin for the bearings which comes from Malaya; asbestos for the brakes from Canada; natural rubber for the tires and tubes from Malaya; and steel—the major ingredient—which is made from chrome from South Africa, manganese from India, and nickel and iron ore from Canada.

Whole industries sometimes develop from a new source of materials, such as the new steel industry north of Philadelphia which has been started recently as a result of arrangements to transport iron ore from Venezuela by boat.

From India has come the important herb Rauwolfia now used to

combat high blood pressure and for mentally disturbed patients in place of electric shock treatment.

So one might continue to enumerate the hundreds of products which come from abroad to be used in the United States.

These foreign countries also serve as important markets for our finished products. Around 6 per cent of our total sales go abroad these days and that percentage often makes the difference between profit and loss. Few people realize that Canada is our best customer, followed closely by South America, and then by Europe.

Similarly the rest of the world is dependent upon us. This fact was dramatized for the writer a few months ago when he was in the Yucatan peninsula of Mexico. This large area was undergoing a depression because we were not buying in large enough quantities the henequen on which Yucatan depends for its livelihood. In a similar way a change in our tariff policy can disrupt the Swiss watch industry. On the other hand, the export of hybrid corn to Italy can revolutionize the growth of that grain in parts of that nation.

Politics and trade often interact on one another. Thus Japan seeks raw materials from China, Manchuria, and Russia and markets for her finished products in those parts of the world, but "cold war" politics prevents her from carrying out this desire and large subsidies from the United States are substituted. The desire for a larger share of the profits of Iranian oil by that nation caused retaliation by the British and one of the world's chief sources of petroleum was cut off for months. A map of the trouble spots of the world and a map of the major resources of the world would reveal a striking similarity if worked out by an enterprising teacher or a class of superior students.

Agriculture

Most of the agricultural products which we produce in the United States are the result of interdependence. Except for corn, all of our cultivated cereals originated in the Old World. The same is true of many of our fruits, which have been brought here from all parts of the world. Even our domesticated animals were brought here from abroad.

Our ideas of irrigation, terracing, and the use of green manures, and more recently our policy of storing grain in the best years for use in lean years, came from China or other Asiatic nations.

Even today we continue to profit from developments in other parts of the world. A new type of rust-proof pepper was recently brought to the United States from Korea by the Food and Agriculture Organization of the United Nations in response to a request for such a product by New England farmers. Brahma bulls from India have been brought to the southwestern part of the United States in recent years and cross-bred with American livestock to develop cattle which can withstand heat.

In these and many other ways we are debtors to the entire world in the field of agriculture.

We have contributed to our world neighbors, too, in many ways, such as through research on the improvement of crops and on the control of diseases. Today, for example, there is joint research between the United States and Peru on the growing of tea, with Guatemala on the improvement of coffee production, with six countries of Latin America on the growing of rubber, and with Nicaragua on the use of the African oil palm and the raising of ipecac, a tropical medicinal plant. Throughout the world the idea of demonstration farms, county agents, and 4-H clubs is spreading, all ideas which have been exported from the United States and adopted or adapted elsewhere.

Art and Architecture

A visit to any art gallery or a walk around almost any large city should reveal the extent of interdependence in these two allied fields. An art museum will have on exhibit the paintings of Dutch, Italian, German, and other European masters and probably the work of Rivera, Orozco, and other modern Mexican mural painters, some of the recent art or wood sculpture from Africa or Haiti, and scrolls and calligraphy from China and Japan.

Our buildings are likely to be Greek or Roman, Tudor or Georgian, with occasionally some Byzantine or Russian designs. On the West Coast one sees the influence of the Japanese in homes or in products within homes, while in the southwest the influence of the Mexicans is often evident.

Science, Medicine, and Mathematics

Few people think of the Moslem world when they think of science, medicine, and mathematics, but we are debtors to Islam as well as to the Greeks and Romans for a wide variety of things which we use daily and consider essential in our lives, ranging from Arabic numerals to algebra and trigonometry, and from astronomy to the reckoning of time and the introduction of writing.

In more recent times we have profited from the scientific work of the German Roentgen, who discovered the X-ray; of the German Koch and his work in bacteriology; of Harvey and Lister in England on the circulation of blood and on antiseptics; of Pasteur in France on the pasteurization of milk; of Oswaldo Cruz in Brazil on the eradication of yellow fever; of Kronenbach in Sweden on brain surgery; and of Noguchi in Japan on yellow fever and venereal diseases.

One might continue to enumerate the advances of science in the far distant past and more recent times, bringing the story up to date with the international control of disease through such a group as the World Health Organization of the United Nations. Germs know no national boundaries and it is only because of the constant vigilance of the World Health Organization and national governments that world-wide epidemics do not plague us.

Music

Music is another field in which the world is interdependent today as it has been in the past. Glance through the programs of a symphony orchestra or even a school glee club and you will discover that there are names of composers from many nations or folk songs taken from many parts of the world whose authors are unknown to us.

Illustrations from Germany and Russia may prove this point quickly and serve as an illustration of how a pupil interested in this field might be encouraged to develop the theme for several countries. A list of German and Austrian musicians familiar to school children here would certainly include Bach, Beethoven, and Brahms, Haydn, Handel (even though English-born), Mozart, Strauss, Schubert, Wagner, and Mendelssohn. A similar list from Russia would include such familiar names as Tchaikowsky, Rimsky-Korsakov, Rubinstein, Moussorgsky, Stravinsky, Rachmaninoff, Prokofiev, Borodin, Shostakovitch, and others.

Religion and Philosophy

As a final illustration of interdependence it should be noted that we in the United States are debtors to the Near East for our two major religions—Judaism and Christianity. Our philosophy of life has also been affected by a large number of European philosophers, Dutch and German, French and English, Italian and Spanish.

As the world grows smaller we become aware of the tremendous influence of Buddha and Confucius, of Lao-Tse and Mencius, of Mohammed and Iqbal, as well as many contemporary thinkers and writers.

So one might continue to enumerate the contributions of the many parts of the world to our growing world culture. Many of these facts will be above comprehension to elementary school and even to most junior high school pupils. Yet they are certainly a part of the rich background from which teachers in these grades need to draw as they introduce boys and girls to the idea of interdependence in our contemporary world. Gifted children, however, can learn much from thorough studies of some of these topics.

Some Contributions of the United States

Studies of interdependence should also stress the fact that the United States has contributed and is contributing many important things to the rest of the world.

In the area of government we have represented for a long period the ideal of democracy to the people of many parts of the globe. We have no monopoly in this field, as Uruguay, the Scandinavian nations, England, New Zealand, Australia, and other nations have made great contributions, too. But the Declaration of Independence, our Constitution, the lives of Jefferson and Lincoln, and the practice of democratic control of the people, by the people, and for the people have inspired the leaders of many countries and millions of people.

In science our mass production and scientific management as well as the tremendous research carried on by government, private industry, and education have aided people in many parts of the world and have been an inspiration for the setting up of laboratories and scientific institutions around the globe.

No nation has developed a more democratic educational system than the United States, faulty as we sometimes think our system is. Public libraries, museums, night schools, and adult education programs, and a score of other developments in public education have likewise been contributed by our nation to the world.

In humanitarian activities and in the place of women in society, the United States has been a leader. Our care of the mentally ill, the blind, the mentally retarded, and our creation of hospitals and public health clinics has been copied in many parts of the earth.

To mention only one more area, we have made tremendous contributions in literature, ranging from the beloved poetry of Walt Whitman to the philosophical writings of Emerson, and from the short story form developed by Edgar Allan Poe to the modern novels of Faulkner, Wolfe, Hemingway, Steinbeck, and others.

Preschool and Primary Grades

As in most other phases of curriculum experiences, emphasis on interdependence with preschool and primary-grade children must be largely focused on the neighborhood and community. Children need to be helped first of all to understand and develop proper cooperative relationships in the home, school, and neighborhood. These are the abc's of international interdependence. Well learned, they can contribute to the rest of the interdependence alphabet.

Children at this stage need to be helped to understand their dependence upon parents, older brothers and sisters, classmates, teachers and other school officials, and neighborhood and community helpers. Since interdependence is a two-way street, they also need to learn how they can help others and to have experiences in which they can assist other people.

At the same time they can learn a little about the interdependence of the world through a variety of experiences. A trip to the post office with a letter can be the occasion for talking about letters which go across the ocean or to neighboring countries or come from abroad. A trip to the zoo can help them to see that animals come from different parts of the world. Making drawings or models of these animals and placing them on a world map can help them to combine geography with the idea of interdependence. A trip to a Chinese laundry or restaurant can let them see the same type of abacus which they use in school in actual use in business. Trips to airports and wharves can help children see the products which are arriving and being sent to people in many parts of the world.

The story of the candy bars which they relish can help young children see that the sugar, the cocoa or chocolate, and even the flavoring have come from across the seas.

Even the vaccination against polio can be used to show how the scientists of several countries cooperated in the study of polio prevention and how the monkeys of India and the Philippines were shipped to the United States to be treated with the vaccine before it was used on human beings.

Teachers will need to use their own ingenuity in developing this concept since there are almost no materials on international interdependence available for the early years. Jerrold Beim's *Two Is a Team* is a classic on intercultural interdependence, showing the cooperation of two boys, one white and one Negro; and Elly McKean's *It's Mine* is an excellent recent volume for young children on learning to share.

On the world there is Madeline Gekiere's *Who Gave Us?*, which tells in the brief text and in large, gay pictures the story of the people, period, and country from which several of our everyday things came. The booklets of the National Dairy Council and other materials on food, cited in Chapter VI, can be helpful in developing the concept of interdependence, as will many of the song and game books cited in various other chapters.

There is need for specific materials in this field for use in the early grades. Enterprising teachers and publishers would perform a much needed service by the preparation of simple accounts on this general theme or on specific aspects of it.

The Middle Grades

Children at this level are often intrigued by where things come from. They can get excited about the development of wheels, the domestication of animals, the discovery of writing and pictures in caves or on stones, reliving the stages of man from primitive times to the present.

Food is a topic of interest and can be developed in detail as a means of showing the world's interdependence. The story of airplanes and air transportation is another topic which delights boys and girls in these years.

As children begin to study other lands and peoples, they can discover the ways in which we have been affected by them and they, in turn, by us, whether it be the story of how the Scandinavians came to the United States and contributed to it, or how we have helped Mexico to recoup its silver-making art or to build dams and irrigation projects.

Some attention can also be given to the conflicts which have arisen out of the fact of interdependence.

Interviews with merchants as to where they sell their products and where they obtain their raw materials can give boys and girls contact with adults and considerable knowledge and understanding of the two-way process of trade. Maps showing this exchange can be helpful, too.

Studying such a simple matter as how a pencil or eraser is made can give children some idea of the many materials needed from abroad to make a common, everyday product.

Many children have put down on paper all the things they have done in a day, listing beside them the debt they owe to somebody, somewhere, and at some time, for the things they have used. This is a useful and interesting idea.

Boys and girls can begin to act upon their interest in interdependence by taking part in Junior Red Cross projects, by collecting money for UNICEF or CARE or some other relief project, by writing to pen pals abroad under adult guidance, or by taking part in school affiliations.

Exhibits of materials which come from abroad that can be found in their homes or in the homes of neighbors and friends can make this theme come to life for many children.

Materials on this topic for the intermediate grades are also scarce. One of the books which can be used is Ruth Brindze's *The Story of*

Our *Calendar*, which gives the history of the calendar from Babylonian times to the present day, with illustrations. Another is Julie Batchelor's *Communication: From Cave Writing to Television*, a book which can also be used with younger children because of its clarity. Several materials are listed in Chapter VI on food, which can be helpful at this point, too.

"The Story of Trade" is the one filmstrip the writer has been able to find which is intended solely for the elementary school, tracing the history of trade from early times to international trade today.

Again a real contribution could be made by persons who prepare stories, booklets, books, films, or filmstrips for this age group on interdependence.

The Upper Grades

For boys and girls of approximately twelve years of age and up there are a number of additional concepts to be stressed in developing the idea of interdependence.

By this time they can understand more fully how science and technology have increased man's dependence upon his fellow human beings and their interest in science can be utilized to the full. Stories of famous scientists can be read, and charts and posters made of the inventions and discoveries and the place from which the scientists came.

Similarly, boys and girls interested in music, art, architecture, and a wide range of other activities can pursue their own individual interests or contribute to group work in the study of countries.

Boys of this age are particularly interested in sports and they may wish to develop a chart of world champions and the nationality of the record holders in various athletic events.

At this upper-grade level much more can be done on trade and its bearing upon jobs in the local community or in the United States. World maps showing the location of resources and charts showing the exchanges of raw materials and finished products can be interesting and promote learning.

Some study can be made, too, of the U. S. Point Four Plan, the Colombo Plan, and the U. N. Social and Technical Assistance Program as means of promoting a more healthy world economy.

As countries are studied, their contributions to world culture can be noted. Some individuals or groups may want to prepare Who's Who lists of the famous contributors from each of the nations considered.

Groups of pupils or an entire class might also want to prepare a large exhibit, similar to the one which the writer viewed at the Philippine Conference in Manila in 1954, with the title of "Our Debt of Gratitude To: . . ." with several countries represented in the subheadings.

A school might well plan a series of exhibits in the main corridor, over a period of months or years, of masterpieces of art. These could be arranged by countries or by themes. Such an exhibit or exhibits might be arranged in conjunction with a local art gallery or museum. Other exhibits might be arranged on music, architecture, and arts and crafts.

Boys and girls in the upper grades should be encouraged to go alone, with their families, in small groups, or as a class to exhibits of this kind in local museums and art galleries.

Among the best resources for this stage of development is Oscar Ogg's The 26 Letters, which tells the story of the alphabet from the writings of early cave men to the development of modern linotype machines. Laurin Zilliacus' Mail for the World is another volume which can be recommended, telling the story of postal interdependence through the Universal Postal Union. The Batchelor volume on Communication: From Cave Writing to Television can also be used with these older pupils. The series of books cited in Chapter IX in the Made in . . . series, will give boys and girls some ideas on the many products which skilled hands in different nations have produced and are still producing.

Melvin Fox's list of United States imports from fifty-nine nations, published in booklet form by the American Association for the United Nations under the title The Interdependence of Nations, should serve as a good reference list for products from abroad, although it is not intended for general reading. Each year the United States Chamber of Commerce prepares a kit of materials on world trade which is available to teachers for a small charge. A few advanced readers will be able to handle some of the materials prepared by the United Nations on this subject.

Six films can be recommended for this age group on various aspects of interdependence. One of these is the Harmon Foundation's film on *China's Gifts to the West*. Although issued several years ago, it is still valuable, giving pictures of paper, gunpowder, porcelain, silks, textiles, dominoes and Mah Jong, decorative designs, and many fruits and flowers as some of the gifts children can best understand. Another film is *Our Shrinking World* which sets the stage for most of what has been said in this chapter about our increasing interdependence.

Four of these films deal with trade. One is *Expanding World Relationships*, tracing the ways in which inventions have developed the need for communication since the days of Jefferson and showing the intensified economic and social interdependence since that early time. Another is *Made in U.S.A.*, in which an automobile is pictured as falling apart piece by piece as the story is told of the area of the world from which the raw materials for it come. A third of these films is *Round Trip: The U.S.A. in World Trade*, an account by manufacturers, laborers, and others in various parts of the world as to what international commerce means to them. In the course of the film the popular fears of foreigners, of cheap labor, and other prejudices are refuted. *World Trade for Better Living* is another film which can be used in portraying this general topic.

"Keystone of Prosperity—America's Foreign Trade" is one of the filmstrips produced by the Office of Education Activities of *The New York Times*, and it has been used with good effect in the upper elementary grades.

This theme of interdependence is so important and so well adapted to the elementary and junior high school grades that it should be developed much further than it has yet been done. Many resources need to be produced on it. This is an area in which teachers, curriculum workers, and publishers need to concentrate in the months and years ahead.

What a nation is, it is difficult to define. Possibly the essential characteristic of national consciousness is a sense of belonging together and of together facing the rest of mankind.

—JAWAHARLAL NEHRU, *Discovery of India*

Love of country is eternal. It is on the same plane as love of family, love of one's native town or village, of all the fundamental realities that in our heart of hearts we hold nearest and dearest. But I am quite sure that there is nothing incompatible between patriotism and humanism—or, if you like, between national and international loyalties. Love of a nation and love of the human race, as one great man once said, can coexist in the same conscience, as naturally as patriotism and love of family, or as patrotism and religious belief.

—LEON BLUM, *For All Mankind*

The paradox of our generation is that all the world has now profited by an education which the West has provided, except . . . the West herself. The West today is still looking at history from that old parochial self-centered standpoint which the other living societies have by now been compelled to transcend. Yet, sooner or later, the West, in her turn, is bound to receive the re-education which the other civilizations have obtained already from the unification of the world by Western action.

—ARTHUR TOYNBEE, *Civilization on Trial*

Culture will then mean the wardrobe which a member of society has at his disposal; education will mean the dressing of him, including the selection of what is most becoming and useful, and the fitting of it to the individual's figure.   —BLISS PERRY, *One World in the Making*

Each culture gives some people, some members of that society a special chance. If we want to tap the whole range, we must tap it through the different cultural expressions of human differences which have been built up for several hundred thousand years.

—MARGARET MEAD, in F. Ernest Johnson's *World Order: Its Intellectual and Cultural Foundations*

Americans have generally accepted diversity as a condition, but only some Americans have embraced it as a value.

—CLYDE KLUCKHOHN, *Mirror for Man*

—————————————— Chapter 9

A World of Many Countries and Cultures

No one knows just how many countries there are in the world to-day. The reason for this is that the word "country" eludes definition. It is not always a territory which is contiguous nor whose people speak the same language, have the same religion, or share the same culture. Perhaps it is better defined in terms of groups of people who have some common traditions, some common purposes and goals, some common symbols, some common land, some common government, and a feeling of belonging together.

The term "culture" is probably even more difficult to define. Clyde Kluckhohn speaks of culture in his *Mirror for Man* as "a way of thinking, feeling, believing. It is the group's knowledge stored up (in memories of men, in books and objects) for future use."

Experts differ on the number of large cultural groups in the world, but there is certainly a minimum of eight. One of these is the Latin culture, comprising Italy, Spain, Portugal, France, Belgium, and Latin America. A second is the Anglo-Saxon culture, consisting of the United Kingdom, Canada, Australia, New Zealand, a part of the Union of South Africa, and the United States. A third is the Germanic group, concentrated in central Europe and including Austria, Germany, The Netherlands, and Scandinavia. A fourth is the Slavic culture, which is the major way of life in the U.S.S.R., Czechoslovakia, Bulgaria, Hungary, and Yugoslavia. A fifth is the Chinese culture, concentrated in China, Korea, Japan, and nearby territories. A sixth is the Indic culture, located in India, Ceylon, Nepal, Burma, Thailand, and to some extent in adjacent areas. The seventh is commonly regarded as the Arabic culture, extending from North Africa to Southeast Asia, with some tangents in southeastern Europe and the U.S.S.R. An eighth is the African culture, concentrated in the area south of the Sahara.

The Importance of Studying Other Countries

Boys and girls eventually need to be introduced to these concepts of countries and cultures as a means of fostering self-enrichment, as one way of understanding their own country better through a knowledge of other nations, as a part of their background in developing better human relations with the people of other countries and cultures, as background for the better understanding of contemporary world affairs, as a part of their preparation for vocations which will take them into other parts of the world, and as an essential part of their training as citizens of the United States and of the world community.

Many concepts need to be developed in schools today as boys and girls are introduced to the variety of countries and cultures around the world. Most of these concepts should be reserved for the middle and upper grades, but a few of them can be touched upon with young children. Looking at the field as a whole, however, the following seem to be major ideas to be developed in elementary and junior high schools:

1. *There are many countries and cultures in the world.* Children need to learn that some of these countries and cultures are large and some small in area and in population. They need to know that some are old and others comparatively new, while some are like new sprouts from old trees.

2. *Each country and culture does some things especially well.* As children study the world, their attention should be called to the fact

that countries and cultures are not perfect. Some take care of old people very well, as in China; others take better care of children, as we do in the United States. Some concentrate on the arts, as the French and Italians seem to do; while others specialize in science and the humanities, as we do in the United States. Some have prejudice against people of lower castes or social and economic rank, as has been the case in India; others have prejudice against people of a certain color, as has been the case in the United States. Boys and girls can be taught to think of countries as irregular shapes and sizes rather than as perfect circles. Each country can learn from the others about certain aspects of life.

3. *Countries and cultures are constantly changing.* The study of history should help children to understand how countries and cultures change. In the period of exploration, for example, China and India were dominant and well developed nations. Then, for a long period, they were less prominent, whereas today they are undergoing drastic changes and again coming to the fore as world powers. As children study the various ways in which countries and cultures change, they should discover that these changes usually come slowly. This should help them to expect less drastic shifts in the world than many Americans hope to see within short periods of time.

4. *Some countries and cultures are more adaptable than others.* Throughout history there have been countries and cultures which have learned how to adapt themselves to changes. They are the ones which have remained important parts of the world for centuries, rather than sliding down the toboggan of history into oblivion. China has been one of those countries, flexible enough to absorb many invaders and to pursue its own ways of living despite outside interference. The United States and Japan are illustrations of countries which in more recent times have learned new ways of living and adapted themselves to changing conditions.

5. *Members of a country or culture are proud of their group.* There are people who are so culture-bound or so nationally-conscious that they sometimes find it difficult to realize that other people are as proud of their countries or cultures as we are of ours. We have to help children to understand the pride of all peoples for their own groups and to develop respect for their feelings. Social scientists call

this feeling "empathy" and consider it among the most important attributes to develop.

6. *We all learn the ways of our country and culture.* Children learn what they live. If they had been born in China, they would speak Chinese, learn from the writings of Confucius, Lao-Tse, and Mencius, eat with chopsticks, and think as Chinese. No matter where a person is born, he tends to learn the ways of that locality or the group into which he is first introduced. Comprehension of this concept should help in assisting children to understand their world neighbors and the ways of living which seem peculiar to outsiders.

7. *There are tremendous variations within countries and cultures.* How easy it is for all of us to generalize. We speak about "the French point of view," "the Russian point of view," of " the Asiatic mind," and "the Latin-American way of doing things." Yet, if we were asked what Americans think about race relations, dancing, or scrapple, we would have to differentiate between many points of view on those topics. Certainly there are some aspects of life on which most of the people of a given country or culture agree, but there are always wide variations on most topics. Children need to be kept from developing stereotypes of people, countries, races, and cultures. They need to learn about the many points of view within large groups of people and of the many different ways of life within any country or culture.

8. *Countries are affected by a variety of factors.* No quick study of any country can help children really understand that nation. There are so many facets to any country that it is impossible to begin to understand them when a day or two is devoted to a country in schools. It is better to select a few nations and to study them intensively than to hop, skip, and jump around the world with a brief stopover in every nation of the globe.

In order to understand any nation, it is important to know its land, its climate, its location, and its resources; its people and their composition; its many ways of living and the reasons for them; its institutions—including its home life, its schools, its government, and its economic organization; its creative activities in the arts; and its religions and values. The history of any country must be explored and its relations with other countries viewed over a long period of time.

Particularly in today's world, it is necessary to see how countries are affected by the power constellation of our time and by their stage of industrialization.

9. *Small countries as well as large ones are important.* Because of our occupation with "bigness" in the United States, we tend to underrate the smaller nations and to minimize their place in the world. Actually it is necessary to develop the concept of the importance of *all* nations, large and small.

Certainly Korea, Israel, and Indo-China illustrate the fact that many of the problems of the world break out in small and seemingly unimportant lands. Likewise small countries have much to offer larger ones in their solutions of problems. Hawaii has much to teach the United States, for example, about race relations. Uruguay is one of the most advanced parts of the world in respect to the welfare of its people. A CIO-AFL mission to Israel in 1953 included in its report the statement that "in some respects, Israel seemed to us to be ahead of the United States. A larger proportion of its workers, both industrial and white collar, are union members than in any other nation. The medical care that the average Israeli receives is probably better and certainly far less expensive than in America today." Scores of other examples could be cited.

One of the trends in the world community today seems to be toward the growing importance of smaller countries. Children should be made aware of this fact and its influence upon the world scene.

10. *Complete understanding of a country or culture is impossible.* Many years ago William James remarked that "every nation has ideals and difficulties and sentiments which are an impenetrable secret to one not of the blood." No teacher, parent, or even anthropologist can completely understand another country or culture no matter how accurate his tools may be. This fact should not prevent anyone from undertaking studies of other countries and cultures, but it might give him encouragement when he becomes confused, or a sense of humility when he believes he has become "expert" about a given area. When one has begun to grasp this important idea, real learning has begun to take place.

Some Criteria for Choosing Countries to be Studied

In the early school years countries as such should not be studied. The concept of a country is too difficult. There can be occasional references to countries, but this should not be a major consideration. In the third or fourth grades there should be more references to countries and an elementary approach to them as units into which the world is divided, but teaching at this stage should be largely on broad topics or themes which cut across countries and cultures and give children a view of transportation, communication, food, family life, and related ideas around the world. There is much to be said for studying countries and cultures which are similar to ours when children first confront these concepts.

Over the twelve years in elementary and secondary schools, however, pupils should have some experience in studying a large number of countries and cultures. Since there are so many nations to become acquainted with, it is important to develop some criteria for choosing the ones to be studied. Among the criteria which should be considered are the following:

1. countries representing each of the eight major cultures of the world;
2. the major world powers, and countries which are likely to become major powers;
3. countries against which children are prejudiced or about which they have learned little;
4. countries which have influenced the United States the most;
5. countries from which the ancestors of a class originated;
6. neighboring nations;
7. countries which are in the news often;
8. countries which illustrate progress in solving world-wide problems;
9. countries on which there are adequate teaching materials;
10. countries about which teachers feel competent to teach.

All of these criteria are not equally important. For example, teachers should be able to teach about any country and number 10 should not be a major factor; but any realistic approach to this topic must take into consideration that there are many teachers at present who are not qualified to teach about every nation in the world community.

Similarly, the criterion of countries which are in the news may be misleading. For example, Guatemala was in the news over a period of months in 1954, but it is doubtful if much time should be spent on that small nation even though it is colorful, fascinating, and important. Some attention can be given to such nations as are in the news, without studying them intensely.

It is obvious, however, that countries like Russia, China, and India would be checked under several of the criteria cited above.

No matter what countries are selected for study, there are certain dangers to be avoided. Among these are the attitude that we have all the answers or that our way of living should be used as a yard-stick with which to measure any nation's progress, the bizarre and glamorous approach, the idea of uncritical good will and sentimentality which says that nations do not have their own troubles, a superficial approach through the one- or two-day studies of countries, and the attempt to get children to find definite answers to the problems of countries when experts are not at all certain as to these problems.

At the heart of any study of another country or culture should be the desire to understand it and appreciate its strengths and weaknesses and its place in the world-wide community of our day. Such an aim may sound simple, but it will call for the most effective teaching that can be carried on.

Preschool and Primary Grades

Although countries are not studied as such in the early school years, some awareness can be developed that the world is divided into parts which are called nations. A few of them can be mentioned and located on the globe which should be available in a primary-grade class as the names of different countries are discovered.

Primary children in these years should be gaining a sense of identification with the United States. They should begin to realize, however, that there are other countries besides their own. They can begin to realize that their story-book friend Heidi lives in a country called Switzerland and that their friend Dee-Dee lives in another part of the globe called China. With careful guidance, Switzerland can become to them a land with many mountains, a great deal of snow, beautiful lakes, interesting tunnels, and such products as cheese, watches, and toys. China can become to them a very large place with many, many people who are like us and also different.

An even better introduction to countries can be through the people children meet from other parts of the globe. Quite quickly the countries from which their friends come can be associated in the minds of children with those friends.

The flags of other nations may be displayed or made, not because they are so important, but because they are symbols or "tags" which help children to identify other parts of the world.

Through these and other experiences, young children can begin to identify the different colors of the world on a map or globe and associate them with people and activities, rather than seeing them merely as bright-colored spots on a big ball.

The Middle Grades

Children of the middle grades can begin to study countries, although it is probably better if such work is postponed at least until the fourth grade.

At this point boys and girls should begin to understand what is meant by countries and to identify them on maps and globes. They should gain some knowledge of the major characteristics of a few nations, preferably ones not too different from their own, and learn about the many factors which have marked their development. They should learn about some of the things each nation does well and how nations are changing, some of them becoming industrialized or semi-industrialized.

Children need to know how proud the people of each country are of their nation, how children learn the ways of their own lands, and how varied conditions are within each of the countries studied.

Above all they should be learning to understand and respect the people of these countries.

The concept of cultures is much too difficult for children in this stage of development and should be postponed at least until the junior high school years, although the similarities between some nations can be discovered earlier.

A wide variety of activities should be used in conjunction with the study of any country, including opportunities to meet people from those lands, films and filmstrips, books about the country, and many activities growing out of reading and other experiences.

Considerable use should be made of maps, some of which should be constructed by the children themselves. Class scrapbooks are preferred over individual notebooks to encourage cooperation and to eliminate or minimize the all too common practice of many parents, with the interest or means, of purchasing materials for their children's scrapbooks in order that Johnny or Susie can have a prettier notebook than the others.

Hearing or singing the music of the nations studied, playing their games, performing a few of their simple dances, trying to reproduce some of their arts and crafts, and to cook according to their recipes, are activities which should be encouraged. Some teachers may find that the playing of national anthems of the countries being studied, with the children listening to the music or marching to it after a brief explanation of it, will help boys and girls to feel as the children of another country feel when their group song is played or sung.

The practice in many schools of introducing China as one of the first countries to be studied seems unrealistic. It has such a long history, such different customs from ours, and such a deep involvement in Confucianism—which young children cannot cope with—that it should be postponed.

Among the materials available for these grades the *World Geography Readers* of the Charles E. Merrill Company are especially recommended. They are brief, readable, well illustrated, and inexpensive. Likewise they exist on most of the countries which will be studied in the middle grades.

Two series of volumes on various countries which are suitable for many middle-grade readers are the books in the New World Neighbor series of D. C. Heath and the Picture Geography series of the Albert Whitman Company. Some pupils can use other volumes listed in the section of this chapter on the upper grades or noted in the Appendix. This is especially true of some of the volumes in the Let's Read About series of the Fideler Company and a few of the books in the Land and People series of Holiday House.

Teachers will find individual books listed in several bibliographies of children's books, such as *Aids to World Understanding for Ele-*

mentary *School Children*, edited by Eva Dratz; *A Bibliography of Books for Children*, published by the Association for Childhood Education; *Books Are Bridges*, prepared by the American Friends Service Committee; and *Literature and Music as Resources for Social Studies* by Ruth Tooze and Beatrice Krone.

It is of course impossible to list here all of the books which might be used, but a few volumes on countries which are similar to our own will be mentioned.

On England Clarke Hutton's *Picture History of Britain* has been widely used. Some pupils can read Geoffrey Trease's *Young Traveler in England and Wales*, even though it is intended for older readers.

On Canada there are Vernon Quinn's *Picture Map Geography of Canada and Alaska*, Lilian Strack's *Crossing Canada*, Clare Bice's *Across Canada*, and H. B. Clifford's *Canada, My Neighbor*.

On Scandinavia Hector O'Neill has produced *The Picture Book of Denmark*, *The Picture Book of Norway*, and *The Picture Book of Sweden*. There is a volume, too, in the Land and People series of Holiday House on Scandinavia.

Typical of the better recent volumes on other countries are Regina Tor's *Getting to Know Puerto Rico*, Lily Edelman's *Japan in Story and Pictures*, and Helen Mears' *The First Book of Japan*.

Illustrative material is available from the "Units of Teaching Pictures" of the Informative Classroom Picture Publishers, on Alaska, Australia, Brazil, Canada, China, the Hawaiian Islands, India, Mexico, South America, and the Soviet Union. Two of the best resource units for these grades are *If You Were a Child in Korea* published by the American Friends Service Committee and *Hawaii for Today's Children: A Resource Unit for Grades 4, 5, and 6*, prepared by the Education Department of the University of Hawaii.

Among the many films on countries, those in The Earth and Its People series of the United World Films, the Films of the Nations series, and the Julien Bryan productions of the International Film Foundation are worthy of special mention.

Many filmstrips are available from the American Geographical Society, the Encyclopedia Britannica, the Informative Classroom Picture Publishers, *The New York Times* (on current events in various nations), the Society for Visual Education, and Young America, to mention companies with series.

Many articles in current events magazines for children should also be used and saved from year to year for future reference.

The Upper Grades

It is chiefly in the upper grades and in junior high schools that children should come to grips with the concept of countries and be introduced to the concept of cultures. Time and space are no longer so confused in the minds of these boys and girls and the importance of world events can be comprehended better by them.

Many of the ideas mentioned in the two previous parts of this chapter will need to be reiterated and reinforced. Such ideas as the changes in countries, their adaptability, the variations within nations, the large number of factors which influence countries, and the importance of small nations can be stressed and many illustrations found of each of these ideas.

The rise of nationalism and some of the problems which it has brought can often be treated in the ninth grade with more gifted pupils. A beginning can be made in an analysis of imperialism and colonialism as important factors in the world scene today. And the interdependence of nations can be highlighted.

Pupils at this point need to begin to think in terms of groups of nations, even though the concept of cultures will be left for detailed discussion to the senior high school years.

Countries which are different from ours should be studied at this point in the curriculum, with special emphasis upon such important nations as Brazil, China, India, Japan, and Russia.

Charts and graphs of income and food as well as the facts of resources and world trade can be used in developing several important concepts. Current events study should be intensified and daily newspapers used frequently. A great deal of reading should be done in a variety of sources, with comparisons of what authors say. Audio-visual materials, trips, and contacts with persons from abroad should not be neglected.

Wherever possible the geography and history of various areas of the world should be combined. Eventually it is hoped that a two-year sequence of world geography and world history can become an integral part of the social studies or core programs of many schools in the eighth and ninth or ninth and tenth grades, with a chronological study within units on different geographical areas growing out of an introductory approach based on current problems in those parts of the world.

There are many series of books or booklets suitable for upper-grade readers. Each of these series emphasizes certain aspects of countries. The volumes in the Holiday House Land and People series are brief, are illustrated with drawings in color, and do not have any of the feeling of textbooks. The books in the Good Neighbor series, limited to Latin America, are also brief, inexpensive, and colorful. The "Made in . . ." series stresses the arts and crafts of countries. Probably the most comprehensive in scope are the Portraits of Nations books. A full listing of the titles in each series is given in Appendix B, as an aid to teachers, librarians, and others.

For folk tales on the various countries the Friendship Press series on "Tales from . . ." is especially good, with volumes on Africa, China, India, Latin-America, and Southeast Asia. The American Geographical Society and Doubleday have just begun a group of excellent booklets with colored pictures to paste into each pamphlet, the *Around the World* series.

There are of course scores of books dealing with countries, which do not appear in any series. Among the many recent volumes are Margueritte Harmon Bro's *Indonesia: Land of Challenge*, Jean Bothwell's *The Story of India*, and Regina Tor's *Getting to Know Puerto Rico*.

There are helpful novels and travel books, poems and essays, biographies, and other types of books on most parts of the world. There are some areas of the world, however, on which books are badly needed. This is especially true of certain countries of the Middle East, on Pakistan, Indonesia, Ceylon, Burma, and Thailand, and on parts of Africa. There was a spate of new books on Latin America a few years ago, but few have appeared in the 1950's to bring the story of these lands up to date.

Films and filmstrips in great abundance are now available for most countries. These have been mentioned in the middle-grades section of this chapter.

Background Materials for Teachers

Every teacher who is helping children to discover the world should subscribe to the Headline series of the Foreign Policy Association, a monthly series of booklets, most of which are on individual countries. Also recommended is *Focus*, a six- to eight-page monthly publication of the American Geographical Society.

Still heavier reading would be the volumes in the Harvard American Foreign Policy Library series, edited by Sumner Welles, with each book bearing the title *The United States and* . . .

Resource units on various countries have been prepared by several companies and organizations, as well as by many school systems, some of which are listed in Appendix A. These may be helpful if used as suggested materials rather than as guides to be strictly followed.

Many of the Embassies and Information Services of governments provide materials free to schools and loan films for a nominal fee. The British and French governments have especially large collections from which teachers may draw. A list of addresses of such governmental sources appears in Appendix C.

Special help to teachers on all countries of the Western Hemisphere except Canada is given by the Pan-American Union. Over the years this organization has produced a wealth of useable materials of many kinds for schools, and teachers should make wide use of their offerings.

An extensive listing may be found in the writer's booklet on *Free and Inexpensive Materials on World Affairs*.

A helpful service could be performed by various organizations if they would prepare kits for teachers on numerous countries selling for one dollar or less. To the writer's knowledge, the World Affairs Council of Northern California is the only group to date which has developed such a service.

Studying other countries and cultures is an enormous topic and teachers need to be clear about their objectives or they will become bogged down in a mass of details. It merits far more attention and far better teaching than has been given it in the past by most schools.

In a society that has discovered the "know-how" of Amalthea's cornucopia, the always ugly inequality in the distribution of this world's goods, in ceasing to be a practical necessity, has become a moral enormity.

—Arnold Toynbee, *Civilization on Trial*

Our ancients said, "People are the foundation of the nation. If the foundation is firm, then the nation will enjoy tranquility." I apply that to the whole world. If the foundation is firm, then the world will enjoy tranquility. But three-fourths of the world's peoples today are underhoused, under-clothed, under-fed, and illiterate. . . . Now so long as that continues to be true, we have a very poor foundation upon which to build the world.

—James Yen, to a UNESCO Seminar, Paris, 1947

A man who does not have enough to feed and clothe himself and his family and to look into the future with a certain amount of confidence may be a dangerous man to his society. Groups of people denied benefits they see other people enjoying may cause trouble. A "have-not" nation endangers the security of its more fortunate neighbors.

—William Buchanan and Hadley Cantril,
How Nations See Each Other

Every gun that is made, every warship launched, every rocket fired signifies, in the final sense, a theft from those who hunger and are not fed, those who are cold and are not clothed.

—Dwight Eisenhower, April 4, 1953

. . . the evil institutions of human society are most likely to be reformed when two conditions are fulfilled. The first is that the institution should be economically unprofitable. The second is that it should be morally intolerable. —Kenneth Boulding, *New Nations for Old*

Industrialization of the underdeveloped areas of the world is perhaps the most formidable task confronting mankind today.

—Harrison Brown, *The Challenge of Man's Future*

Food is the starting place. If we cannot work together there, we cannot work together on anything.

—John Boyd-Orr

——————————————————— Chapter 10

A World of Poverty and Plenty

During their earlier years children need to be introduced to a nonthreatening world. But what a distorted view of the world they would have if their education about the world ended there!

Unfortunately the world in which they live now and will continue to live is a world of both poverty and plenty. This is not a pretty picture to paint or to view, but eventually children must see it, understand it, be challenged by it, and learn how they can help now and in the years ahead to improve it.

Parents and teachers will do well to postpone the full view of this picture of poverty, disease, malnutrition, ignorance, injustice, and illiteracy. Children have enough problems of their own to solve in obtaining security and a place in the sun, without adding more weight to their shoulders. Yet, gradually, children must discover this unequal world in all its ugliness.

By the time they have reached the junior high school, they ought to have been confronted with the fact that most of the world is ill-fed, ill-housed, ill-clothed, illiterate, and ill, together with what these facts imply. Without such basic knowledge of our global

147

society, how can they understand the appeal of communism to millions of persons, how can they understand the revolutions around the world today, how can they understand the wars which continue to break out here and there, how can they understand the problems in connection with United States foreign policy, and how can they understand a large proportion of the work of the United Nations?

There are many ramifications to this theme of poverty and plenty, but there are also a few central concepts which should help parents and teachers to see the woods rather than hundreds of trees, saplings, and shrubs. These central ideas should enable persons working with children to develop some focal points in this difficult but important aspect of the world scene.

Most important is the idea that poverty exists in every country of the world. Abysmal, unbelievable poverty is widespread, involving approximately two-thirds of the world's people. Tonight two out of every three persons in the world will go to bed hungry either because there is not enough food or because it is so poorly distributed.

On the top rung of the ladder of caloric intake, with 3000 or more calories per person per day, stand Argentina, Australia, Canada, Denmark, Finland, Iceland, Ireland, The Netherlands, New Zealand, Norway, Sweden, Switzerland, the United Kingdom, and the United States. On the bottom rungs of the ladder stand the rest of the world with their near-starvation rations. This is a staggering and sobering statement about our world today.

Two-thirds of the world has an average life expectancy of around thirty years as compared with sixty-five or more in such countries as The Netherlands, Australia, New Zealand, the Scandinavian countries, the United Kingdom, and the United States.

The figures of annual per capita income for various parts of the world are also arresting. The most recent United Nations figures place the United States at the top with $1453 per person per year, followed by Western Europe with $473, Latin America with $152, Africa with $118, the Middle East with $89, South Asia with $55, and Southeast Asia with $30. Since these figures were released, the income per person in the United States has risen to over $2300 per person per year. Even making allowance for many differences not taken into account by these figures, the gulf between us and the rest of the world is alarmingly wide. What this means in housing, health, clothing, education, and other aspects of life can be judged more concretely if one attempts to make out a yearly budget for a family of five, six, or seven with around $50 per person. In this connection it is important to bear in mind that the figures given above are averages, because millions of persons earn far less than the figures given.

Allied to this fact of low income is the realization that the rich countries are growing proportionately richer and the poor countries poorer.

In this connection it is important for children to discover that all nations are not similarly endowed. Many of them have rich resources which can be developed; China, India, Ethiopia, and Nigeria are four such examples. The economic potential of others, such as Pakistan and Paraguay, is relatively low. It is true that the United States has become the richest nation of the world partly because of the inventive genius and hard work of its people. It is well to remember, however, that this country is also richly endowed with natural resources.

Boys and girls should become aware that the ugly aspects of life in our world today are often evidence that people have not cared about their world neighbors. Much of the squalor of the world is the result of selfishness and greed in its worst forms. Where people have neglected to care for the earth, have squandered its resources, or have prevented others from having a decent level of living, poverty, disease, ignorance, malnutrition, and similar deplorable conditions have resulted.

Children should learn, too, that such extreme poverty does not need to exist. In all parts of the world people have begun to realize that basic fact and are acting upon it. Perhaps the Bandung Conference of 1955 was one of the most dramatic symbols of the revolt against poverty and its fellow-travelers, inasmuch as a desire for better standards of living was one of the factors which bound the representatives of the Asian and African countries together at that meeting.

Closely related to the foregoing concepts is a fifth: such conditions of poverty are a threat to world peace and security. Under-

150 INTRODUCING CHILDREN TO THE WORLD

developed areas of the world are open to exploitation and to rivalries between major powers. Eventually such rivalries lead to tensions or war. Often the people of these underprivileged areas become restless, demanding their rights and thus causing further imbalance in the world. A recognition of these facts led to the formation of several of the specialized agencies of the United Nations as a part of that organization's attempts to promote peace and security, whether through the Food and Agriculture Organization, the World Health Organization, or the Trusteeship Council.

A sixth idea to be developed is the fact that there are many ways of alleviating poverty. These range all the way from communism to capitalism, with a large part of the world making its approach through some form of socialism. Children need to understand that, whatever their political and social implications, each of these forms of economy is being used in the attempt to raise standards of living. They should also discover how each of these economic ideologies is competing in the international market place for the chance to prove that its way is best.

Boys and girls need to know, moreover, that much progress is being made in improving living standards, even though more progress in more places and at a faster rate is desperately needed. They should learn about the Technical Assistance Program of the United Nations, the Colombo Plan of the British Commonwealth, the Point Four Program of the United States, and the work of many individual governments. Attention should also be called to the work of nongovernmental organizations.

Wherever possible examples of what children are doing to raise the standards of living of the world should be cited. One of the most easily understood ways is the work of children in Israel in planting hundreds of thousands of trees to help hold the water and soil of that long eroded land. An outstanding example of what one child can do is the story of a young girl in Norway at the time of Albert Schweitzer's visit there to receive the Nobel Peace Prize. Wondering what she could do to help, she wrote a letter to the labor paper, *Arbeiderbladet*, suggesting that a special fund be raised to give to Dr. Schweitzer for his work in Africa. Within three days $43,000 had been pledged.

Closely allied to this last concept is the idea that there are many ways in which improvements may come, ranging from such simple changes as adding metal points to wooden plows to large loans for the building of dams and factories.

Another idea which should be developed, even though it can be done only in an elementary way, is that all people do not want to change. Many persons find it difficult to alter their ways of living. Likewise, all kinds of problems result from urbanization, industrialization, and even from seemingly slight changes in agriculture and sanitation.

Finally, boys and girls need to be given opportunities to act upon their new-found knowledge about the world of poverty and plenty. Schools need to keep in mind their responsibility to provide even small projects by which children and youth can contribute to the aid of others less fortunate than themselves.

Obviously most of these concepts cannot be developed in detail, but a beginning can be made in elementary and junior high schools.

Children need to learn about the world of poverty and plenty in simple language, with vivid illustrations, in an atmosphere of caring and loving. Otherwise these concepts can cause damage, such as a sense of guilt about the squalor, suffering, and strife in the world, or a feeling of frustration because the child does not know what he can do about such conditions.

Teachers also need to bear in mind the fact that all of the world's problems cannot be solved by economic measures. Perhaps one of the gravest dangers today in the United States is the feeling that almost any problem can be solved with money and technical assistance. People need to be helped to lead more productive lives, but they also need to be helped to lead more purposeful lives.

Preschool and Primary Grade Children

Poverty and plenty as words mean nothing to young children, but as concepts in everyday living they may mean much. Early in life boys and girls learn that some children in their own neighborhoods and communities have more money than others, live in better homes, have more food, go to more places, and do more things.

Teachers should not develop in detail the concepts listed in this chapter, but they should begin to help form the basic attitudes on which others will build general ideas about the world of poverty and plenty. Children need to be permitted and encouraged by parents and teachers to accept other people no matter what their economic or social status may be. They need to know some of the reasons people are poor and to understand that poor people are not necessarily ignorant or without ability. Furthermore they should learn early that poverty is not a sound basis upon which to judge people. They need to learn that poor people have contributed much to the world and that some of them have even become famous, like Booker T. Washington and Vincent Van Gogh. They need to understand that people need help of many kinds and that they can help each other.

As they read accounts of children in other lands, look at pictures, and see films and filmstrips about them, boys and girls can begin to realize that their peers in other parts of the world are also rich or poor. Through such a story as that of Antonia in *The Poppy Seeds*, they can learn how other children have helped to make their communties a better place to live.

Through books such as Munro Leaf's *Fair Play* and *Let's Do Better* they can begin to appreciate the importance of justice long before they hear the term used. Similarly, they can develop a desire to help in small ways. Through school-wide projects with the neighborhood or community, they can participate in helping to improve the places in which they live. And through sharing in school or community projects for the Red Cross, UNICEF, UNESCO, the American Friends Service Committee, or other world-wide service organizations, children can begin to identify themselves with people around the globe, learning to help people in trouble no matter where they are.

Most of all, they need to live in an atmosphere where kindness and friendship are practiced and poverty entails no penalties.

The Middle Grades

Much more can be done in the middle grades toward developing the concepts mentioned already in this chapter. These boys and girls can learn about the existence of poverty and plenty in the world either through units on various phases of life around the world or by their study of countries. They can begin to understand why some people and nations are poor and others rich and how this has caused trouble not only between people but between nations. Most of all, they can learn something about the resources of the various countries studied and how nations are trying to better living conditions for their citizens. Through service projects they can help other people locally and nationally and in some cases internationally.

Stories, books, current events papers, films and filmstrips, pictures, the construction of typical homes and villages in dioramas, and the making of simple charts and graphs will expose children to these ideas.

There is a great need for many kinds of materials to develop the concepts of a world of poverty and plenty with this age group. *People Are People* is one excellent series of filmstrips to illustrate these ideas. Some of the materials in the *Junior Red Cross Journal* are helpful as are some of the articles and pictures in current events papers.

More books are needed such as Claire and George Louden's *Rain in the Winds: A Story of India*. In this book Moti, an elephant, is rented to a visitor to an Indian village in return for much-needed rice and water. The original owner's son, Arun, sets out to find Moti and finally locates the elephant working on an irrigation dam. The story is delightfully told, yet introduces children to important ideas about Indian village life and attempts to improve living there. The first part of the book is printed in brown and the second part in brown and green to carry out the theme of new life for Indian villages through irrigation projects.

Some of the materials mentioned in Chapter XIII, on "International Conflict and Cooperation," can also be used in connection with this theme, such as the book and filmstrip *A Garden We Planted Together*.

The Upper Grades to a World of Poverty and Plenty

Primarily the concepts outlined in this chapter should be studied in the upper grades and in senior high schools. A unit on A World of Poverty and Plenty would be quite appropriate in the junior high school either in a core program or in a social studies class. Much use can be made of committee projects and individual reports on various phases of this theme, especially for gifted pupils.

Files of source materials should be started by teachers and pupils, bringing together clippings from newspapers, magazines, and current events papers which illustrate this basic concept.

Here is another field which publishers might well explore with the purpose of producing picture sets and pamphlets for the upper grades.

Considerable attention should be given in these upper-grade years to general conditions around the world in regard to income, food, health, housing, and education. Comparative charts and graphs illustrating these phases of life in many countries can be helpful and lead to discussions as to why people and nations are rich and poor and what happens as a result of poverty locally, nationally, and internationally.

Such factors as the location of countries, their basic resources, their stage of industrialization, their history as colonial powers or as colonies, their transportation facilities, their educational opportunities, and their customs and traditions should be examined.

Some attention can be given to the idea that the gap between rich and poor countries is widening despite improvements in the economically underdeveloped nations. Stress should be laid on the fact that poverty does not need to exist and that economic, social, and political dislocations occur as a result of squalor, malnutrition, disease, ignorance, and illiteracy.

Prominence needs to be given to the progress that is being made in many parts of the world and to some of the problems that increased standards of living bring in their wake. Among the many methods being used to improve general conditions around the world are the use of domestic and foreign capital; loans by the United Nations Bank, governments, and private investors; the use of submarginal land and the improvement of agriculture in many ways; the building of irrigation projects and industries; the improvement of farm tools and machinery; the introduction of better seeds and methods of farming; research of many kinds; the improvement of village and city sanitation and housing; programs of fundamental education; the education of nurses and doctors; and the use of planning in communities, nations, and the world.

Boys and girls need to know that people are helping themselves and are not merely relying on gifts from abroad to raise general economic conditions in their communities and countries.

The concept of the disruptions which follow such changes is a difficult one for upper-grade children to grasp and should not be developed in detail, although it should be introduced at this point.

With upper-grade children there should be great emphasis upon service projects. The desire of the early adolescent "to do something" and his interest in identifying with adults should be capitalized upon in projects ranging from the Heifer project to the Magazines for Friendship program and from UNICEF drives to participation in World Health Day, United Nations Day, and Pan-American Day. In situations where junior high school graduating classes make a gift to the school at commencement, consideration should be given to gifts that will help people in some other part of the world, the particular area to be determined by the pupils.

A few materials have begun to appear which are suitable for this age group, but there is plenty of room for new resources to develop the general concept of a world of poverty and plenty. Margueritte Harmon Bro's book *Su-Mei's Golden Year* is the story of a young Chinese whose father proposes the use of modern agricultural methods to the villagers. They turn him down; but nevertheless Su-Mei plants, cares for, and then saves the experimental plot of wheat and proves his father right. A somewhat similar story takes place in Guatemala in Mary and Conrad Buff's *Magic Maize* where Fabian, an Indian boy, plants the new corn of the "gringos" and shows the farmers of his area how they can improve their output. This book is enhanced by the full-page color drawings of life in Guatemala. Some students will profit from Arthur Goodfriend's book *The Only War We Seek*, portraying low living standards around the world graphically and poignantly. Others may enjoy Christy Borth's *Pioneers of Plenty* or Cynthia Bowles' *At Home in India*.

Among the books on the work of the United Nations are Graham Beckel's *Workshops for the World*, Dorothy Canfield Fisher's *Pool* of *Knowledge: How the United Nations Share Their Skills*, and Elizabeth Yates' *Rainbow Round the World* (on UNICEF).

Films such as *Indonesia Builds a Better Life*, and the UNESCO production *World Without End* (on Mexico and Thailand) can be used with most junior high school groups. The U.N. film *A Village Awakens* tells the story of a road built in a Greek village, as the beginning of a series of local improvements. A similar film on Nigeria is *Daybreak in Udi*, in which a maternity hospital is built by the local Africans.

A good filmstrip is "East Africa Tackles the Land Problem."

Posters and charts from the specialized agencies of the U.N. can be effective in presenting some of the problems of poverty around the world and some of the progress that is being made. Materials from the information offices of several governments also describe progress. Pictures from the *UNESCO Courier* and from current magazines and newspapers can be clipped and used on bulletin boards and in opaque projectors.

Better learning will usually take place when pupils prepare such materials themselves. Added incentive will be given if the best materials are saved and used in succeeding years with other classes.

Children should be encouraged to take part in some action projects for improvements in other parts of the globe. They may want to send a plow to an underdeveloped area through CARE, participate in the Pan-American Union's program to distribute Fundamental Education booklets on pure water or safe milk in Latin America, prepare and send school supplies to Italy and Korea through the American Friends Service Committee, or help to build a house in Korea.

As background for their work in this field teachers will find such volumes as Chester Bowles' *Ambassador's Report* (on India) and Earl Hanson's *Transformation: The Story of Modern Puerto Rico* full of valuable information on what two nations are doing to improve conditions.

In our relations with other nations we of the United States are peculiarly handicapped in our understanding of the world of poverty and plenty. As Justice Douglas has pointed out in his volume on

Strange Lands and Friendly People, "to Asians America is too powerful to co-operate and too rich to understand them."

Everything that can be done to help children (and adults) to understand the world of poverty and plenty needs to be done and done now. This is a difficult concept to develop but an important one for the well-being of the United States and of the world community.

Where the mind is without fear and the head is held high;
Where knowledge is free;
Where the world has not been broken up into fragments by narrow
domestic walls;
Where words come out from the depths of truth;
Where tireless striving stretches its arms towards perfection;
Where the clear stream of reason has not lost its way into the dreary
desert sands of dead habit;
Where the mind is led forward by Thee into ever-widening thought
and action—
Into that heaven of freedom, my Father, let my country awake.

—RABINDRANATH TAGORE

I deeply believe in the capacity of democracy to surmount any trials that
may lie ahead, provided only we practice it in our daily lives. And among
the things we must practice is that, while we seek fervently to ferret
out the subversive and anti-democratic forces in the country, we do not
at the same time, by hysteria, by resort to innuendo and smears, and
unfortunate tactics, besmirch the very cause we believe in, and cause a
separation among our people, cause one group and one individual to
hate another based on mere attacks, mere unsubstantiated attacks upon
their loyalty.

—DAVID E. LILIENTHAL, *Creed of an American*

If we are to win the cold war, we must start at home with a new dedica-
tion to the ideal of democracy. Here is a great chance for the schools of
our country to create a new generation which knows the meaning of
democracy. The schools should teach our children why our ancestors
came to this country, why they sought freedom from European domination, and what the Constitution, and particularly the Bill of Rights,
means to us as individuals. We must ourselves have a clear understanding
of and faith in the ideals which are the foundation of our nation before
we can persuade other peoples to follow our leadership rather than that
of Moscow. Thus a sound education in our own national heritage is a
first requirement in an effective system of education for good international relations.

—OLIVER CALDWELL, *Education in a Free World*

Chapter 11

A World with Many Forms of Government

Charges and countercharges hurled back and forth by the governments of the Middle East over a border incident, changes of cabinet ministers in Great Britain, or elections in Indonesia, visits of Ministers of Foreign Affairs from Germany or Japan to Washington, campaign speeches in the United States filled with references to foreign policy—these and scores of similar events are featured over television, headlined in the newspapers, and bandied about over the coffee cups in homes throughout the United States.

The children may be reading comic books, pleading for another program on television, or fighting over whose turn it is to do the dishes. Nevertheless, they hear these strange expressions and take in far more than adults surmise.

Some boys and girls let these matters slide as just so much adult patter. Others are bewildered by the scraps of information they have heard and failed to piece together. A few are intrigued by the little they have learned and are ready for more—if teachers or parents have time or the needed background to help them understand these current events.

Eventually all boys and girls need to learn about the role of governments in many parts of the world today, including the government of their own nation. Introducing them to this aspect of life in the world community will not be easy, but neither can it be ignored. Governments are increasingly important and boys and girls need to learn as much about them as their maturity permits, with actual experiences in government as much as possible and within the scope of their abilities.

No introduction to the world today is complete until children have begun to understand the variety of governments in the world, some of the more elementary interactions between them, and the place they play in the lives of everyone on this globe.

Some Basic Concepts to be Developed

By the end of the junior high school years there are a large number of concepts about government which pupils should have grasped.

Grouped together and arranged somewhat in the order of their difficulty, the following concepts seem important for exploration in the elementary and junior high school years. The phraseology in which they are couched is of course intended for teachers and will need to be adjusted radically for younger pupils. The ways in which these ideas may be developed will be left to later parts of this chapter. Here, then, are some of the basic concepts about governments for teachers to bear in mind in introducing children to the world:

1. Groups of people everywhere organize themselves into governments. People do this today and have always done so.
2. These governments are very important. They are organized to help people in many ways, with some governments more concerned about their citizens than others.
3. We live in a democracy where people decide things for themselves or through elected representatives. Our government attempts to abide by the will of the majority, with protection for its minorities.
4. We should be proud of our democratic way of life and want to make the United States an even better place in which to live.
5. Many of our ideas of government were obtained from people in other countries and several nations have adopted aspects of our government in their countries.
6. There are many forms of government in the world today, includ-

ing monarchies, constitutional monarchies, social democracies, capitalistic democracies, fascist regimes, and Communist governments.

7. The form of government in any country is determined by many factors, among which are its economic status, its religion or religions, and its history.

8. Several nations have recently won their independence and have set up their own governments. Others are still demanding independence and a chance to form their own independent regimes.

9. There is a great deal of competition around the world today between the various forms of government. This competition has caused "cold wars" and actual warfare.

10. All governments have problems to solve and will continue to have problems in the future. Governments, however, do solve some problems.

11. Over the centuries governments have been organized for larger and larger groups of people, ranging in size from clans and tribes to whole nations.

12. There are some regional governmental organizations in the world today, plus the United Nations and its agencies.

There are of course additional concepts which a few pupils can handle. One is the fact that many countries have a democratic tradition, especially at the local level, whether they are democratic in their national government or not. Another is the fact that radical changes in governments often disrupt existing societies and that changes in national governments do not always bring changes at the village or town level for a long time. Still another concerns the various ways in which parties are organized in democratic nations, ranging from those organized around ideas to those developed around the personalities of leaders. These and similar concepts cannot be developed with most pupils, but they can be challenging to superior students.

The over-all aims in introducing children to governments here and abroad are to help boys and girls to see the necessity of some kind of government, to see the variety of governments in the world and some of the reasons for them, and to begin to understand why Americans feel that the democratic way of life is the most desirable pattern eventually for all people everywhere.

Only a few of these ideas can even be introduced in the preschool and primary grades. Most of them can be introduced in the intermediate grades and the first four developed somewhat. By the time pupils have reached the upper grades all of these ideas can be introduced and developed at some depth.

Preschool and Primary Grade Children

A major aim of the preschool and primary grades is to foster good group living. All the experiences which children have in these years can contribute to the development of social relationships, whether they are reliving home situations, acting out visits to the grocery store or doctor's, playing games, singing or doing rhythms, or sitting around in a reading circle while the teacher tells them stories or reads aloud to them.

Such activities may seem far removed from the study of governments around the world, but these experiences in living with others are the abc's of government. Through them children learn the give and take of everyday living, learn to make rules and to abide by them, learn to respect constituted authority—and sometimes learn that there are penalties attached to disobedience of the laws of the classroom and school.

Children in these early years need to learn to think about the rights of others through a variety of shared experiences. They need to be given opportunities to propose alternative activities and to vote on them. At the same time they need to be introduced to the method of consensus, whereby a variety of activities is planned to meet the individual differences of large groups. This approach is an even more complicated one than voting and is a more refined application of the theory of democracy in action.

Children need to learn through experience and through discussion that government also involves responsibilities. Teachers concerned with this important phase of democratic living will provide as many different opportunities in the classroom as is possible so that all the boys and girls can take their part in helping the group.

As these experiences are planned and carried out, teachers and pupils can learn that people everywhere organize themselves into groups, which are like clubs or classes, and make laws or rules for themselves.

On trips to school and to various places in the community they can see that governments help people in various ways, from providing traffic lights and policemen to inspecting the milk they drink and the candy they eat.

By voting and by consensus, children can learn the ways of democracy long before they have any real understanding of the term itself.

Through celebrations and discussions, songs and dramatics, they can develop pride in their own community, state, and nation. Current events can show them that there are problems with which governments wrestle, whether they are trying to integrate the schools or provide better garbage collection and cleaner streets.

As introductory studies are made of children in other parts of the world, the idea that they live under governments can be introduced. Children can also learn that their friends in other parts of the world are proud of their countries and their governments, without having to know just what kind of governments they live under or how they work.

The resources for such elementary studies of government are the classroom, school, and community, and the group activities that go on in these basic social groups. Books about children in other lands will not tell specifically about governments in those nations, but they sometimes show the ways in which children in other lands regard their own countries.

Three books used successfully by teachers in the primary grades in this general area are Edith Lowe's *Animal Parade*, Mina Turner's *Town Meeting Means Me*, and Munro Leaf's *Fair Play*.

Questions will certainly arise in most classrooms about communism, socialism, and other big words which children hear from time to time. Teachers can answer such questions briefly by saying that they are names for the ways in which people in some parts of the world vote and run their government. It is not the teacher's responsibility in these early years to elaborate on these ideas or to condemn them in words or tone of voice. Such indoctrination is contrary to the concept of democracy whereby people have a chance to examine the merits and demerits of an idea before passing judgment on it.

The Middle Grades

Several of the concepts which have been introduced in the pre-school and primary grades can be developed at greater depth in the intermediate grades and most of the other concepts listed in the early paragraphs of this chapter can be introduced at this level, especially by the fifth grade.

As boys and girls start their studies of various countries around the world they will discover that people everywhere organize themselves into governments now and have done so in the past. They will learn that some groups of people are organized as families, with the elders making the rules or laws. They will learn that there have been kings in many parts of the world and that there are still several countries with kings and queens, even though some of them do not have much say in the government, as in England and in the Scandinavian countries. They will learn that railroads, mines, telephone and telegraph companies, and other businesses in some nations are owned solely by the governments or at least in part by them, an introduction for them of the idea of socialism. They will also come across the concept of communism as they make their way around the world and read and hear about current events in various parts of the globe.

As children discover that there are different forms of government in the world, they need to be helped to understand why these many forms of organization developed. Without delving deep into the history of these countries, children can learn that there are many ways of organizing groups, just as they have different ways of making decisions in the classroom, on the playground, in the school, and in the community. These different ways have grown up as a result of the history of the various countries, as a result of the schools they have had or because they did not have schools, as a result of their ideas about religion, or because of their wealth or lack of wealth.

Certainly the governments of the world cannot be understood without knowing something about the industrial revolution and colonialism. Boys and girls in the elementary and junior high school grades are not ready for a full-scale study of these important and difficult terms, but they can learn that the factories of England and other countries needed raw materials and that people went to Africa and Asia to obtain these materials, taking over the governments of large areas in the process.

They can also learn something of the resentment and bitterness of people who do not rule themselves and the demand for independence. Probably the best way to explain this concept is to relate it to their desire to help in making the rules of their classroom or school or to have some small part in decisions made in their families.

As children begin their study of the United States and its history, they can see how our democratic government arose and how its leaders got many of their ideas from ancient Greece, from Rome, from England, from France, and from other parts of the world.

As they study the life of the early American Indians they can learn that some groups of Indians had a democratic form of government, even though teachers will not want to belabor this idea.

Through their elementary study of American history, boys and girls can begin to understand how our idea of democracy has grown. One vivid illustration would be to see who could vote in colonial days and who can vote now, letting children discover that the vote was largely limited to white men, persons over twenty-one years of age, property holders, and church members. By comparisons with the situation today, they can see that democracy is an idea which grows from generation to generation and that we have not reached perfection in applying it even now.

The elementary study of current events in the community, state, and nation can help children to discover that governments wrestle with all kinds of problems and solve many of them after years and years of working on them. Children need to learn early that there are problems still to be solved and that there always will be problems.

Current events can also open up in a simple way the competition around the world between various forms of government. Only if children have learned how people around the globe live can they understand even in a rudimentary way why there is such a thing as communism in the world. Without going into details about the theories behind this form of government, children in the fourth or fifth grades can understand that people who are poor and not used to deciding things for themselves often believe that a government of this kind will work faster to bring them better conditions of living—even though performance is not always as great as the promises made to them.

In these years children can also learn that new forms of governments have been developed as people settled down to live in villages and towns instead of wandering from place to place as the nomadic peoples did for long periods of time. They can learn that some nations are relatively new and that regional governmental organizations are quite new. Certainly they will need to learn something about the United Nations and its agencies, a subject which is developed in Chapter 13.

Materials for the middle grades on these concepts are still limited. So far as the writer can find, there is no book which tells in simple terms about governments in various parts of the world. Geography and history textbooks touch on this topic and some of the books on individual countries mention governments. But the resources for developing this concept through written materials, films, filmstrips, and other materials are strictly limited.

Teachers will find Erich Kastner and Walter Trier's *The Animal Conference* and the Giant Golden Book on *The Animal Fair* helpful in developing the concepts mentioned in this chapter. They will want to encourage class councils and participation in school government. They will want to make use of election time to show in a simple way how our government functions. They will want to encourage children to share in decisions democratically and to take their share of responsibility in classroom duties, helping with school programs of many kinds, taking part in safety patrols, or participating in service projects undertaken by the entire school or community. In this as in other phases of life, children learn what they live. More real experience in democratic living will go on in the day-to-day experiences of the home and school than in discussions about democracy as a way of life.

The Upper Grades

By the time boys and girls reach the upper grades, and especially the eighth and ninth years in school, they can really come to grips with the concepts outlined in this chapter. Every one of these ideas should be handled in these upper years even though the treatment will often have to be simple. Superior students should be given many opportunities to delve deep into several of these concepts, being challenged far more than some of them are at present.

It will be far easier for these older boys and girls to grasp the importance of governments past and present. Time and space are more meaningful to them and their wider experience in the world will help them to know that people cannot do just as they want but must have rules. As they study different governments they can learn how the concern of nations for their citizens varies.

Pride in their own country is an aim which should be stressed in all grades. At the junior high school level boys and girls can begin to see our own nation as others see us. They can be proud of the respect we have won in many parts of the world for our concept of democracy, our scientific know-how, our health and sanitation standards, our agriculture, our area planning such as the Tennessee Valley Authority, our education, and other phases of American life.

At the same time they need to know that many people abroad are critical of us. Only by knowing some of the points on which we are criticized can they understand international relations and seek to improve their own country. They can see that because of our place in the world and our form of government we live in a "goldfish bowl" or behind a picket fence rather than a high wall, in full view of the world.

Among the aspects of life on which we are criticized are our treatment of Negroes and other dark-skinned people, our curbs on freedom and our witch hunts, our frequent support of colonialism in such parts of the world as North Africa, and our concern about money and power. Pupils may want to read some of the critical statements of people in other parts of the world about us and teachers will undoubtedly want to explain these feelings. This is difficult without seeming unpatriotic to some, but capable teachers can present these as the comments of some of our world neighbors and help pupils understand why they feel as they do.

Wherever possible, boys and girls should be given opportunities to participate in action projects at their level of maturity, whether they be school traffic surveys, petitions for more playground space in the community, assistance in programs of integration in the schools, or a host of allied projects for the betterment of life locally and nationally.

As children compare and contrast the United States with other nations, they should learn about some of the factors which have led to the rapid rise of the United States as a nation. Among these are our geographical position, our land and resources, our climate, our educational system and democratic ideals, our development of good transportation and communication facilities, our hard work and inventive genius, our one national language, and our form of government.

In their history work they should learn of the debt which we owe to the people of other nations for our concepts of democracy and they can learn with pride of the influence of American democracy upon other countries, which ranges from admiration around the world for such figures as Jefferson, Lincoln, Wilson, and Franklin D. Roosevelt to the adaptation of many of our ideas of government in other lands.

The idea that there are many forms of government in the world and that these governments are in competition or conflict with each other must be faced in these upper grades. The writer has found it easier to develop these concepts if two approaches are used. One is to get pupils to try to think as though they were citizens for a short time of another nation. The boy or girl who realizes that he or she was introduced early in life to the importance of the Emperor by such festive occasions as the Japanese Doll Festival, when each child plays with the dolls representing this important family, will begin to understand how the children of Japan have been indoctrinated on the centrality of the Emperor and his family. If they realize that such children were taught in school to revere this person and to sing songs and take part in celebrations about the Emperor, they will begin to realize how the worship of the Emperor developed.

Or, if they try to make out a budget for an entire family on $150 to $250 a year, they will be more likely to understand the feeling of a Chinese peasant when he hears the promises of the Communists to give him land and raise his standard of living.

The other recommended approach is the use of a long line or continuum which represents the many governments of the world, ranging from fascist regimes on the one end to Communist governments on the other, with the various forms of democracy in the middle. If teachers want to show the similarities between fascist and Communist governments, they may find it better to use a horseshoe-like illustration, with fascism and communism coming closer together than on a continuum.

Teachers do not need to give pupils the idea that they approve of these various governments just because they are trying to understand why they exist in certain parts of the world. In fact, it is only the person who is firm in his adherence to democracy who can be free to understand the existence of other forms of government.

In this regard teachers will want to present the claims of democracy as the only form of government yet devised by mankind in which each person's capacities are developed to the highest possible point, in order that every person can contribute to the general welfare and share in the benefits of a democratic society.

In presenting such controversial issues, teachers would do well to develop the kind of rapport in the school and community which permits them to teach in this way. They have the right to speak freely and frankly, but they must earn the right to be listened to. This right is earned in large part by developing good rapport with parents and other adults in the community, with administrative officers in a school, and with pupils. Support for such teaching comes with active participation by teachers in community organizations which uphold and encourage the right in a democracy to analyze controversial issues without being accused of subversion.

Upper-grade children need to know, too, that all governments are confronted with problems at the local and national level and in their world relationships. In the social studies field and in current events pupils should study some of these current problems and their possible solutions as well as understanding some of the problems which have been solved in the past.

They should realize that as people come closer together in the world, they find it necessary to have rules or laws for ever-wider groups and to regulate such aspects of life as trade and commerce in larger and larger circles. Pupils should be introduced at least to such developments as the Benelux Organization, the Organization of American States, the European Coal and Steel Community, the Arab League, the Colombo Plan, the British Commonwealth of Nations, and the United Nations and its specialized agencies.

It is also important for them to know that misinformation about our government and our misinformation about other governments is a cause of friction in the world.

The teacher and current events materials of many kinds are the greatest resources now available for developing with upper-grade pupils the concepts mentioned in the foregoing paragraphs. It is therefore important that teachers have a wide background themselves and that they use a wide variety of sources for their background, not limiting themselves to magazines and newspapers of any one point of view. *Time, Newsweek,* and *U.S. News and World Report* need to be balanced by such magazines as *The Progressive, The Nation, The New Republic,* and *The Reporter.* Wherever possible teachers should read either *The New York Times* or the *Christian Science Monitor.*

Many pupils will find Minoo Masani's *The Growing Human Family* and Ralph and Adelin Linton's *Man's Way from Cave to Skyscraper* helpful on ways in which governments have developed over the centuries. Chapters in books in the Let's Read About . . . and the Portraits of Nations series will give pupils some background on governments in various nations. Textbooks in geography and history can serve for many as the basic materials. Current events papers and clippings from old issues of these magazines will also be useful. Newspapers should be used by many pupils. Ruth Wagner and Ivah Green's *Put Democracy to Work* is highly recommended for the junior high school age.

The thrilling story of the rise of new nations or the extension of democracy in old nations can often be told best through biographies. Among these are Nina Baker's *Juarez, Hero of Mexico* or Randall E. Stratton's and Howard E. Wilson's *Juarez of Mexico,* Cornelia Spencer's *Romulo: Voice of Freedom* and Rachel Baker's *Chaim Weizmann: Builder of a Nation.*

A few films are available for use with superior students in the junior high school grades, such as *General Election* and *How Britain Votes*, or *Government of Japan*, produced by the U.S. Army.

Most important, however, are the opportunities for pupils to learn democracy by living it in the home, classroom, school, and community.

Religions may be compared to a series of roads on which human beings are traveling. Our road is not the only one. There are others, starting from different places and going through different territory, but they all lead toward the same goal. What the goal is we cannot see, but we know that it is a good place. Perhaps the travelers on each of the roads think that theirs is the only way, but there are many crossroads connecting one highway with another, so that no road is entirely independent of the rest. There are side roads, too, abandoned and overgrown with weeds and brambles. If we follow one of these roads we may find that it leads to a deserted ruin, but even from the ruin we can learn something of the people who once lived there. They were human like ourselves, and they too once thought that their road was the best way to the place we are all seeking. The study of religion is an attempt to follow our own road and to explore the crossroads leading to the others. It may help us to understand the other travelers.

—DELIGHT ANSLEY, *The Good Ways*

We now realize that those who, a few years ago, pictured all of the world's religions as essentially similar, were oversimplifying the facts. We are learning that the price of tolerance is not necessarily the loss of our convictions. We can best express our love to the Hindu and others, not by pretending that basically we believe the same thing, but by honestly examining our differences and retaining respect and love for one another despite them.

—WILLIAM HORDERN, *A Layman's Guide to Protestant Theology*

We now know that science cannot bring the completion of human culture without the constraining influence of values that in effect are religious.

—RALPH T. FLEWELLING, in *Learning and World Peace*

We need a world faith, a community of universal interests and ideals. This can come imperialistically, as one faith does to death the other faiths in a long struggle. . . . Or it can come by the method of free inquiry, ever rooted in the concern for the common good. In this case, the concrete religions, even while seeking universality, will implement whatever general goodwill may already be found. The second approach is ours.

—NELS F. S. FERRÉ, in *Learning and World Peace Conference on Science, Philosophy, and Religion*

Chapter 12

A World with Many Religions and Value Systems

What an interesting variety of people there is in the world community today! Each of the two and a half billion residents of the earth has his own value system. It may have been greatly influenced by one of the world's major religions or philosophies, but it is unique to him, having been shaped and reshaped by all the experiences of his life.

It is impossible and unnecessary to understand all these individual philosophies, but it is important and possible to understand something about the major value systems which influence millions of people around the globe.

Actually such knowledge is basic to international understanding and cooperation and should be the first lesson in the primer of world affairs. How can anyone really understand other individuals without knowing the value system on which they act? Yet, such understanding is so complicated and so difficult that it must be postponed in large part until a person is relatively mature.

Any program which attempts to introduce children to the world must cope with the problem of helping them understand the major religions and value systems now extant. This is a difficult aspect of any program in world-mindedness, but any program is incomplete without it.

Some Basic Concepts to Develop

Reduced to its most simple forms, any program should include the development of at least the following ten concepts:

1. *There are many religions and philosophies of life in the world today.* Quite naturally children tend to think that all people in the world believe and act very much as they do. They learn quite early to expect some variations to accepted codes of conduct even within their own families, but they have no conception of the great variety of beliefs people around the world hold.

As they read about people in other parts of the globe and their ways of living, they are bound to hear about Hindu temples, Shinto shrines, Moslem mosques, and other places of worship. In books, films and filmstrips, photographs, museums, art galleries, magazines and newspapers, and over the radio and television they will pick up ideas about such seemingly strange customs as the veneration of cows in India, the practice of purdah in Moslem countries, and the colorful parades and festivals of the Buddhists at the time of burial of their people.

Children will want to know about these various religions and their beliefs and practices. It is the duty of society to help them to understand this important aspect of life known as religion, whether the schools, homes, churches, or other agencies carry or share the responsibility for their introduction to the major faiths of the world.

At first simple answers can be given, helping children to learn that the people of the world worship in many different ways, just as the people of their community do.

Eventually children need to know that there are several major religious groups and philosophies of life in the world community. Children who are interested in figures will want to know how many people there are in each of these major groups. A precise answer cannot be given, but such figures as the following, from the *Encyclopedia Britannica*, can be used:

Christian		741,985,482
Roman Catholic	421,340,901	
Eastern Orthodox	127,629,986	
Protestant	193,104,595	
Moslem		315,699,103
Confucian		300,289,000
Hindu		255,715,506
Buddhist		150,300,000
Primitive		121,150,000
Taoist		50,053,000
Shinto		25,000,000
Jewish		11,303,350
Zoroastrian		124,890
Others or none		347,397,969

Boys and girls should learn at least the basic beliefs of each of the world's major groups, without being subjected to the minutiae of theological discussion. They should also know that the original beliefs and practices have been modified by the followers of each of these main groups and that the original teachings of their great leaders have been corrupted by centuries of compromise.

In today's world children also need to have considerable understanding of communism and its major tenets, both theoretical and actual, as one of the most important philosophies or ways of life now practiced in the world community.

Children should also learn that there are many differences within each of these groups. Perhaps it is sufficient for them to understand that there are orthodox or conservative groups, persons or groups holding middle-of-the-road positions, and liberals in each of the major faiths, whether it is Judaism, Islam, Buddhism, or Christianity.

Introductions to these leading ways of life around the world need to be carried on frankly and as objectively as possible, with a goal of understanding why people believe and act as they do. It will not be possible for children to understand all the various beliefs and practices of these various groups, but they can at least learn that "that is the way they think things should be done." Perhaps that is all that can be expected in such an intricate and involved topic as religion with children.

2. *There are a few basic values which almost all of these groups*

promote. It may be a temptation to some well-meaning teachers to try to show that all these religions are basically alike, but it is untrue and should not be done. The recognition of differences and the attempt to help children understand them is a central concept in this controversial field.

Despite their many differences, however, all of these groups have a few points in common. All or almost all of them have some sacred writings, some sacred places, some outstanding leaders, some holy days, and some important symbols. All of them teach loyalty to the family unit, even though that unit varies from group to group. All of them teach obedience to authority although the form of obedience and the authorities differ. All of them uphold honesty, kindliness, and justice as they interpret those concepts.

As a part of their attempt to see the common beliefs of mankind, older children should read and discuss the Charter of the United Nations and the Declaration of Human Rights. In those two documents most of the nations of the world have set forth their common values, even though they may give only lip service to them at the moment, just as we have paid only lip service in the past to certain parts of our own Constitution with its important Bill of Rights.

3. *These religions and value systems mean much to people.* Boys and girls should begin fairly early to appreciate how much a person's religion means to him, no matter to which of the world faiths he adheres. They should realize that persons in each of these large groups are not equally devout or consistent in the practice of their beliefs. Nevertheless, these ways of life have great meaning to millions of persons.

In large parts of the world the temple, mosque, synagogue, or shrine is the center of the life of the community. From birth to death people are influenced by their religious faith. They obtain their ideas of what is right and wrong from their religion and carry on its practices in varying degrees of faithfulness. So important is the allegiance of many persons to their faith that they are willing to undergo all kinds of ridicule or persecution. History and even current events are filled with examples of such devotion which will give a sense of reality to this concept of the importance of religious belief.

4. *There have been terrible conflicts in the name of religion and*

some conflicts still exist. Closely allied to this third point is the fact that some of the most violent conflicts in world history have been beween religious groups or over religion. The wars between Christians and Moslems, the Hundred Years War, the more recent hostilities between Arabs and Jews over Palestine, and the violent outbreaks in India at the time of partition between Moslems on the one hand and Hindus and Sikhs on the other are but four examples of this fact. These are unhappy chapters in the history of mankind, but important for children to know. Nor are our hands clean in the United States, despite a rather good record of religious tolerance. There have been such episodes as the hanging of Quakers on the Boston Common in colonial days, the persecution of Mormons in various parts of the United States before they moved to what is now Utah, anti-Semitism at various points in our history, and the sordid history of the Ku Klux Klan in fairly recent times.

5. *There is a growing movement around the world for inter-religious cooperation.* A story of which we can be proud is the growing movement toward understanding and cooperation between religious faiths. This ranges from the union of most Protestants into one major group in such countries as Canada, India, and Japan, to the formation of the World Council of Churches. Another chapter is the growing understanding between Christians and Jews in the United States and abroad, fostered by such organizations as the National Conference of Christians and Jews and the World Brotherhood of Christians and Jews.

6. *Religion is often an important factor in local, national, and international politics.* As children learn about politics, they will need to become aware of the important influence religion has. At times the influence of religion has been for the good; at other times it has been the cause of friction or of conflict. One example of its beneficial effects in politics would be the fact that most of the values in Western democracies come from our Judaic-Christian tradition with its stress on the importance of individuals, its concern for handicapped persons, its emphasis upon equal rights for women, and its respect for minorities. Examples of its harmful effects might include the conflicts between the church and anticlerical adherents in many parts of Latin America, the tendency of Hinduism for a long period

to accept the caste system and the poverty of its people, or the lack of concern of most Christians in the United States for the development of full equality for Negroes after the freeing of the slaves in 1863.

No real understanding of French politics, of events in the Middle East or Southeast Asia, of Argentina, or of almost any other part of the world today can be gained without an understanding of the place of religion. Children should not be subjected to long accounts of this topic, but they need to see it as another of the many important factors which determine policies around the globe.

7. *Some religions have a missionary outlook.* One of the most important facts to grasp regarding religions is the fact that some feel that their way of life is so valuable that it should be shared with others, leading to the establishment of missions in various parts of the world. This has characterized the Moslem and Christian groups particularly. Often much good has resulted from such missions, in the establishment of schools and hospitals, in raising the place of women in certain societies, and in bringing new concepts of life to people. But there has been a negative side, too, in the disruption of the existing fabric of society, in the hostility and conflict which has often accompanied such movements, and in the governmental control by foreign powers which has so often accompanied religious activity. Even today there is conflict between Christians and Moslems in parts of Africa as a result of missionary activities.

8. *Most religions have had a great spiritual leader.* Among the great men of all times have been such religious leaders as Buddha, Confucius, Jesus, Lao-tse, Mohammed, and Zoroaster. Children should become acquainted with these outstanding persons and some of their major teachings, as well as such recent figures as Gandhi, Schweitzer, and Kagawa.

9. *Ways of worship and religious symbolism vary from group to group.* Boys and girls will frequently be interested in the ways of worship of the world's leading religions and in the symbolism of these various groups. Actually these approaches can often be the best ways of introducing children to the beliefs and practices of religious faiths. The celebration of the birthday of Krishna in the Hindu faith, the Id festival in Islam, the processions in honor of Buddha's birthday,

observance of Hanukkah or Yom Kippur in the Jewish faith, or of Christmas or Easter by Christians can lead children easily and naturally into the beliefs of the groups themselves. The same can be said of the symbols used in worship, whether they are the Sacred Ark or the Torah of the Jews, the altar and cross of the Christians, the statues and family shrines of the Buddhists, or the mosques of the Moslems.

10. *Children need to develop their own codes of values with the help of the various agencies of society.* The task of teachers in American schools is not to indoctrinate children on the merits of any religious group. But teachers have a responsibility to help children to learn some of the basic values of our society and to examine and develop their own value systems through reading, discussion, and more particularly through the quality of living that goes on in classrooms and schools. Schools in our society need to work with other agencies of their communities in fostering a fine quality of living which places emphasis upon the development of every person so that he may contribute his best to the common good and share in its benefits.

Some Suggested Experiences for Children

Even before they come to school, children have begun to form basic attitudes about people of other religions and value systems. They have begun to establish their own codes of action, learned in part from the family and in part from the neighborhoods in which they live. They have also begun to form attitudes toward authority and about cooperation and competition.

In their early years at school a grave responsibility rests with teachers to help them to accept people on their own merits rather than upon the basis of color, creed, social or economic status, nationality, or political belief. Such attitudes are even more easily caught than taught. Teachers need to probe their own prejudices and try to eliminate them so that they will be free to develop in children these basic attitudes of respect and appreciation for people despite different backgrounds.

Opportunities for developing such values occur in many ways in the preschool and primary grades. The food children eat sometimes causes comment and can become the subject for discussion as it relates to religious customs and beliefs. Sometimes children have picked up names which they hurl at each other without any understanding of their meaning. Without condemning children for their use of such derogatory terms, teachers can help them to realize that these are words which hurt other people and should not be used. The approach of holidays can be utilized to help children accept the fact that different people have different holidays. In many cases these days can be celebrated simply as excellent learning situations.

In scores of day-to-day situations, teachers can help children to develop the values which our society deems important. Competitiveness on more and more occasions can give way to cooperativeness. Final authority can remain with the teacher, with increasing opportunities for children to make decisions and to assume leadership. Children can solve many problems by gathering facts and diverse opinions, examining them, and reaching conclusions as to the most effective action to take. They can learn responsibility by sharing in the work of the classroom and school, often rotating these responsibilities so that a favored group does not develop. Likewise they can begin to see how other people feel by spontaneous dramatizations and later simple forms of sociodrama. Opportunities can be found to let each child have some areas of living in which he or she excels, with the emphasis upon many forms of success rather than merely success in reading, writing, and arithmetic, or athletics.

Such approaches apply not just to the preschool and primary grades but to every grade level in elementary and junior high schools. Some values are learned early, but the obligation for developing the finest type of living possible rests with the teachers of every subject field and of every class, as well as with all the persons with whom children come in contact in these formative years.

As children read about their peers in other parts of the world, questions will arise about the religions of these children. These can be answered simply at first, with the explanation that people in different parts of the world have different churches just as we do in our own community. As the pupils grow older, they can be introduced gradually to the many religious groups in the United States and in the world through a variety of experiences.

Wherever possible, visits should be arranged to several places of worship, with explanations of their ways of worship and beliefs, as simply and as warmly told as possible.

In connection with such studies, some children may want to make reproductions in clay or wood of the churches they have visited or read about. Or they may want to paint pictures of these religious shrines. Older children may want to collect, mount, and exhibit pictures of some of the famous places of worship around the world.

Many children enjoy seeing some of the objects used in worship, learning at the same time something of their significance. These may be the sacred books of the various faiths or the vestments used in different ways of worship. Some children will find enjoyment and profit in making transparencies, like the windows of a cathedral.

Older boys and girls often enjoy making collections of the most famous or representative sayings of different religions. This can serve as motivation for considerable reading about the religions of the world. A caution is probably in order at this point, for boys and girls will need considerable help in such a project, as many of the sayings they read demand more background than most children and young people will have.

Plays and pageants, especially at the time of special religious holidays, can be valuable learning experiences. Films and filmstrips on this topic are not abundant, but there are a few which can be used. An organization like the National Conference of Christians and Jews can be especially helpful in locating such materials.

More specialized work can be introduced with older pupils interested in art, music, and architecture, by having them visit art galleries and museums to see the originals or reproductions of famous paintings with religious themes, by having them listen to recordings of religious music or sing some of the simple tunes, and by encouraging them to collect and exhibit pictures illustrating the influence of religion on architecture in many parts of the world.

Some map study can be carried on in the intermediate grades by having children locate the churches in their community and by having them place on maps of the United States symbols of people and places connected with our religious history. With older pupils world maps can be made which show the extent of the world's leading religions and places associated with major events or personalities of the various world religions. There are a few biographies and novels with religious themes which can be read by older pupils with good reading ability, either as individuals or as part of committee reports.

Studies of history should reveal the great contributions made by religious groups to the world and also the conflicts which have occurred between these major religions. Discussions rather than debates are recommended on the constructive and destructive aspects of missions. The collection of news clippings and the discussion of important news items regarding religion in the world today should be encouraged.

Some attention should be given by teachers to words and terms which children will need to understand on this topic, inasmuch as words like monotheism, polytheism, communion, the Torah, theocracy, denomination, and mosque will be new to most pupils.

Some pupils may want to write brief statements of "This I Believe," especially if they have read parts of the current books by that title edited by Edward R. Murrow, or similar volumes by other persons. The development of a chart of the "trees" of religions and their offshoots can also be helpful.

These, then, are some of the activities which can be carried on with profit by children of various age levels, under the competent and understanding guidance of parents, teachers, and other persons who work with children and youth.

Resources on Religions and Value Systems

Despite its importance as a part of education and especially as a part of education about the world community, there is not a great deal of material for use by children on this important topic. As schools take up this subject more and more, there will be an increasing need for good materials, which publishers should be able to supply in the years just ahead.

As an introduction Mabel Pyne's The Story of Religion, published in 1954, can be used with children as young as the third grade. This is the only book of its kind for younger children.

Among the best books for older pupils are Delight Ansley's The Good Ways, which tells about the major religions of the world in simple story form, and the books by Florence Mary Fitch on *Allah: The God of Islam, One God: The Ways We Worship Him* (on Catholicism, Protestantism, and Judaism), and *Their Search for God: Ways of Worship in the Orient* (on Hinduism, Confucianism, Taoism, Shintoism, and Buddhism).

More difficult are Roland Bainton's *The Church of Our Fathers*, on the history of Christianity; Lewis Browne's *This Believing World*, on all the world faiths; Ruth Cranston's *World Faith*; and Joseph Gaer's *How the Great Religions Began*, now in a paper-bound edition. Ruth Smith has compiled selected writings from the major religions in *Tree of Life*, suitable for better readers among the older pupils.

Some pupils will be able to read such novels as Sholem Asch's *The Apostle, Mary*, and *The Nazarene*, Franz Werfel's *Song of Bernadette*, the more simple accounts by Lloyd Douglas of *The Big Fisherman* and *The Robe*. Librarians can help children to find other novels which are suited to their individual interests and capacities.

Katherine Shippen's *Moses* and some of the biographies of famous religious leaders such as Gandhi, Schweitzer, and Kagawa can be used, while an occasional student will enjoy Roland Bainton's *Here I Stand*, a prize-winning biography of Martin Luther.

Three films have been used with particular success on this general theme of world religions. One is *Fire Upon the Earth*, a history of Christianity in color; a second, *One God*, based upon the Fitch volume by that title; and the third *Your Neighbor Celebrates*, an account of the major Jewish festivals. The story of "One God: The Ways We Worship Him" has also been published as a filmstrip. Charts of "Three Great Faiths Worshipping God" are sold by the National Conference of Christians and Jews. "One God: The Ways We Worship Him," is also available as a Kapp Record, with music.

These are some of the materials which may be used with pupils to help them understand the religious beliefs and practices of their neighbors around the world. In the final analysis, however, it is the parents, teachers, and other persons with whom boys and girls come in contact who will largely shape their value systems and their outlook on the people of other faiths. In developing the concepts mentioned in this chapter there should be even more cooperation with community agencies than on other topics treated in this volume.

If we want an abiding peace, we must build an international community. It is a vast task and the building will take a long time. But we can lay the cornerstone . . . , and can set up an organization to continue the job of construction.

—ROBERT MacIVER, *Toward an Abiding Peace*

When men learn to work together, they inch along toward learning to think together.

—HARRY OVERSTREET, *The Great Investment*

It is impossible for one to be an internationalist without being a nationalist. Internationalism is possible only when nationalism becomes a fact, i.e. when people belonging to different countries have organized themselves and are able to act as one man. It is not nationalism, that is evil, it is the narrowness, selfishness, exclusiveness which is the bane of modern nations which is evil.

—MAHATMA GANDHI

We the people of the United Nations determined to save succeeding generations from the scourge of war, which twice in our lifetime has brought untold suffering to mankind, and to reaffirm faith in fundamental human rights, in the dignity and worth of the human person, in the equal rights of men and women and of nations large and small, and to establish conditions under which justice and respect for the obligations arising from treaties and other sources of international law can be maintained, and to promote social progress and better standards of life in larger freedom, and for these ends to practice tolerance and live together in peace with one another as good neighbors, and to unite our strength to maintain international peace and security, and to ensure, by the acceptance of principles and the institution of methods, that armed force shall not be used, save in the common interest, and to employ international machinery for the promotion of economic and social advancement of all peoples, have resolved to combine our efforts to accomplish these aims.

—Charter of the United Nations

Young Americans, as part of their education for citizenship, should have opportunities to learn in school why their country is following a policy of international cooperation, how that policy works, and what it means to have their country a member of the U.N. and UNESCO. Teaching about such things is an obligation resting upon all public schools in the United States.

—EDUCATIONAL POLICIES COMMISSION, *The United Nations, UNESCO and American Schools*

—————————————————— Chapter 13

A World of Conflict and Cooperation

Who is there today who escapes the concept of conflict? It takes many different forms, from the temper tantrums of children and the sharp words of adults to propaganda campaigns of nations and cold and hot wars. But whatever its form, it is omnipresent, insistent, perpetual.

Much as we might like to hide this part of life from children, we cannot. It is a reality which they discover early and which must be reckoned with in introducing them to the world. They need to know that it is a part of life, taking different forms with different people, in different places, and at different times. They need to know its costs and consequences to individuals and nations. And they need to learn that conflicts will continue even though the nature of these outbreaks may change and some of the worst conflicts be reduced or even eliminated.

Cooperation is a concept which is less obvious to most people. It, too, is an essential part of the fabric of life. It is occurring constantly, ranging from simple acts of friendship in homes and schools to international relief and the exchange of ideas, products, and skills. Whatever forms it takes, it, too, is omnipresent, insistent, perpetual.

Much more emphasis needs to be placed on this concept than is now being done in schools. Children need to learn how much cooperation there is in their world at the community, national, and international levels. They need to practice the skills of cooperative living in the home, in the school, and in the community. They need to discover how many aspects of their daily lives are due to cooperation.

At the international level they need to learn how much cooperation there is, from the dispatching of letters around the world to the protection of people from contagious diseases. They need to know that cooperation is increasing at the international level. They should learn early that war is not inevitable and that peace is possible. They should begin to understand the long story of man's attempts to attain a peaceful world-wide society and some of the hurdles yet to be cleared before it is attained. They should eventually be confronted with the ghastly alternatives to cooperation between nations and what these alternatives mean to them. They should be encouraged to make the small contributions to cooperation which they can make now and to develop a desire to make larger contributions in the future.

Preschool and Primary Grades

Early in their lives children are introduced to the concept of conflict. They are often surrounded by it, affected directly or indirectly by it—and are sometimes the cause of it.

One of the tasks of the home and school is to help children to understand that there are often disagreements among people, that all disagreements are not bad, and that there are ways of solving troubles between people without resorting to violence.

Wise parents and teachers can help children early to learn the ways of peace. Adults will want to minimize the possibilities of conflict wherever possible by seeing to it that children are not too tired to play and work with others, that there are enough blocks or paint brushes so that children are not tempted to quarrel over these possessions, or that large enough areas of work are provided so that close physical contact does not cause tensions, quarrels, and fist-fights. Adults will also need to be aware constantly of the need for children to have a large measure of success in a variety of ways so that they will not take out their frustrations in aggressive behavior.

But children cannot and should not be protected from all possible causes of conflict. They need to be helped in avoiding and settling disputes by learning to make their own rules and to abide by them, by learning to talk about their troubles and to air their grievances before they become too big to handle, by learning to withdraw from the group when they cannot get along with others, by learning to get rid of their anger through games, music, clay modeling, and other devices, and by learning to take their troubles at times to other pupils or adults.

Young children can learn that cooperation pays dividends in time, energy, and in fun. Such lessons do not come easily, but the degree to which they are learned is one measure of success of the early years at home and at school.

Through almost all of the activities in the preschool and primary grades the lesson of cooperation can be learned, whether children are helping each other with boots and coats, pushing a large load together, putting toys away together, playing house or doctor, taking trips on make-believe airplanes, or helping each other with reading, writing, or arithmetic.

These are the first steps in learning to live cooperatively in the world community. There is little or no value in studying the history of international cooperation or the mediating functions of the United Nations if the pattern of living that is ingrained in pupils is one of accepting conflict as inevitable and quarrels and fights as part of the routine of life.

In the early years at school almost all of the experiences to develop the concept of cooperation should be concrete, first-hand ones. Stories, however, can reinforce learning by helping children to see how other children solved their problems. Such books as Vana Earle's *My Friend Johnny*, the Beims' *Two Is a Team*, Hogan's *Nappy Has a New Friend*, Leaf's *Fair Play*, Nemec's *Let's Take Turns*, or Tworkov's *The Camel Who Took a Walk* can help children to see the importance of cooperation and to learn some of the skills of living together without being subjected to a barrage of words and moralizing by parents and teachers.

International conflict and cooperation should be largely ignored in these early years. Where the adult community foists upon children such experiences as air-raid drills, teachers and parents will need to be imaginative in allaying the fears of children and making a game of such practices rather than enlarging their fears or moralizing with them about the need for peace in the world.

Sometimes children will be affected by relatives who are sent away on military duty to other parts of the world. At such times teachers and parents will need to talk about where these relatives or friends are going and what they will do. Children are often helped by acting out such situations or by drawing, painting, or modeling what they are thinking. At other times they merely need the sympathetic ears of adults while they talk and ask questions. Time, the love and affection of adults and their peers, and plenty of pleasant activities can also work wonders.

Children in these early years will often be aware that their elders are celebrating United Nations Day or Week, taking part in a folk festival, or debating some aspect of foreign policy in a civic organization. Teachers should not ignore the interest of children in these adult activities. They should plan experiences which help children to share so far as possible in related experiences.

The display of the United Nations flag and the flags of other countries, a birthday party with the appropriate number of candles for the U.N., and the singing of such songs as Irving Caesar's "Songs of Friendship" may give children a feeling of belonging to the adult world. They may also take part in conjunction with older boys and girls in drives for UNICEF or UNESCO, learn a little about the Universal Postal Union in connection with their study of the post office, or hear or read about the U.N. building or some of the things that organization does for children around the world.

More important are the introduction of stories about the Christ of the Andes statue (celebrating the end of hostilities between Chile and Argentina) or the Peace Arch and garden between Canada and the United States. These are concrete and tangible evidences of international cooperation and more easily grasped than technical assistance and arguments over the veto power!

Almost the only resource for children on the United Nations is the book and filmstrip *A Garden We Planted Together*, an allegory of the aims and functions of the U.N. In it a group of children decide to make a garden in a weedy, stony field. They make a plan which they call "The Charter of the Garden" and work together. When problems arise, they share their seeds and jobs according to the rule book. In the final parts of the story, the parallel between the garden and the United Nations is pointed out briefly but distinctly.

A play, *One World for Joan* (available from the American Association for the United Nations), is intended for the first grade, telling how children are brothers and sisters around the world.

In such ways as these, children can be introduced early to conflict and cooperation and in a very elementary way to international conflict and international cooperation.

The Middle Grades

As boys and girls in the middle grades are introduced to a larger world than their local community, they need to discover that within our own nation and other nations as well as between countries there is also conflict and cooperation.

The examples of conflict from the past and the present are numerous. Textbooks stress them. Newspapers and television and radio emphasize them. The conversation of many adults accentuates this phase of life. It is therefore doubly important that teachers point out the many instances of cooperation within and between countries. They may point to the fine interracial cooperation in Hawaii and Brazil, the good relationships between people of diverse backgrounds in Switzerland and in the United States, the cessation of open hostilities between Moslems and Christians in most parts of the world even though they were long bitter enemies, the work of the national and international organizations of Christians and Jews, and the long history of collaboration between nations in health, labor, and many other fields. Children at this stage of their schooling may be interested to know that their fathers and mothers belong to local branches of organizations which are international in character, such as the Rotary or Kiwanis clubs, the American Association of University Women, the American Association for the United Nations.

Opportunities for learning the skills of cooperation through experience in planning class and school programs, working on units in committees, participating in the school government, taking responsibility on the playground and on trips should be increased at this point.

Children can also learn what happens when people do not cooperate. A fight on the playground, a plan for a party which doesn't "click," or a class or school council meeting which doesn't go off properly are only three out of scores of opportunities in the day-to-day life of school children which can be examined as illustrations of lack of cooperation. When children discover what has gone wrong and why, better learning takes place than when the teacher turns preacher and tells them what she knows about the reasons for their failures.

Stress at this stage of school should be on the story of international cooperation rather than upon the United Nations and its agencies. The story of the peaceful separation of Norway and Sweden at the turn of the present century, the story of the undefended border between the United States and Canada, and the work of Count Bernadotte and Ralph Bunche in mediating the conflict between Arabs and Jews are three of the best examples of this much neglected aspect of world history. The work of such organizations as the Red Cross and CARE can also be introduced.

Since symbols mean much to children, use can be made of the Red Cross flag and of such celebrations as Pan-American Day, World Friendship Day, World Health Day, and United Nations Day and Week. Wherever possible children should be involved in school-wide and community projects.

Some introduction should be made to the United Nations and its specialized agencies. Most children in the middle grades are not yet ready for a study of the United Nations as a whole; the emphasis should probably be upon the work of such agencies as the Food and Agriculture Organization and the World Health Organization, since their efforts are more easily understood than the work of other parts of the U.N.

The work of UNESCO may be introduced, although its concentration upon fundamental education, clearing house activities, and scientific and cultural cooperation make it difficult to dramatize and explain to young children. There is the further handicap of inadequate materials for boys and girls of this age, a fault which should be corrected by the preparation of simple materials on this important organization.

There is a decided lack of adequate resources on all phases of international cooperation for the middle grades. Probably the best source of materials at present are the current events magazines, which should be filed away for future reference after they are used.

Even the two accounts of the United Nations for this age group are poor. Lois Fischer's *You and the United Nation* is most frequently used, but it is now out of date, includes such impossible words for children as "aggressiveness," "hostility," and "frustrations," and abounds in illustrations which stress the stereotypes of people of other nations. Clara O. Wilson's *Working Together in the United Nations* is a simple account, but it also uses the same kind of stereotypes in its illustrations.

The one really fine book for this age on the U.N. is Dorothy Canfield Fisher's *A Fair World for All: The Meaning of the Declaration of Human Rights*, suitable for many fifth- and sixth-grade readers.

There is a great need for simple, accurate, and interesting accounts of the U.N. and some of its agencies.

Pictures, charts, and posters of the U.N. and its specialized agencies should be used on bulletin boards, through opaque projectors, and as motivation for discussions.

Boys and girls at this age may be interested in making the U.N. flag from the patterns available from the National Committee on Boys and Girls Club Work or in cutting out the colored flags of member states from posters issued by the U.N. and mounting them on toothpicks, matches, or small sticks.

Two plays which may be used with this age group are *Nancy's Dream*, a story about UNICEF and *The Martian Schemers*, in which visitors from Mars learn about the specialized agencies of the U.N.

A three-dimensional model of the United Nations buildings is also an excellent teaching device which can be purchased from the U.N. Bookshop and mounted by the children themselves. From the construction of this model should arise many questions about the organization.

The Upper Grades

By the time boys and girls reach the upper grades, they should be ready for a more intensive study of international conflicts and cooperation.

The causes of conflict between individuals and groups locally and nationally should be explored and the causes of international conflict added. Boys and girls need to know that there are many reasons for international tensions and wars, including such factors as propaganda, the personal ambition of rulers, religious differences, feelings of inferiority among nations which find compensation in aggressive actions, incompetent diplomacy, the desire for more land or resources or markets, ideological differences, and even education in the importance of force as a means of settling disputes. The study of history should illuminate these and other factors.

At the same time boys and girls need to know something of man's long search for international cooperation and peace and his partial success in achieving these goals. Textbooks tend to ignore this aspect of world community and teachers will need to supplement them.

Often a unit on International Conflict and Cooperation can bring together these two strands in world history in an interesting manner.

Boys and girls in these years should be encouraged to take part in community action programs for the Red Cross, CARE, and other relief groups. They can also join with senior high school pupils in sponsoring the exchange of older students through such organizations as the American Field Service and the American Friends Service Committee.

Boys and girls should also be encouraged to listen to radio programs and to view television broadcasts on world needs and to analyze the background of the commentators. They should use current events magazines and begin to make real use of the daily news-papers. Occasionally they can take part in pageants and plays, arrange debates and panels, and even appear on local radio and TV stations on international themes. A few may attend student conferences on international relations or make visits to International Houses on the campuses of nearby colleges.

Since biography is a strong interest at this stage, the lives of per-sons like Pierre Ceresole, the founder of the Work Camp Move-ment; Gandhi; Madame Curie; Albert Schweitzer; Fridtjof Nansen; and Albert Einstein should be read.

Resources on different aspects of international cooperation are fairly plentiful for the upper grades and are being produced in much greater quantity as time moves along.

On the story of international cooperation there are at least three good books and a pamphlet. One of these is Minoo Masani's The Growing Human Family. Another is Tom Galt's The Story of Peace and War. Perhaps the best account is James Avery Joyce's World in the Making: The Story of International Cooperation. Good readers will be able to use Samuel Steinberg's Peace in the Making.

The field of biography includes Alden Hatch's Young Willkie, Eleanor Doorly's The Radium Woman: A Life of Marie Curie, Joseph Gollomb's Albert Schweitzer, Anna G. Hall's Nansen, J. Alvin Kugelmass' Ralph Bunche: Fighter for Peace, Marshall Mc-Clintock's Trygve Lie, Shakuntala Masani's Gandhi's Story and Nehru's Story, and Catherine Peare's Albert Einstein and Mahatma Gandhi. Among the books of collective biography are Paul de Kruif's popular accounts of Hunger Fighters, Men Against Death, and Microbe Hunters, and the writer's Twelve Citizens of the World. Teachers interested in other titles may want to refer to the writer's article on "World Heroes" in Social Education for April, 1952.

Short accounts of world heroes are sometimes included in an-thologies for the upper grades. An example of this is the section on "Heroes of Service" in the Scott Foresman book Paths and Path-finders, which has brief accounts of Louis Braille, Jane Addams, Wilfred Grenfell, and Walter Reed.

A few schools may want to use the recorded organ music of

Schweitzer in connection with studies of his life, or the message of Gandhi now available on a Victor record.

A film presenting the story of the undefended border between the United States and Canada, entitled *Border Without Bayonets*, is also appropriate for this age level.

By the time boys and girls reach the upper grades they are ready for a fairly intensive examination of the United Nations and its agencies. In such studies several pitfalls should be avoided. One is the danger of emphasizing structure so that children associate the U.N. solely with a chart of its divisions and subdivisions. Another is the danger of concentrating on the highly involved and controversial work of the General Assembly and Security Council. A third is to present the U.N. as an organization with its headquarters in New York City, without showing its influence upon people around the world, including the pupils studying it. A fourth is the use of materials written for older boys and girls or even adults. A fifth is the cursory glance at the U.N. during U.N. Day or Week, without any attention to it at other times throughout the year. Finally, there is the danger of studying the U.N. from a purely intellectual approach rather than as an intellectual and emotional experience.

Speaking more positively there are at least seven major aims of any thorough study of the U.N. system. Children need to know the *purposes* as outlined in the Preamble to the Charter, with the emphasis upon achieving peace and security, furthering human rights, and promoting social and economic progress in larger freedom. Boys and girls should learn that this organization is man's greatest effort thus far to organize a large part of the world for peace and justice. Perhaps the greatest difference between the League of Nations and the United Nations is the total approach of the latter, including emphasis upon food, health, education, labor, and other phases of life as well as upon political problems.

Furthermore children need to know about the *power* of the U.N., realizing that it is not a world government and that it does not deprive nations of their own power or sovereignty. In fact its greatest weakness lies in its lack of power to act.

In the third place, boys and girls need to know something about the *programs* and *progress* of the U.N. Far too few people know what it has accomplished from the winning of independence for Indonesia, Libya, and Eritrea to its tremendous work in agriculture, health, food, and education.

In the fourth place, pupils need to know some of its *problems*, which range from its lack of real power to the inability to find personnel who combine all the attributes of citizens of the world—including competence in their field, language skills, human relations abilities, and a broad knowledge and understanding of many countries and cultures.

Furthermore, children need to know a little about its *potentialities*, discussing whether it might someday grow into a world government and analyzing the advantages and disadvantages of such a development.

Much of the work of the U.N. can be understood by upper-grade boys and girls through the biographies of some of its leaders, such as Franklin D. Roosevelt, Carlos Romulo, Sir John Boyd Orr, Mrs. Pandit, Trygve Lie, Dag Hammarskjold, Ralph Bunche, and others. Children need to know a few of these *personalities* associated with the U.N. and to realize what they have contributed to mankind.

Finally, boys and girls need to understand that even though the United Nations is an intergovernmental organization its progress is determined in the long run by the *people* of the world, acting through their governments and through nongovernmental organizations.

There are many ways in which the United Nations may be studied in the upper grades. Some teachers may want to emphasize current happenings in the U.N. and its agencies, letting any study of the U.N. system as a whole serve as background for these current events.

Others may want to trace a single issue from its inception through its completion, such as the winning of independence for Indonesia or the troubles in Palestine.

A highly recommended method is to obtain an over-all picture of the United Nations as a class group, followed by committee studies of some of the agencies.

A large number of activities can be carried on profitably in connection with any study of the United Nations. Charts and posters can be collected, posted, and studied by a class or by committees.

Large charts can be made of some of the outstanding accomplishments of the U.N. and its agencies. Time lines of its history are often helpful. Bulletin boards and scrapbooks on various phases of the organization can be kept and filed for use by later classes. Biographies of a few leading personalities can be obtained and reported in interviews or skits to the class. Maps of places where the U.N. is working can be obtained or made. Plays and radio programs can be obtained or developed and in some cases given to a school, a Parent-Teacher organization, a civic club, or over a local radio station.

Those pupils who learn best through their hands should be encouraged to prepare replicas of the U.N. building in wood, glass, or clay; to make posters about the U.N. or one of its agencies; or to prepare dioramas of the work of some part of the U.N. system.

Trips to the United Nations are possible for a few groups and should be carefully planned in advance if they are to be successful.

In conjunction with all these activities there should be a great deal of reading and a wide use of pictures, films, and filmstrips.

Fortunately there is considerable material on the United Nations system for upper-grade pupils. Among the books are Tom Galt's *How the United Nations Works*, Eleanor Roosevelt and Helen Ferris' *Partners: The United Nations and Youth*; and Graham Beckel's *Workshops for the World*, a practical account of the work of the agencies.

Katherine Shippen's *Pool of Knowledge* tells briefly several stories of technical assistance. *Mail for the World: From the Courier to the Universal Postal Union* is a small book by Laurin Zilliacus on the activities of one of the specialized agencies and can be used very well with the UNESCO publication *Round the World With a Postage Stamp* and the film *United Nations, N.Y.*

Two books on UNICEF are Kathleen McLaughlin's *New Life in Old Lands* and Elizabeth Yates' *Rainbow Round the World: A Story of UNICEF*.

United Nations, N.Y. by Dorothy Sterling and Myron Ehrenberg is largely a pictorial story of the U.N. headquarters, with some text.

Booklets for grades six through nine are also fairly plentiful. Perhaps the most comprehensive of these is *How Peoples Work Together: The United Nations and the Specialized Agencies*, prepared by the United Nations, with many fine photographs. Less expensive are the yearly issue of *Scholastic* magazine on "Paths to World Peace" and the booklet of the American Education Press on *The United Nations: A Handbook of the U.N.*

Ruth Wagner and Ivah Green's *Put Democracy to Work* puts the emphasis on what is being done and can be done to foster world peace. With this some teachers may want to use the allegory in Eric Kastner and Walter Trier's *Animals' Conference.*

A few plays for this age group are available from the American Association for the United Nations and the scripts of various radio programs may be obtained from the United Nations.

The two best over-all accounts of the U.N. in films are *Workshop for Peace* and *Grand Design. World Without End* is a remarkable production of UNESCO on fundamental education in Mexico and Thailand, while *The Children* and *Assignment Children* (starring Danny Kaye) are useful on UNICEF.

There are a great many filmstrips now on more specialized tasks of the United Nations, available through the McGraw-Hill Publishing Company.

Teachers will find two compact and inexpensive aids to teaching about the U.N. in Eva Dratz's *Guide to Teaching about the United Nations and World Affairs* and the writer's *Studying the United Nations and Its Specialized Agencies.* On the topic of human rights there is Wilhelmina Hill and Helen Mackintosh's *How Children Learn About Human Rights* and a UNESCO booklet with the title *A Teacher's Guide to the Declaration of Human Rights. A Junior High School Looks at UNESCO* is a valuable account of the work of the Alice Deal Junior High School in Washington, D.C., written by Delia Goetz.

For trips to the United Nations there is a leaflet issued by the Committee on International Relations of the National Education Association on *Planning Your Trip to the U.N.*

Teachers will find in *United Nations Plays and Programs,* co-authored by Aileen Fisher and Olive Rabe, some fine materials.

Kits of materials are always useful and may be obtained free of charge or inexpensively from the American Association for the United Nations, the Committee on International Relations of the

National Education Association, U.S. Committee on U.N. Day, UNICEF, the UNESCO Relations Staff of the U.S. Department of State, and the United Nations Book Store in the U.N. headquarters (addresses for which are given in Appendix C).

Of special value to teachers is the magazine *UNESCO Courier*, issued monthly and available through the Columbia University Press.

Teachers wishing to gain more background on the extensive work of the United Nations may want to read A. H. Feller's *United Nations and World Community*, John McLaurin's longer and more critical account in *The United Nations and Power Politics*, Clark M. Eichelberger's *UN: The First Ten Years*, or the shorter and less expensive account contained in the pocket book by David Cushman Coyle on *The United Nations and How It Works*. One of the best booklets on this subject is *The United Nations: Action for Peace: A Layman's Guide*, by Marie and Louis Zocca. Teachers will find very helpful the *Box Score on the U.N.: 1945–1955* prepared by Robert Reid of the Committee on International Relations of the National Education Association.

You probably won't believe this, but today there are no new worlds to discover. If we want a new world, we must improve the one we already have. —ADMIRAL BYRD

Time no longer works for peace. Time today works against peace.
—NORMAN COUSINS, *Modern Man Is Obsolete*

I look forward to the time when men will be as ashamed of being disloyal to humanity as they are now of being disloyal to their country.
—WOODROW WILSON, at the Paris Peace Conference

The past is gone and static. Nothing we can do can change it. The future is before us and dynamic. Everything we do will affect it. Each day brings with its new frontiers, in our homes and in our businesses, if we will only recognize them.
—CHARLES F. KETTERING

Mankind is now in one of its rare moods of shifting its outlook. The mere compulsion of tradition has lost its force. It is our business . . . to re-create and re-enact a vision of the world, including those elements of reverence and order without which society lapses into riot, and penetrated through and through with unflinching rationality. Such a vision is the knowledge which Plato identified with virtue. Epochs for which, within the limits of their development, this vision has been widespread are the epochs unfading in the memory of mankind.
—ALFRED NORTH WHITEHEAD, *Adventures in Ideas*

Because I have confidence in the power of truth and of the spirit, I believe in the future of mankind.
—ALBERT SCHWEITZER

Teachers are privileged to walk through their communities with boys and girls, to lift with them forever the old drawbridges of ignorance, misconceptions, and prejudice which served only to separate and divide mankind, and to raise in their place strong, new spans of knowledge, understanding, and human sympathy, which unify the human family.
—LORETTA KLEE SCHELL, in Howard Anderson's
Approaches to an Understanding of World Affairs

It is not incumbent on you to complete the work; neither are you free to desist from it altogether.
—HILLEL THE ELDER

Chapter 14

Conclusion

Some people say that the world is growing smaller and in a sense that is true. Yet, in another sense the world is constantly growing larger. One can no longer be a competent citizen, parent, or teacher merely by knowing about one's home community, state, and nation. One must also know a great deal about the world.

And the world with which one must be conversant is composed of approximately one hundred countries and two and a half billion persons. These people live in a wide variety of places and lead lives which are similar in some ways but dissimilar in a great many others.

Ours is a world of crisis and it may continue so for a long time to come. The only thing which seems certain about the world at times is change, and even the tempo of change is accelerated.

It is no simple task to introduce boys and girls to this vast, complicated, chaotic, changing world community. It cannot be done by adding another subject to the already overburdened curriculum; it must be done by having the world dimension added to all phases of existing subjects. It cannot be done by the social studies field alone; it must be done by work in all fields. It cannot be done by the

201

memorization of isolated facts about the world; it must be done by emphasis upon the formation and change of attitudes, the acquisition of skills, and the development of some big concepts.

Primarily the introduction to the world must come in the homes of pupils. If there is to be a healthy world society it must be founded upon healthy subsocieties, of which homes are the most important.

Then the introduction must be furthered in schools and communities where individuals are accepted despite differences and the potentialities of each person are developed to the highest possible point.

To be effective these introductions to the world must be made by parents and teachers who are themselves world-minded or growing toward that important goal. They must have faith in themselves and confidence in the ability of men and women to move toward a world of peace and justice for all the inhabitants of this earth. They need patience, perspective, and persistence as well as skill in opening windows to the wide world for young people. They need a deep religious faith or philosophy of life which undergirds their efforts to help create a better world community and gives them faith in the eventual triumph of right no matter what the temporary obstacles may be.

Then, too, they need a great deal of knowledge about the world and a few major goals or objectives, such as we have tried to outline in this book, so that they and their children or pupils will not get lost in a mass of unimportant details.

Unfortunately the events which have catapulted the United States into a position of world leadership and placed a new and tremendous responsibility upon parents and teachers find most of us unprepared for this new, exciting, and frightening task. The easy answer is to long for a return of the good old days when teaching was supposedly less difficult. But no one can actually return to those days, especially not teachers, who are expected to live in the world of their day and to help their pupils to live in it effectively. Moreover, teachers should be leaders in their home communities, living on the frontier and helping others to live there.

Consequently parents and teachers need to add a new dimension to their lives, to gain a planetary perspective. This means growth, and growth often takes its toll in time, energy, money, and psychological adjustment. Getting to know this wide world of ours is not an easy task. Let us not disillusion ourselves on that point.

But getting to know the world and its inhabitants can be an exciting adventure, too. As we have taken at least ten trips around the world in the various chapters of this book, we have seen that it is a fascinating place, with all manner of people, all kinds of occupations, many means of travel and communication, several forms of government and quite a few major religions, full of fun and beauty as well as plagued with poverty and conflict.

Fortunately parents and teachers can learn about this world of ours with their children and pupils. They do not have to be authorities on every aspect of it; in fact, more learning on the part of their young charges sometimes takes place if their elders are not too expert. Learning about the world on the part of adults may mean adjustments in summer school plans or in the type of reading material perused and studied in the all too few spare moments in the evening, over weekends, and during vacation times.

But such readjustments will pay off in huge dividends. Living can be more expansive and teaching more stimulating if one knows a great deal about what is going on in the world community. There will be new people to meet in books and in person, new friendships, a better understanding of the news in papers, on the radio, and on television. There will be new countries to explore in travel or on the magic carpets of books, films, museum and art exhibits, and pictures. There may be new opportunities for leadership in curriculum change, in local clubs and organizations, in churches, labor, business, or professional groups. Certainly there will be the thrill and self-confidence which comes in teaching something with which one is conversant and about which one is competent.

Since this job of introducing children to the world is such a tremendous task, parents and teachers need to be clear about their objectives, intelligent in the choice of appropriate experiences, and competent in the selection of the resources to be used. This, too, will take time and effort, but there is certainly no group of persons in the country better able to grow in world-mindedness than teachers. With the exception of a few persons, they are intelligent, dedicated individuals, capable of adjustments to new situations.

In a program of such scope, it is well to bear in mind that the heart of any program of developing international understanding is the ability to associate differences with friendliness rather than hostility. That is the bull's eye of the teaching target in human relations, whether it be in the classroom, community, nation, or world community. With this in mind parents and teachers will readily see how basic the mental hygiene approach is in developing world-minded boys and girls. Only those who are secure themselves can accept differences. The base of any program of introducing children to the world is therefore the same as the base for any educational program—developing maturity, changing egocentric individuals into sociocentric people, stimulating growth.

The little that parents and teachers can do may seem trivial to them. In such moments it may be well to remember the truth so simply stated in the African proverb: "A river is made great by its little streams."

Within the last few years there has been a noticeable increase in the interest of people in programs about the world. So great has that interest become that some pressure groups have been frightened and have resorted to oppressive measures to try to curb its further development.

Teachers are always subject to attack when they are out on the frontier. They will do well to build their relationships in the school where they teach and in the community where they live in order that they may pursue their objectives with the support of parents and other citizens. They will also do well to associate themselves with like-minded teachers and other adults in community and national organizations devoted to building a better world. There is real strength and support in such associations.

Teachers occasionally need to be reminded of their responsibilities as citizens. No school program about the world can advance far beyond the stage of development of the citizens of the local community in which the school is located. For the sake of improved programs in the schools as well as for the sake of better local enlightenment, teachers need to examine seriously their role in community affairs.

A greater responsibility and a greater opportunity lies with the schools of the United States in the next few years than in any generation in our history. The changes in the next decade or two may well set a pattern for a long time to come. The times therefore demand world-minded teachers who are concerned about introducing the next generation in a competent, effective, and understanding way to the world community in which they are living and will continue to live well into the twenty-first century.

What more exciting task is there for teachers today than to broaden their own horizons in order that they may introduce children to the wide world about them as their community and their home? In the words of a sage of the past, "It is not incumbent on you to complete the work; neither are you free to desist from it altogether."

APPENDIXES

Appendix A. Materials for Teachers

Books

Anderson, Howard R., ed., *Approaches to an Understanding of World Affairs* (Washington: National Council for the Social Studies, 1954), 478 pp. Especially Chap. 16: "Developing International Understanding in the Elementary School," by Loretta Klee Schell.

Arndt, C. O., and Everett, Samuel, eds., *Education for a World Society* (N.Y.: Harper, 1951), 273 pp.

Burrows, Alvina T., *Teaching Children in the Middle Grades* (Boston: Heath, 1952), 280 pp.

Everett, Samuel, and Arndt, C. O., eds., *Teaching World Affairs in American Schools* (N.Y.: Harper, 1956), 270 pp.

Kenworthy, Leonard S., *World Horizons for Teachers* (N.Y.: Teachers College, Columbia, 1952), 171 pp.

Kohn, Clyde F., ed., *Geographic Approaches to Social Education* (Washington: National Council for the Social Studies, 1948), 299 pp. Especially Chap. 18: "Geographic Instruction in the Primary Grades," by Thomas F. Barton, and Chap. 19: "Geographic Instruction in the Intermediate and Upper Grades," by Clyde F. Kohn.

Preston, Ralph, ed., *Teaching World Understanding* (N.Y.: Prentice Hall, 1955), 207 pp. Especially Chap. 2: "Studying Other Countries and Peoples in the Elementary School," by Leonard S. Kenworthy.

Snyder, Harold, *When Peoples Speak to Peoples: An Action Guide to International Cultural Relations for American Organizations, Institutions, and Individuals* (Washington: American Council on Education, 1953), 245 pp.

Stendler, Celia B., and Martin, William E., *Intergroup Education in Kindergarten-Primary Grades* (N.Y.: Macmillan, 1953), 151 pp.

Tooze, Ruth, and Krone, Beatrice, *Literature and Music as Resources for Social Studies* (N.Y.: Prentice Hall, 1955), 457 pp.

Washburne, Carleton, *The World's Good: Education for World-Mindedness* (N.Y.: John Day, 1954), 301 pp.

West, Edith, ed., *Improving the Teaching of World History* (Washington: National Council for the Social Studies, 1949), 275 pp. Especially Chap. 5: "Other Lands and Peoples in Programs for the Primary Grades," by Margaret McGrath; Chap. 6: "World History, Peoples, and Cultures in Programs for Intermediate and Junior High School Years," by Corinne Harper; and Chap. 18: "Reading Materials for the Elementary School," by Alice R. Brooks.

Pamphlets

Allport, Gordon W., *The Resolution of Intergroup Tensions* (N.Y.: National Conference of Christians and Jews, 1952), 49 pp.

Beauchamp, Mary, and others, *Building Brotherhood: What Can Elementary Schools Do?* (N.Y.: National Conference of Christians and Jews, 1952), 64 pp.

Beust, Nora E., *Books to Help Build International Understanding* (Washington: U.S. Office of Education), issued yearly. Free.

A Bibliography of Books for Children (Washington: Association for Childhood Education International, 1954), 109 pp.

Books Are Bridges (Phila.: American Friends Service Committee, 1953), 54 pp.

Dratz, Eva M., *Guide to Teaching About the United Nations and World Affairs* (N.Y.: American Association for the United Nations, 1955), 44 pp.

Educational Leader (Pittsburg, Kansas: Kansas State Teachers College), special issues of July 1, 1952; January 1, 1954; and April 1, 1954.

Goetz, Delia, *World Understanding Begins with Children* (Washington: G.P.O., 1949), 30 pp.

Hill, Wilhelmina, and Mackintosh, Helen K., *How Children Learn about Human Rights* (Washington: G.P.O., 1951), 16 pp.

Kenworthy, Leonard S., *Asia in the Social Studies Curriculum* (Brooklyn: The Author, 1951), 44 pp.

———, *Free and Inexpensive Materials on World Affairs* (Brooklyn: The Author, 1953), 96 pp.

———, *Studying the United Nations* (Brooklyn: The Author, 1953), 44 pp.

———, *Studying the U.S.S.R.* (Brooklyn: The Author, 1952), 40 pp.

Unesco, *In the Classroom with Children Under Thirteen Years of Age* (Paris, 1949), 63 pp. Through the Columbia Univ. Press.

———, *The Influence of Home and Community on Children Under Thirteen Years of Age* (Paris, 1949), 53 pp. Through the Columbia Univ. Press.

———, *A Handbook on the Teaching of Geography* (Paris, 1951), 101 pp. Through the Columbia Univ. Press.

———, *The Universal Declaration of Human Rights: A Guide for Teachers* (Paris, 1953), 87 pp. Through the Columbia Univ. Press.

Magazines

Childhood Education, 1200 15th St., N.W., Washington 5, D.C.

Elementary School Journal, 5750 Ellis Ave., Chicago 37, Ill.

Focus, American Geographical Society, Broadway at 156th St., N.Y.C. 22.

Geographic School Bulletin, The National Geographic Society, 16th and M Sts., N.W., Washington 6, D.C.

Headline Books, Foreign Policy Ass., 345 East 46th St., N.Y.C. 17.

International Conciliation Pamphlets, Carnegie Endowment, 345 East 46th St., N.Y.C. 17.

Journal of Geography, 3333 Elston Ave., Chicago 18, Ill.
Social Education, 1201 16th St., N.W., Washington 6, D.C.
Unesco Courier, Columbia University Press, 116th and Broadway, N.Y.C. 27.
World Airways Teacher, 28-19 Bridge Plaza North, Long Island City 1, N.Y. Free.

Resource Units

Britannica Junior, Encyclopedia Britannica, 425 North Michigan Ave., Chicago 11, Ill.: The Eskimos, Holland, China and Japan, Cold Lands and Hot Lands, Central and South America.
Compton's Pictured Encyclopedia, F. E. Compton and Co., 1000 North Dearborn St., Chicago 10, Ill.: Primary grades: Airplanes; Intermediate grades: Brazil, Canada, Mexico; Upper grades: Alaska and the Hawaiian Islands, Studying the Sky, The United Nations.
Fitzsimmons, Lorraine, Hawaii for Today's Children: A Resource Unit for Grades 4, 5, and 6 Educ. Dept., Univ. of Hawaii, Honolulu; 1954, 65 pp.
Guide to Korea, American Friends Service Committee, P.O. Box 966 M, Pasadena 20, Cal., 1954, 34 pp.
Instructor Units, F. A. Owen Publishing Co., Dansville, N.Y.: On Africa, Australia, Canada, Eskimos, Holland, India, Japan, Mexico, North America, South America, Brazil, Venezuela and the Guianas, Switzerland, Old World Gifts, World Peace, World Trade.
Let's Face the Facts and Act: A Curriculum Bulletin on the United Nations for Elementary Schools, St. Paul Public Schools, St. Paul, Minn., 1948, 147 pp.
We Are World Citizens, Bay City Public Schools, Bay City, Mich., Grades 4–7, Vols, 1 and 2.
The World Book Encyclopedia Reference Library, Field Enterprises, Inc., Educational Division, Merchandise Mart Plaza, Chicago 54, Ill.: Sixth grade: United Nations; Seventh grade: Latin America, Argentina, Brazil.

Equipment

Atlasphere balloon globe, The Blaine Company, 130 W. 42nd St., N.Y.C. 36.

Appendix B. Materials for Boys and Girls

(Note: P in listings indicates material suitable to primary grades; M for middle grades; U for upper grades.)

Chapter 4.   The Earth as the Home of Man

References for Teachers

Blough, Glenn O., and Huggett, Albert J., *Elementary School Science and How to Teach It* (N.Y.: Dryden, 1951), 310 pp.

Burrows, Alvina, *Teaching Children in the Middle Grades* (Boston: Heath, 1952), 280 pp.

Craig, Gerald S., *Science for the Elementary School Teacher* (Boston: Ginn, 1947), 561 pp.

The Earth's Surface (Dansville, N.Y.: Owen Publishing Co.). An Instructor Unit.

Primary grades

Bendick, Jeanne, *All Around You: A First Look at the World* (N.Y.: Whittlesey, 1951), 48 pp.

Hogan, Inez, *World Round* (N.Y.: Dutton, 149), 64 pp.

Little Wonder Books (Columbus, Ohio: Merrill Books):
Life in the Sea, 1954, 24 pp.
Where Animals Live, 1953, 24 pp.

Pease, Josephine, *This Is the World* (N.Y.: Rand McNally, 1947), 72 pp.

Schlein, Miriam, *Go with the Sun* (N.Y.: Scott, 1952), 36 pp.

―――, *The Sun Looks Down* (N.Y.: Abelard, 1954), 48 pp.

Schneider, Herman and Nina, *Follow the Sunset* (N.Y.: Doubleday, 1952), 44 pp.

―――, *You Among the Stars* (N.Y.: Scott, 1951), 62 pp.

Tresselt, Alvin, *Follow the Wind* (N.Y.: Lothrop, 1950), 26 pp.

―――, *Rain Drop Splash* (N.Y.: Lothrop, 1946), 29 pp.

Webber, Irma E., *Anywhere in the World* (N.Y.: Scott, 1947), 64 pp.

―――, *Bits That Grow Big* (N.Y.: Scott, 1949), 64 pp.

―――, *Travelers All* (N.Y.: Scott, 1944), 32 pp.

―――, *Up Above and Down Below* (N.Y.: Scott, 1943), 32 pp.

Werner, Elsa J., *The Golden Geography: A Child's Introduction to the World* (N.Y.: Simon and Schuster, 1952), 96 pp.

Middle grades

Andrews, Roy Chapman, *All About Dinosaurs* (N.Y.: Random, 1953), 146 pp.

Buck, Pearl S., *The Big Wave* (N.Y.: John Day, 1948), 61 pp.

Clymer, Eleanor, *Make Way for Water* (N.Y.: Messner, 1953), 63 pp.

Cormack, M. B., *The First Book of Stones* (N.Y.: Watts, 1950), 93 pp.

Edelstadt, Vera, *Oceans in the Sky* (N.Y.: Knopf, 1946), 58 pp.

Fahs, Sophia, *Beginnings of Earth and Sky* (Boston: Beacon, 1949), 154 pp.

Frost, Frances, *Rocket Away* (N.Y.: Whittlesey, 1953), 48 pp.

Holling, Holling C., *Minn of the Mississippi* (Boston: Houghton, 1951), 85 pp.

————, *Paddle to the Sea* (Boston: Houghton, 1942), 63 pp.

————, *Sea Bird Flying* (Boston: Houghton, 1948), 58 pp.

————, *Tree in the Trail* (Boston: Houghton, 1942), 63 pp.

Huntington, Harriet, *Let's Go to the Brook* (N.Y.: Doubleday, 1952), 88 pp.

————, *Let's Go to the Desert* (N.Y.: Doubleday, 1949), 90 pp.

————, *Let's Go to the Seashore* (N.Y.: Doubleday, 1941), 88 pp.

Lane, Ferdinand, *All About the Sea* (N.Y.: Random, 1953), 148 pp.

Lewellen, John, *The True Book of Moon, Sun and Stars* (Chicago: Childrens Press, 1954), 46 pp.

Neurath, Marie, *I'll Show You How It Happens* (N.Y.: Chanticleer, 1949), 32 pp.

Norling, Jo and Ernest, *The First Book of Water* (N.Y.: Watts, 1952), 45 pp.

Petersham, Maud and Misha, *Story Book of Earth's Treasures* (Philadelphia: Winston, 1935), 128 pp.

Potter, Edna, *Land from the Sea* (N.Y.: Longman's, 1939), 62 pp.

Pough, Frederick H., *All About Volcanoes and Earthquakes* (N.Y.: Random, 1953), 149 pp.

Payne, Mabel, *A Little History of the Wide World* (Boston: Houghton, 1947), 36 pp.

Tannehill, Ivan R., *All About the Weather* (N.Y.: Random, 1953), 148 pp.

White, Anne Terry, *All About the Stars* (N.Y.: Random, 1954), 144 pp.

————, *All About Our Changing Rocks* (N.Y.: Random, 1955), 150 pp.

Zim, Herbert S., *Dinosaurs* (N.Y.: Morrow, 1954), 64 pp.

————, *The Sun* (N.Y.: Morrow, 1953), 51 pp.

————, *What's Inside the Earth* (N.Y.: Morrow, 1953), 32 pp.

Upper grades

Coy, Harold, *The Real Book of Rivers* (N.Y.: Garden City and Watts, 1953), 192 pp.

Epstein, Samuel, and Williams, Beryl, *The Real Book about the Sea* (N.Y.: Watts, 1954), 223 pp.

Evans, Eva Knox, *Why We Live Where We Live* (Boston: Little, Brown, 1953), 151 pp.

Fenton, Carroll and Mildred, *The Land We Live On* (N.Y.: Doubleday, 1944), 88 pp.

————, *Riches from the Earth* (N.Y.: John Day, 1953), 159 pp.

————, *Worlds in the Sky* (N.Y.: John Day, 1950), 96 pp.

"The Great Waste Lands" in *Lands and Peoples*, Vol. 7 (N.Y.: Grolier Society, 1955), pp. 331–342.

Hyde, Margaret O., *Atoms Today and Tomorrow* (N.Y.: Whittelsey, 1955), 143 pp.

Lewellen, John, *You and Atomic Energy and Its Wonderful Uses* (Chicago: Childrens Press, 1949), 52 pp.

Little Wonder Books (Columbus, Ohio: Merrill Books):
Early Life on the Earth
The Earth

McNeil, Marion G., *Between Earth and Sky* (N.Y.: Oxford, 1944), 64 pp.

Pan American Union Commodity series, 1942–1947, 14–30 pp.
On cacao, coffee, copper, quinine, rubber, sugar, tin, tagua, tonka beans, and yerbe mate.

Parker, Bertha M., *Beyond the Solar System* (Evanston: Row Peterson, 1942), 36 pp.

———, *The Earth's Changing Surface* (Evanston: Row Peterson, 1942), 36 pp.

———, *The Earth a Great Storehouse* (Evanston: Row Peterson, 1941), 36 pp.

Reed, W. Maxwell, *Earth for Sam* (N.Y.: Harcourt, 1930), 387 pp.

———, *Stars for Sam* (N.Y.: Schuman, 1952), 190 pp.

———, and Bronson, Wilfrid S., *Sea for Sam* (N.Y.: Harcourt, 1935), 360 pp.

Riedman, Sarah R., *Water for People* (N.Y.: Schuman, 1952), 151 pp.

Roeder, William S., *Geography and Human Affairs* (N.Y.: Oxford Book, 1951), 60 pp.

Schneider, Herman and Nina, *Rocks, Rivers and the Changing Earth* (N.Y.: Scott, 1952), 181 pp.

"The Strength of Running Waters" in *Lands and Peoples*, Vol. 7 (N.Y.: Grolier Society, 1955), pp. 343–352.

Williams, Lou, *A Dipperful of Stars: A Beginner's Guide to the Heavens* (Chicago: Follett, 1950), 180 pp.

Wyler, Rose, and Ames, Gerald, *Life on the Earth* (N.Y.: Abelard, 1953), 143 pp.

———, *Planet Earth* (N.Y.: Schuman, 1952), 156 pp.

———, *Restless Earth* (N.Y.: Abelard, 1954), 156 pp.

Zim, Herbert S., and Cooper, Elizabeth K., *Minerals: Their Identification, Uses, and How to Collect Them* (N.Y.: Harcourt, 1943), 368 pp.

Films

Airplane Changes Our World Map (Ency. Brit. Films, 1942), 11 min.
The Desert (Filmsets, 1942), 8 min., silent, black and white.

Deserts (Gateway, 1953), 10 min., sound, black and white.

The Dutch Way (Films of the Nations, 1949), 22 min., sound, black and white.

Earth and Its Seasons (Knowledge Builders, 1938), 10 min., sound, black and white.

Earth—Rotation and Revolution (Edited Pictures System, 1939), 9 min., sound, black and white.

Earth—Surface and Climate (Edited Pictures System, 1939), 12 min., silent, black and white.

The Earth's Skin (Almanac Films, 1952), 10 min., sound, black and white.

Energy in Our Rivers (Coronet, 1948), 10 min., sound, black and white.

Land Behind the Dykes (United World, 1949), 20 min., sound, black and white.

Life in the Sahara (Ency. Brit. Films, 1932), 15 min., silent, black and white.

New Earth (Films of the Nations, 1944), 22 min., sound, black and white.

Our Earth (Ency. Brit. Films, 1937), 11 min., sound, black and white.

The Seasons (Teaching Film Custodians, 1948), 20 min., sound, black and white.

The Sun's Family (Young America, 1950), 11 min., sound, black and white.

Water (United World, 1948), 11 min., sound, black and white.

We Visit the Seashore (Young America, 1949), 10 min., sound, black and white.

What Is a Map? (Young America, 1949), 10 min., sound, black and white.

What Makes Day and Night? (Young America, 1947), 11 min., sound, black and white.

What Makes a Desert? (Young America, 1949), 11 min., sound, black and white.

World We Live In (Knowledge Builders, 1939), 10 min., sound, black and white.

Filmstrips

"About Our Earth" (Curriculum, 1947), 26 frames.

"Day and Night" (Young America, 1949), 34 frames.

"Flat Maps of a Round World" (Popular Science, 1948), 56 frames.

"Global Geography Short Cuts" (Telecurve, 1949), 96 frames.

"How Our Earth Began" (Curriculum, 1947), 32 frames.

"How We Think Our Earth Came to Be" (Jam Handy, 1947), 62 frames.

"Maps and Men" (Popular Science, 1948), 44 frames.

"Maps and Their Meaning" (Popular Science, 1948), 53 frames, color.
"Oil: Stake in the Cold War" (N.Y. Times, 1952), 53 frames.
"Our Changing Earth" (Curriculum, 1947), 28 frames.
"Our Earth Is Changing" (Jam Handy, 1947), 68 frames.
"Our Earth Is Moving" (Curriculum, 1947), 23 frames.
"We Live on a Huge Ball" (Popular Science, 1948), 52 frames.
"The World We Live In" (Life), 60–70 frames each, color:
    "The Canopy of Air," "The Earth Is Born," "The Face of the Land,"
    "The Miracle of the Sea," "Reptiles Inherit the Earth."

Chapter 5. Two and a Half Billion Neighbors

Primary grades

Beim, Lorraine and Jerrold, *The Burro That Had a Name* (N.Y.: Harcourt, 1939), 62 pp.
———, *Lucky Pierre* (N.Y.: Harcourt, 1940), 62 pp.
———, *Sasha and the Samovar* (N.Y.: Harcourt, 1944), 68 pp.
Belpre, Pura, *Perez and Martina* (N.Y.: Warne, 1932), 79 pp.
Bemelmans, Ludwig, *Madeline* (N.Y.: Simon and Schuster, 1939), 48 pp.
———, *Madeline's Rescue* (N.Y.: Viking, 1953), 56 pp.
Best, Allena, *Penny Whistle* (N.Y.: Macmillan, 1941), unpaged.
Brown, Jeanette P., *Rosita: A Little Girl of Puerto Rico* (N.Y.: Friendship Press, 1949), 60 pp.
Carmichael, William, *Lee Fong and His Toy Junk* (N.Y.: McKay, 1955), 32 pp.
Clark, Ann N., *Looking-for-Something* (N.Y.: Viking, 1952), 56 pp.
Creekmore, Raymond, *Ali's Elephant* (N.Y.: Macmillan, 1949), 40 pp.
———, *Fujio* (N.Y.: Macmillan, 1951), 44 pp.
———, *Little Fu* (N.Y.: Macmillan, 1947), 40 pp.
Crespi, Zhenya G., *Manuelito of Costa Rica* (N.Y.: Messner, 1940), 40 pp.
Crist, Eda and Richard, *Chico* (Phila.: Westminster, 1951), 80 pp.
D'Aulaire, Ingri and Edgar, *Nils* (N.Y.: Doubleday, 1948), 42 pp.
———, *Ola* (N.Y.: Doubleday, 1932), 55 pp.
Davis, Norman, *Picken's Great Adventure* (N.Y.: Oxford, 1949), 43 pp.
Davis, Robert, *Pepperfoot of Thursday Market* (N.Y.: Holiday, 1941), 157 pp.
Garrett, Helen, *Angelo, The Naughty One* (N.Y.: Viking, 1944), unpaged.
Halladay, Anne N., *Toshio and Tama: Children of the New Japan* (N.Y.: Friendship Press, 1950), 126 pp.
Joseph, A. W., *Sondo, A Liberian Boy* (Chicago: Whitman, 1936), 32 pp.

Kingman, Lee, *Ilenka* (Boston: Houghton, 1945), 48 pp.
Lattimore, Eleanor, *Peachblossom* (N.Y.: Harcourt, 1943), 96 pp.
Liang, Yen, *Tommy and Dee-Dee* (N.Y.: Oxford, 1953), 32 pp.
Lide, Alice A., *Yinka-tu the Yak* (N.Y.: Viking, 1938), 63 pp.
Millen, Nina, *A Sari for Sita* (N.Y.: Friendship Press, 1938), 36 pp.
McMeekin, Isabel M., *A First Book About Babies: All Around the World* (N.Y.: Watts, 1950), 42 pp.
Morrow, E. R. C., *The Painted Pig* (N.Y.: Knopf, 1930), 32 pp.
O'Donnell, Mabel, and Bloss, Margaret, *Chinese Children, English Children, French Children, Italian Children, Japanese Children, Norwegian Children, Spanish Children,* and *Swiss Children* (Evanston: Row Peterson, 1951), 36 pp. each.
Politi, Leo, *Little Leo* (N.Y.: Scribner's, 1951), unpaged.
Watts, Mabel, *The Patchwork Kilt* (N.Y.: Aladdin, 1954), 42 pp.
Yashima, Taro, *The Village Tree* (N.Y.: Viking, 1953), 34 pp.
Young, Evelyn, *The Tale of Tai* (N.Y.: Oxford, 1950), 34 pp.
————, *Wu and Lu and Li* (N.Y.: Oxford, 1939), 28 pp.

Middle grades

Angelo, Valenti, *Nino* (N.Y.: Viking, 1938), 244 pp.
Atwater, Claire N., *Manoel* (N.Y.: Longmans, 1940), 67 pp.
Batchelor, Julie F., *A Cap for Mul Chaud* (N.Y.: Harcourt, 1950), 58 pp.
Benedict, Ruth, and Weltfish, Gene, *In Henry's Backyard: The Races of Mankind* (N.Y.: Schuman, 1948), 54 pp.
Bishop, Claire H., *Pancakes Paris* (N.Y.: Viking, 1947), 62 pp.
Bothwell, Jean, *Little Boat Boy: A Story of Kashmir* (N.Y.: Harcourt, 1945), 252 pp.
————, *Little Flute Player* (N.Y.: Morrow, 1949), 159 pp.
————, *Sword of a Warrior* (N.Y.: Harcourt, 1951), 228 pp.
Buck, Pearl, *The Water-Buffalo Children* (N.Y.: John Day, 1943), 60 pp.
————, *Yu Lau: Flying Boy of China* (N.Y.: John Day, 1945), 60 pp.
Buff, May, *The Apple and the Arrow* (Boston: Houghton, 1951), 74 pp.
Carveth, Lysle, *Jungle Boy* (N.Y.: Longmans, 1945), 103 pp.
Collin, Hedwig, *Wind Island* (N.Y.: Viking, 1945), 96 pp.
Crane, Alan, *Nick and Nan in Yucatan* (N.Y.: Nelson, 1945), 30 pp.
Darling, Marjorie, *Journey to Ankara* (N.Y.: Macmillan, 1954), unpaged.
D'Aulaire, Ingri and Edgar, *Children of the Northlights* (N.Y.: Viking, 1935), 40 pp.
Evans, Eva Knox, *All About Us* (Irvington-on-Hudson: Capitol, 1947), 95 pp.

Hoffman, Ruth and Helen, *Little Arab Ali* (Phila.: Lippincott, 1941), 47 pp.

Lattimore, Eleanor, *Little Pear* (N.Y.: Harcourt, 1931), 144 pp.

———, *Little Pear and His Friends* (N.Y.: Harcourt, 1934), 178 pp.

———, *Peachblossom* (N.Y.: Harcourt, 1943), 96 pp.

———, *The Questions of Lifu* (N.Y.: Harcourt, 1942), 104 pp.

———, *The Story of Lee Ling* (N.Y.: Harcourt, 1940), 114 pp.

———, *Three Little Chinese Girls* (N.Y.: Morrow, 1948), 128 pp.

Liu, Beatrice, *Little Wu and the Watermelons* (Chicago: Follett, 1954), 96 pp.

Mirsky, Reba P., *Thirty-One Brothers and Sisters* (Chicago: Wilcox and Follett, 1952), 190 pp.

Mirza, Youel B., *Children of the Housetops* (N.Y.: Doubleday, 1939), 248 pp.

Schwalje, Earl and Marjory, *Cezar and the Music-Maker* (N.Y.: Knopf, 1951), 77 pp.

Solem, Elizabeth F., *We Learn About Other Children* (Chicago: Ency. Brit., 1954), 316 pp. Composite volume of all the books in their World's Children Series.

Steintorf, Louise, *Children of North Africa* (Phila.: Lippincott, 1943), 184 pp.

———, *Children of South Africa* (Phila.: Lippincott, 1945), 175 pp.

Von Hagen, Victor W., *Chico of the Andes* (N.Y.: Nelson, 1943), 196 pp.

Washburne, Heluiz, *Rhamon: A Boy of Kashmir* (Chicago: Whitman, 1939), 127 pp.

———, and Anauta, *Children of the Blizzard* (N.Y.: John Day, 1952), 192 pp.

Wimberley, Pearl K., *Child of Colombia* (N.Y.: Dutton, 1944), 176 pp.

Upper grades

Alpenfels, Ethel, *Sense and Nonsense About Race* (N.Y.: Friendship Press, 1946), 48 pp.

Benedict, Ruth, and Weltfish, Gene, *The Races of Mankind* (N.Y.: Public Affairs Committee, 1947), 32 pp.

Bishop, Claire, *Twenty and Ten* (N.Y.: Viking, 1952), 76 pp.

Bro, Margueritte Harmon, *Su-Mei's Golden Year* (N.Y.: Doubleday, 1950), 246 pp.

Brown, Rose, *Two Children of Brazil* (Phila.: Lippincott, 1940), 229 pp.

Buckley, Peter, *Cesare of Italy* (N.Y.: Watts, 1954), 88 pp.

———, *Luis of Spain* (N.Y.: Watts, 1955), 87 pp.

———, *Michel of Switzerland* (N.Y.: Watts, 1955), 88 pp.

Clark, A. M., *Santiago* (N.Y.: Viking, 1955), 189 pp.

————, *Secret of the Andes* (N.Y.: Viking, 1952), 130 pp.

Crockett, Lucy H., *Pong Choolie, You Rascal* (N.Y.: Holt, 1951), 246 pp.

————, *Teru, A Tale of Yokohama* (N.Y.: Holt, 1950), 213 pp.

————, *That Mario* (N.Y.: Holt, 1940), 181 pp.

Davis, Robert, *Pepperfoot of Thursday Market* (N.Y.: Holiday, 1941), 187 pp.

Eberle, Irmengarde, *Big Family of Peoples* (N.Y.: Crowell, 1952), 243 pp.

Edel, May, *The Story of People: Anthropology for Young People* (Boston: Little, Brown, 1953), 197 pp.

Evans, Eva Knox, *People Are Important* (Irvington-on-Hudson: Capitol, 1951), 87 pp.

Fitinghoff, Laura M., *Children of the Moor* (Boston: Houghton, 1927), 282 pp.

Gatti, Attilio, *Kamanda, An African Boy* (N.Y.: McBride, 1941), 148 pp.

————, *Saranga, The Pygmy* (N.Y.: Scribner's, 1940), 226 pp.

Goetz, Delia, *Other Young Americans* (N.Y.: Morrow, 1948), 256 pp.

————, *Pandita: A Little Girl of Guatemala* (N.Y.: Harcourt, 1941), 180 pp.

"How the Races of Man Developed," *Life Magazine*, May 10, 1953, pp. 101–106.

Kenworthy, Leonard S., "Two and a Half Billion Neighbors," *American Red Cross Journal*, February 1953, pp. 4–6.

Lewis, Elizabeth F., *Ho-Ming: Girl of New China* (Phila.: Winston, 1934), 266 pp.

————, *Young Fu of the Upper Yangtze* (Phila.: Winston, 1932), 263 pp.

Lindegren, Signe, *Ingrid's Holiday* (N.Y.: Macmillan, 1932), 238 pp.

Masani, Minocheher R., *The Growing Human Family* (N.Y.: Oxford, 1951), 127 pp.

Meader, Stephen, *Trap Lines North* (N.Y.: Dodd, Mead, 1948), 268 pp.

Montague, Ashley, *Modern Man* (Chicago: Science Research, 1956), 48 pp.

Pollock, Katherine, *The Gaucho's Daughter* (Boston: Heath, 1941), 56 pp.

Sower, Phyllis, *Elephant Boy of the Teak Forest* (N.Y.: Messner, 1949), 169 pp.

Spyri, Johanna, *Heidi* (Boston: Houghton, various editions).

Steichen, Edward, *The Family of Man* (N.Y.: Museum of Modern Art, 1955), 192 pp.

Turngren, Annette, *Flaxen Braids* (N.Y.: Nelson, 1937), 249 pp.

What Is Race? (Paris: Unesco, 1952), 86 pp. Through the Columbia Univ. Press.

Films

Boundary Lines (Association Films, 1947), 10 min., color.
Brotherhood of Man (Brandon, 1946), 10 min., sound, color.
Bushman Goes Home (Australian News and Information, 1947), 10 min., sound, black and white.
Children of Africa (Harmon, 1939), 30 min., silent, black and white.
China's Children (Harmon, 1932), 15 min., silent, black and white.
Children of Russia (International Film Foundation, 1946), 13 min., sound, black and white.
A Day With English Children (Coronet, 1948), 10 min., sound, black and white.
Eric and Anna in the Country (Scandia, 1948), 23 min., sound, black and white. Sweden.
Happy Valley (Canadian Travel, 1948), 10 min., sound, color. Nova Scotia.
The Malay Peninsula (Coronet, 1948), 10 min., sound, black and white or color.
Nomads of the Jungle (United World, 1948), 20 min., sound, black and white. Malaya.
Peoples of Canada (National Film Board of Canada, 1947), 21 min., sound, black and white.
Tina, A Girl of Mexico (Frith, 1946), 16 min., sound, color.
Tomorrow's a Wonderful Day (Hadassah, 1949), 45 min., sound, black and white. Israel.
Encyclopedia Britannica, Neighbors of Europe series, 11 min., sound, black and white:
Children of Holland, Children of Switzerland, English Children, French Children, Italian Children, Norwegian Children, and *Spanish Children.*
———, North American Neighbors series:
Eskimo Children, French-Canadian Children, Mexican Children, and *People of Mexico.*
———, South American Neighbors series:
Argentina, Brazil, Chile, and *Peru.*
———, Neighbors of Asia and Africa series:
Children of China, Children of Japan, Giant People (The Watusi of Africa), *People of China, People of the Congo,* and *Pygmies of Africa.*
———, Island Neighbors series:
Children of the Canals of England and *People of Hawaii.*

Filmstrips

"About People" (Anti-Defamation League, 1948), 63 frames, color.

"Canadian Eskimo" (National Film Board of Canada, 1949), 30 frames.

"The Canadian People" (National Film Board of Canada, 1945), 60 frames.

"Children of Japan" (Baptist South, 1949), 36 frames.

"English Children" (Stillfilm, 1948), 30 frames.

"Jiro and Hanako of Japan: Work and Play" (Yale Divinity, 1950), 39 frames, color.

"Ling-wu and Che-Tsoo of China" (Eye Gate, 1952), 23 frames, color, P.

"Man One Family" (Film Publishers, 1948), 57 frames.

"Sumo, A Boy of Africa" (Methodist Church, 1950), 57 frames.

Encyclopedia Britannica, Children of Many Lands series, black and white:

"Children of China," "Children of Holland," "Children of Switzerland," "English Children," "Eskimo Children," "French Children," "French-Canadian Children," "Irish Children," "Japanese Children," "Mexican Children," "Norwegian Children," and "Spanish Children."

Eye Gate House series on Children, P:

"Ahmed and Adah of the Desert Lands," "Ling-wu and Che-tsoo of China," "Toyo and Yuki in Japan," and "Wambo and Tawa of the Hot Lands."

Popular Science series on Swedish Children:

"Snipp, Snapp, Snurr," seven different filmstrips in color; "Flicka, Dicka, Ricka," six different filmstrips in color.

Stillfilm series on Children, P:

"Ahmed" (Arab children), "Chang" (Malay boy), "English Children," and "Mexican Children."

Young America, Children of Latin America series, color:

"Vacation on the Pampas" (Argentina), "Chico Learns to Read" (Brazil), "Jose Harvests Bananas" (Guatemala), "Market Day at Cuzco" (Peru), "Fiesta Day" (Mexico), and "The Silver-Studded Belt" (Chile).

————, Children of the Orient series, color:

"Koko of the Philippines," "Selim of Egypt," "Ming Li of China," "Ali of Saudi Arabia," "Ramesh of India," and "Gali of Turkey."

Magazines

Articles on the children of other lands are often found in *Child Life*, *The Children's Digest*, *Jack and Jill*, *The Junior Red Cross Journal*, *Story Parade*, and other magazines.

Chapter 6. Ways of Living Around the World

FOOD

References for Teachers

Food and People series of Unesco: *Are There Too Many People?; Distribution of the World's Food; Food, Soil, and People; Food and the Family; Food and Social Progress; The U.N. Sets the Table* (N.Y.: Manhattan Publishing Co.).

Food for All: A Sixth Grade Experience (Washington: Department of Elementary School Principals, 1951), 32 pp.

Stevens, Grace A., "Foods for the World from the Americas," *Social Education*, January 1945, pp. 20–22.

Primary and middle grades

Carpenter, Frank, *How the World Is Fed* (N.Y.: American, 1935), 284 pp.

Hollos, Clara, *The Story of Your Bread* (N.Y.: International, 1948), 44 pp.

Howard, Ethel K., *How We Get Our Food* (N.Y.: Harcourt, 1939), 111 pp.

Jupo, Frank, *Nothing to Eat But Food* (N.Y.: Aladdin, 1954), 48 pp.

National Dairy Council series on food:
   Hello, Alaska, Hello from New Zealand, Hello from South America, It's Always Breakfast Time Somewhere, and *Milk Around the World* (Chicago: National Dairy Council, 1947–1948).

Petersham, Maud and Misha, *The Story Book of Corn* (Phila.: Winston, 1936), 32 pp.

———, *The Story Book of Food* (Phila.: Winston, 1936), 128 pp.

———, *The Story Book of Rice* (Phila.: Winston, 1936), 32 pp.

———, *The Story Book of Wheat* (Phila.: Winston, 1936), 32 pp.

———, *The Story Book of Food from the Field* (Phila.: Winston, 1936), 128 pp.

Webster, Hanson, and Polkinghouse, Ada, *What the World Eats* (Boston: Houghton, 1938), 380 pp.

Upper grades

Boswell, Victor R., "Our Vegetable Travellers," *National Geographic,* August 1949.

Davidson, Bill, "Bread from the Sea," *Reader's Digest,* June 1954.

Eberle, Irmengarde, *Basketful: The Story of Our Foods* (N.Y.: Crowell, 1946), 246 pp.

Giles, Dorothy, *Singing Valleys: The Story of Corn* (N.Y.: Random, 1940), 361 pp.

Hancock, Ralph, *Foods from Latin America* (Columbus: Merrill Books, 1946), 32 pp.

"India's Rice Revolution," *Reader's Digest*, September 1954.

Long, Eula F., *Chocolate: From Mayan to Modern* (N.Y.: Aladdin, 1950), 207 pp.

Lucas, Jannette, *First the Flower, Then the Fruit* (Phila.: Lippincott, 1943), 72 pp.

———, *Fruits of the Earth* (Phila.: Lippincott, 1942), 71 pp.

———, *Where Did Your Garden Grow?* (Phila.: Lippincott, 1939), 63 pp.

Muller, Edwin, "Can We Farm the Ocean?" *Reader's Digest*, December 1954.

Riedman, Sarah, *Food for People* (N.Y.: Abelard, 1954), 192 pp.

Williams-Ellis, Amabel, *The Puzzle of Food and People* (N.Y.: Manhattan, 1951), 58 pp.

The World's Favorite Recipes (Washington: U.S. Committee for U.N. Day, 1955), 16 pp.

Films

Bananas, Yes (United Fruit Co.), 10 min., black and white.

Battle for Bread (U.N. Film Division, 1949), 16 min., sound, black and white.

Canadian Wheat Story (Young America, 1946), 6 min., sound, black and white.

Grain That Built a Hemisphere (Institute of Inter-American Affairs, 1943), 11 min., sound, color.

Rice Farming in Japan (Michigan Univ., 1953), 12 min., sound, color.

55,000 for Breakfast (Canadian Film Board, 1949), 11 min., sound, black and white.

Tea—Rice—Cocoanuts (Filmsets, 1942), 8 min., black and white.

The World Is Rich (Brandon, 1947), 43 min., sound, black and white.

World of Plenty (British Information Services, 1949), 45 min., sound, black and white.

Filmstrips

"Agriculture" (Eye Gate, 1952), 24 frames, color.

"Agriculture in the Philippines" (American Geo. Society, 1954), 30 frames, color.

"Crops of the Americas" (Photolab, 1948), 41 frames, black and white.

"Early Man and His Food" (Popular Science, 1947), 40 frames, black and white, P.

"Rice in Monsoon Asia" (American Geographical Society, 1954), 30 frames, color.

"World Food Supply and the United Nations" (McGraw-Hill, 1949),
67 frames, black and white.
Encyclopedia Britannica, Food and People series:
"Production of Foods," "Distribution of Foods," "Science and Agri-
culture," "Consumption of Foods," and "Fundamentals of Diet,"
black and white, M.
Popular Science, Food Around the World series:
"Food Makes History," "Our Food Comes from All Parts of the
World," and "Food Habits and Customs."
McGraw-Hill, Latin America, The Land and Its Gifts series:
"Coffee Brazil Fills the Pot," "For America's Sweet Tooth, How
We Get Our Sugar," and "Bananas Grow Upside Down."

CLOTHING

Books

Beskow, Elsa, *Pelle's New Suit* (N.Y.: Harper, 1929), 16 pp. P.
Bradshaw, Angela, *World Costumes* (N.Y.: Macmillan, 1953), 191 pp.
U.
Haire, Frances H., *The Folk Costume Book* (N.Y.: Barnes, 1937), 150
pp. U.
Jordan, Nina, *Homemade Dolls in Foreign Dress* (N.Y.: Harcourt,
1939), 246 pp.
Jupo, Frank, *Nothing to Wear But Clothes* (N.Y.: Aladdin, 1953), 48
pp. M.
Petersham, Maud and Misha, *The Story Book of Clothing* (Phila.:
Winston, 1933), 32 pp.
    Also similar books on cotton, rayon, silk, and wool, M.

Filmstrips

"The History of Clothing" (Society for Visual Education, 1950), 71
frames, black and white.
"The Story of Clothing" (Currriculum Filmstrips, 1950), 25 frames,
color.

Picture units

"The Clothing of Other Peoples: I and II" (Creative Educational So-
ciety).
"Clothing Long Ago" and "Clothing in Other Lands" (Informative
Classroom Picture Publishers).

Slides

"Clothes Around the World" (American Friends Service Committee).

HOUSES AND HOME LIFE
Primary grades

Beim, Lorraine and Jerrold, *The Little Igloo* (N.Y.: Harcourt, 1941), 72 pp.
Henry, Marguerite, *Auno and Tauno: A Story of Finland* (Chicago: Whitman, 1948), 32 pp.
Iwamatsu, Jun, *Plenty to Watch* (N.Y.: Viking, 1954), 39 pp.
Jannes, Elly, *Elle Kari* (N.Y.: Macmillan, 1952), 44 pp.
Ketchum, Jean, *Stick-in-the-Mud: A Tale of a Village, A Custom and a Little Boy* (N.Y.: Scott, 1953), 39 pp.
MacIntyre, Elizabeth, *Susan, Who Lives in Australia* (N.Y.: Scribner's, 1944), 32 pp.
Yashima, Taro, *The Village Tree* (N.Y.: Viking, 1953), 36 pp.

Middle grades

Acacio, Arsenio, *Work and Play in the Philippines* (Boston: Heath, 1944), 80 pp.
Bartusek, Libushka, *Happy Times in Czechoslovakia* (N.Y.: Knopf, 1940), 62 pp.
Bose, Irene, *Totaran: The Story of a Village Boy in India Today* (N.Y.: Macmillan, 1943), 118 pp.
Buck, Pearl S., *One Bright Day* (N.Y.: John Day, 1950), 60 pp.
Buff, M. M. and C., *Kobi: A Boy of Switzerland* (N.Y.: Viking, 1934), 128 pp.
Burns, William A., *A World Full of Homes* (N.Y.: Whittlesey, 1953), 120 pp.
Clark, Ann Nolan, *Magic Money* (N.Y.: Viking, 1950), 121 pp.
Collin, Hedvig, *Wind Island* (N.Y.: Viking, 1945), 96 pp.
Creekmore, Raymond, *Fujio* (N.Y.: Macmillan, 1951), 40 pp.
Crespi, Zhenya, *Manuelito of Costa Rica* (N.Y.: Messner, 1940), 40 pp.
Crockett, Lucy, *Lucio and His Nuong: A Tale of the Philippine Islands* (N.Y.: Holt, 1939), 54 pp.
DeAngeli, Marguerite, *Up the Hill* (N.Y.: Doubleday, 1942), 88 pp.
Edelman, Lily, *Japan in Story and Pictures* (N.Y.: Harcourt, 1953), 56 pp. Chap. 3, "Inside Japanese Homes."
Ege, Nezahet, *Turgut Lives in Turkey* (N.Y.: Longmans, 1939), 230 pp.
Fennimore, Stephen, *Bush Holiday* (N.Y.: Doubleday, 1949), 242 pp.
Greenberg, Evelyn, *The Little Tractor Who Traveled to Israel* (N.Y.: Behrman, 1949), 48 pp.
Hamsun, Marie, *Norwegian Family* (Phila.: Lippincott, 1934), 342 pp.
————, *Norwegian Farm* (Phila.: Lippincott, 1933), 343 pp.
Hoffman, Gloria, *Home at Last: A Story of Children in Israel* (N.Y.: McKay, 1951), 48 pp.

Liu, Beatrice, *Little Wu and the Watermelons* (Chicago: Follett, 1954), 96 pp.
Lownsberry, Eloise, *Marta, the Doll* (N.Y.: Longmans, 1946), 118 pp.
McDonald, Lucile, *Sheker's Lucky Piece* (N.Y.: Oxford, 1941), 79 pp.
Mears, Helen, *The First Book of Japan* (N.Y.: Watts, 1953), 68 pp.
Parish, Helen, *At the Palace Gates* (N.Y.: Viking, 1949), 64 pp.
Petersham, M. and M., *The Story Book of Houses* (Phila.: Winston, 1933), 32 pp.
Sower, Phyllis A., *Elephant Boy of the Teak Forest* (N.Y.: Messner, 1949), 169 pp.
Stern, Elizabeth K., *Red Jungle Boy* (N.Y.: Harcourt, 1937), 82 pp.
Voronkova, L., *Little Girl from the City* (Boston: Little, Brown, 1948), 165 pp.
Wiese, Kurt, *The Chinese Ink Stick* (N.Y.: Doubleday, 1929), 199 pp.
Wood, Esther, *Pedro's Coconut Skates* (N.Y.: Longmans, 1938), 191 pp.

Upper grades

Adams, R. C., *Sky High in Bolivia* (Boston: Heath, 1942), 64 pp.
Bazin, Rene, *Juniper Farm* (N.Y.: Macmillan, 1928), 180 pp.
Bemelmans, Ludwig, *The High Wind* (N.Y.: Harper, 1954), 113 pp.
Benary-Isbert, Margot, *The Ark* (N.Y.: Harcourt, 1953), 246 pp.
———, *Rowan Farm* (N.Y.: Harcourt, 1954), 277 pp.
Comfort, Mildred, *Temple Town to Tokyo* (Chicago: Beckley-Cardy, 1952), 143 pp.
De Jong, Dola, *The Level Land* (N.Y.: Scribner's, 1943), 164 pp.
———, *Return to Level Land* (N.Y.: Scribner's, 1947), 152 pp.
How Did They Live series (London: Gawthorne), 48 pp. each:
    On China, Egypt, India, Java, Mexico, Peru, Rhodesia, and Sumer. Available through the British Book Centre.
How We Live (N.Y.: Scholastic Magazines, 1949), 16 pp.
Irwin, William and Dorothy, *Australia and New Zealand* (N.Y.: Macmillan, 1950), 312 pp.
Kennedy, Jean, *Here Is India* (N.Y.: Scribner's, 1945), 154 pp.
Nevins, Albert J., *The Adventures of Wu Han of Korea* (N.Y.: Dodd, Mead, 1951), 244 pp.
Pollock, Katherine G., *The Gaucho's Daughter* (Boston: Heath, 1941), 56 pp.
Reiss, Malcolm, *China Boat Boy* (Phila.: Lippincott, 1954), 157 pp.
Singh, Reginald, *Gift of the Forest* (N.Y.: Longmans, 1942), 296 pp.
Stewart, Marguerite, *Boys and Girls of the Orient* (St. Louis: Webster, 1946), 278 pp.
Waln, Nora, *House of Exile* (Boston: Little, Brown, 1935), 337 pp.
Wernher, Hilda, *My Indian Family* (N.Y.: John Day, 1945), 298 pp.

Yutang, Lin, *My Country and My People* (N. Y.: John Day, various editions), 382 pp.

Films

Arabian Bazaar (Ency. Brit., 1953), 12 min., sound, color.
Asian Earth: The Life Story of a Hindu Mother (Atlantis, 1954), 22 min., sound, color.
China's Home Life (China Films, 1932), 15 min., silent, black and white.
A Day with English Children (Coronet, 1948), 10 min., black and white or color.
The Forgotten Village (Brandon, 1941), 67 min., black and white, sound.
In and Around Amsterdam (Films of the Nations, 1948), 10 min., sound, black and white.
Rural Life of Mexico (Coronet, 1945), 11 min., sound, black and white.
Village Life of India (Teaching Film Custodians, 1935), sound, black and white.
Young Uruguay (United World, 1943), 17 min., sound, black and white.
Coronet Film, *Life in Other Lands* series, one reel each, black and white or color:
    Life in a Fishing Village (Sweden), *Life in Hot, Wet Lands* (The Congo Basin), *Life in Lowlands* (The Netherlands), *Life in Mountains* (Switzerland), *Life in Northern Lands* (Norway), *Life in the Nile Valley* (Egypt), *Life of Nomad People* (Africa), *Life on a French Farm, Modern France: The Land and the People*, and *Spain: The Land and the People.*
International Film Foundation series, 2 reels each, black and white, available through McGraw-Hill:
    Japanese Family, Pacific Family, Peiping Family, and *Sampan Family.*
United World Film series, two reels each, sound, black and white:
    Good Neighbor Family (Latin America), *Lima Family* (Peru), and *Montevideo Family* (Uruguay).

Filmstrips

"All Kinds of Houses" (Canadian Film Board, 1951), 39 frames, color.
"High Sheep Station" (New Zealand Embassy), 33 frames, black and white.
"History of Shelter" (Society for Visual Education, 1949), 70 frames, black and white.
"Home, School and Church" (Yale Divinity School, 1950), 39 frames, color.

"How Man Has Learned to Shelter Himself" (Popular Science, 1948), 40 frames, black and white.
"Life on a New Zealand Dairy Farm" (New Zealand Embassy), 37 frames, black and white.
"Ling-wu and Che-Tsoo of China" (Eye Gate, 1952), 23 frames, color.
"Man's Shelter Today" (Popular Science, 1948), black and white.
"Maori Houses of the Village" (New Zealand Embassy), 36 frames, black and white.
"Story of Houses" (Eye Gate, 1952), 9 filmstrips, each with 23 frames, color:
> "Castle and Manor House," "Dwellers in Tents," "The First Homes," "The First Permanent Homes," "Homes in the United States—Old and New," "Houses of the American Indians," "Houses Around the World," "More Strange Houses," "Strange Houses."

Curriculum Films, Janet Visits Europe series, color, 24 frames each:
> On France, Holland, Italy, Scotland.

———, Our South American Neighbors series, color:
> On Agriculture, Amazon Village, Highland Indians, The Land, Lowland Indians.

Popular Science, Home Life series, color:
> On England, France, Holland, Italy, Scandinavia, and Switzerland.

Young America, Families of the World series, black and white:
> On China, Czechoslovakia, Egypt, England, Equatorial Africa, France, Germany, Italy, Japan, Mexico, and Pakistan.

———, People Are People series, black and white:
> "How They Farm; Their Food, How They Bathe," "At Bedtime, How They Shop;" "Their Kitchens, How They Play;" "Their Laundry, How They Get Around," "How They Worship, How They Study; At Home."

Picture units and cut-outs

"Children and Their Homes" (Friendship Press).
"Homes Around the World" (Creative Educational Society).
Presbyterian Board of Missions, "Cut'n' Fold series, Homes Around the World":
> On India, Japan, Northern Alaska, the Philippines, Puerto Rico, Southern Alaska, Syria-Lebanon, and West Africa.

TRANSPORTATION

References for Teachers

Arey, Charles K., *Elementary School Science for the Air Age* (N.Y.: Macmillan, 1942), 145 pp.
Mehrens, Harold, *Adventures in Aviation Education* (Washington: American Council for Education, 1951), 401 pp.

Primary grades

Jensen, Paul, *Golden Book of Airplanes* (N.Y.: Simon and Schuster, 1953), 28 pp.
McCullough, John G., and Kessler, Leonard, *Farther and Faster* (N.Y.: Crowell, 1954), 62 pp.
Smith, Marie, *Joe's Story of the Airport* (N.Y.: Scribner's, 1951), 24 pp.

Middle grades

Allison, Dorothy K., *Helpful Helicopters* (Los Angeles: Melmont, 1954), 24 pp.
Buehr, Walter, *Through the Locks: Canals Today and Yesterday* (N.Y.: Putnam, 1954), 64 pp.
Gateway Books (New York: Random House):
    Famous Airports of the World, Famous Bridges of the World, Famous Harbors of the World, Famous Railroad Stations of the World, Famous Subways and Tunnels of the World.
Hancock, Ralph, *Travel in Latin America* (Columbus: Merrill Books, 1948), 48 pp.
Neurath, Marie, *Rockets and Jets* (N.Y.: Lothrop, 1952), 36 pp.
Petersham, M. and M., *The Story Book of Transportation* (Phila.: Winston, 1933), 32 pp.
———, *The Story Book of Wheels* (Phila.: Winston, 1935), 32 pp.
Rosanov, Sergei, *Adventures of Misha* (N.Y.: Stokes, 1938), 83 pp.
Simon, Mina L., *Beasts of Burden* (N.Y.: Lothrop, 1954), 81 pp.
Trevar, Lloyd, *Sky Highways* (Boston, Houghton, 1954), 61 pp.

Upper grades

Adams, Jean, and others, *Heroines of the Sky* (N.Y.: Doubleday, 1942), 295 pp.
Coblenz, Catherine C., *The Pan American Highway* (Washington: Pan American Union, 1947), 16 pp.
Coe, Douglas, *Road to Alaska* (N.Y.: Messner, 1943), 175 pp.
Coggins, J., and Pratt, F., *Rockets, Jets, Guided Missiles and Space Ships* (N.Y.: Viking, 1951), unpaged.
Lazzari, Pietro, *Transportation in the Other Americas* (Washington: Pan American Union, 1947), 16 pp.
Lewellen, John, *Birds and Planes: How They Fly* (N.Y.: Crowell, 1953), 134 pp.
———, *You and Space Travel* (Chicago: Childrens Press, 1951), 60 pp.

Films

Airport Activities (Academy, 1952), 17 min., sound, black and white, P. and M.

An Airplane Trip (Ency. Brit., 1938), 11 min., sound, black and white, P. and M.

Anyway to Get There (Teaching Film Custodians, 1933), 9 min., sound, black and white, M. and U.

Giants of the Jungle (Teaching Film Custodians, 1939), 11 min., sound, black and white, M. and U. On elephants.

International Airport (U.S. Rubber, 1949), 15 min., sound, black and white, U.

Filmstrips

"Let's Visit an Ocean Liner" (Popular Science, 1948), 40 frames, black and white, P. and M.

"Maori Canoes for Transportation" (New Zealand Embassy), 39 frames, black and white, U.

"River Boats, Llamas and Airplanes" (McGraw-Hill, 1949), 30 frames, color, U.

"Transportation Around the World" (Popular Science, 1949), black and white, M.

"What Do They Mean to Us?" (Curriculum Films, 1950), 27 frames, black and white, P. and M.

Young America, History of Transportation and Communication series, black and white:
"History of Air Transportation," "History of Communication," "History of Land Transportation," "History of Ocean Transportation."

Eye Gate, Story of Transportation series, color:
"Animals in Transportation," "Modern Land Transportation," "Railroads in Transportation," "Roads, Bridges, and Tunnels," "Transportation by Water," "Transportation in the Air," "Transportation on Foot," "Wheels in Transportation."

Picture Unit

"Transportation: India: Ancient and Modern" (Informative Classroom Picture Publishers).

COMMUNICATION

Primary and middle grades

McSpadden, Joseph, *How They Carried the Mail* (N.Y.: Sears, 1930), 305 pp.

Neurath, Marie, *Around the World in a Flash* (N.Y.: Lothrop, 1954), 36 pp.

Schloat, G. Warren, *Adventures of a Letter* (N.Y.: Scribner's, 1949), 48 pp.

Wiese, Kurt, *You Can Write Chinese* (N.Y.: Viking, 1945), 64 pp.

Upper grades

Batchelor, Julie, *Communication: From Cave Writing to Television* (N.Y.: Harcourt, 1953), 116 pp.

Bauman, Hans, *Caves of the Great Hunters* (N.Y.: Pantheon, 1954), 160 pp.

Brindze, Ruth, *The Story of Our Calendar* (N.Y.: Vanguard, 1949), 63 pp.

Floherty, John, *Men Against Distance: The Story of Communication* (Phila.: Lippincott, 1954), 148 pp.

McSpadden, J. Walker, *How They Sent the News* (N.Y.: Dodd, Mead, 1953), 254 pp.

Ogg, Oscar, *The 26 Letters* (N.Y.: Crowell, 1948), 254 pp.

Stevenson, Orlando, *Talking Wire: The Story of Alexander Graham Bell* (N.Y.: Messner, 1947), 207 pp.

Films (See also Transportation)

Chinese Writing (Harmon, 1949), 22 min., color, U.

The History of Writing (Ency. Brit., 1950), 25 min., black and white, M. and U.

The Story of Communication (Instructor Films, 1949), 20 min., black and white, U.

Filmstrips

"Early Communication" (Curriculum Films, 1950), 27 frames, color, P. and M.

Eye Gate, The Story of Communication series, black and white, M. and U:

"Communication by Electricity," "Communication by Sight," "Communication by Sound," "Mail Goes Through," "Messages," "Modern Means of Communication," "Paper and Books," "Signs and Symbols," and "Speaking and Writing."

SCHOOLS

Primary and middle grades

Acker, Helen, *School Train* (N.Y.: Abelard, 1953), 118 pp. Canada.

Bunce, William, *Here Comes the School Train* (N.Y.: Dutton, 1953), 63 pp. Canada.

Edelman, Lily, *Japan in Story and Pictures* (N.Y.: Harcourt, 1953), 56 pp. Chap. 2, "In Japanese Schools."

Lattimore, Eleanor, *Peachblossom* (N.Y.: Harcourt, 1943), 96 pp. Chap. 7, "The School for Little Girls."

Upper grades

Bro, Margueritte Harmon, *Indonesia, Land of Challenge* (N.Y.: Harper, 1954), 263 pp. Chap. 7, "A Nation at School."

Buckley, Peter, *Cesare of Italy* (N.Y.: Watts, 1954), 88 pp. Chap. 2.

————, *Luis of Spain* (N.Y.: Watts, 1955), 87 pp. Chap. 4.

————, *Michel of Switzerland* (N.Y.: Watts, 1956), 88 pp. Chap. 4.

Ekrem, Selma, *Turkey: Old and New* (N.Y.: Scribner's, 1947), 186 pp. Chap. 4, "A Nation Goes to School."

Goetz, Delia, *Let's Read About South America* (Grand Rapids: Fideler, 1950), 128 pp. Chap. 14, "Going to School in South America."

McNally, E. E. G., *This Is Mexico* (Boston: Dodd, Mead, 1947). Chap. 3, "When Boys and Girls Are at School."

Nourse, Mary, and Goetz, Delia, *China: Country of Contrasts* (N.Y.: Harcourt, 1944), 229 pp. Chap. 8, "China at School."

Raman, T. A., *Let's Read About India* (Grand Rapids: Fideler, 1950), 128 pp. Chap. 15, "Education in India."

Shapovalov, Michael, and Walsh, Warren B., *Let's Read About Russia* (Grand Rapids: Fideler, undated), 142 pp. Chap. 12, "Going to School in Russia."

Spencer, Cornelia, *Let's Read About China* (Grand Rapids: Fideler, 1940), 128 pp. Chap. 15, "Going to School."

Tarshis, Elizabeth, *The Village that Learned to Read* (Boston: Houghton, 1941), 158 pp. (Mexico).

Films

Indonesia Learns (U.N. Film Division, 1952), 10 min., black and white.

School in the Mailbox (Australian News and Information, 1947), 18 min., black and white.

Schools of Mexico (Coronet, 1945), 10 min., black and white.

Young Australia at School (Australian News and Information, 1948), 9 min., color.

Filmstrip

"Our School Life" (Teaching Aids Laboratory, 1955). Japan.

Recording

"Schoolbells in the Desert" (New York: Unesco). Middle East refugee schools and what Unesco is doing.

Chapter 7. A World of Fun and Beauty

(Because of the topical treatment in this chapter, the bibliography is arranged according to topics in alphabetical order.)

General and miscellaneous

Keene, Frances W., *Fun Around the World* (Pelham, N.Y.: Seashore Press, 1955), 128 pp.

Soong, Maying, *The Art of Chinese Paper Folding for Young and Old* (N.Y.: Harcourt, 1948), 132 pp.

Wiese, Kurt, *You Can Write Chinese* (N.Y.: Viking, 1945), 64 pp.

ANIMALS

Bridges, William, *Zoo Babies* (N.Y.: Viking, 1941), 160 pp. M.

Credle, Ellis, *My Pet Peepelo* (N.Y.: Oxford, 1948), 62 pp. M.

D'Aulaire, Ingri and Edgar, *Animals Everywhere* (N.Y.: Doubleday, 1954), 32 pp. P.

Ditmars, Raymond L., *Twenty Little Pets from Everywhere* (N.Y.: Messner, 1943), 64 pp. P.

Flack, Marjorie, *The Story of Ping* (N.Y.: Viking, 1933), 32 pp. P.

Flaherty, Frances, *Sabu, The Elephant Boy* (N. Y.: Oxford, 1937), 61 pp. U.

Frisch, Wilhelmine, *The Storks of Lillegard* (Indianapolis: Bobbs-Merrill, 1950), 231 pp. U.

Hawkins, Sheila, *Animals of Australia* (London: Puffin Books, 1949), 32 pp. M. Through Penguin Books.

Irwin, William and Dorothy, *Australia and New Zealand* (N.Y.: Macmillan, 1950), 312 pp. U. Chapters on "The Wonderful Animals of Australia" and "Birds That Work and Play."

Lowe, Edith, *Animal Parade* (Kenosha, Wisc.: Samuel Loew Co., 1951), 24 pp.

Mann, William M. and Lucile Q., "Around the World for Animals," *National Geographic Magazine*, June 1938. U.

Neurath, Marie, *The Wonder World of Animals* (N.Y.: Lothrop, 1952), 36 pp. P.

Provenson, Alice and Martin, *The Animal Fair* (N.Y.: Simon and Schuster, 1952), 76 pp. M.

Purcell, John W., *True Book of African Animals* (Chicago: Childrens Press, 1954), 46 pp. M.

Schlein, Miriam, *Elephant Herd* (N.Y.: Scott, 1954), unpaged. P.

Slaughter, Jean, *Horses Around the World* (Phila.: Lippincott, 1955), 88 pp. U.

Sojo, Toba, *The Animal Frolic* (N.Y.: Putnam, 1954), unpaged. P.

Von Hagen, Victor W., *South American Zoo* (N.Y.: Messner, 1946), 182 pp. M.

Film

Kruger National Park (Nu-Art, 1946), 10 min., sound, color.

Filmstrip

"Work Animals Around the World" (Curriculum Films, 1952), six filmstrips on different animals.

Picture Units

"Animals of Other Lands" (Creative Educational Society).
"Australian Animals," a chart, is available from the Australian News and Information Bureau.
"Children and Their Pets" (Friendship Press), 10″ x 12″ pictures.

ART AND CHILDREN'S DRAWINGS

Chase, Alice, *Famous Paintings* (N.Y.: Platt and Munk, 1951), 103 pp. M-U.
Cohn, Norma, *Little People in a Big Country* (N.Y.: Oxford, 1945), 31 pp. M.
Cothren, Marion B., *Pictures of France by Her Children* (N.Y.: Oxford, 1950), 32 pp. M.
Gibson, Katharine, *Pictures to Grow Up With* (N.Y.: Studio, 1942), 151 pp. U.
———, *More Pictures to Grow Up With* (N.Y.: Studio, 1946), 144 pp. U.
Miller, M. D., and Rutter, F., *Child Artists of the Australian Bush* (N.Y.: British Book Centre, 1950), 80 pp. U.

Slides

Slides and paintings by children are available on loan from the American Friends Service Committee and exhibits of children's art are available from the Junior Red Cross.

BEAUTY OF NATURE

Film

Japan in Cherry Blossom Time (Fitzpatrick, 1935), 10 min., sound, black and white or color.

Filmstrip

"Scenic Wonders of North Island" (New Zealand Embassy), 36 frames.

CLOTHING (See also Bibliography on page 224)

Beskow, Elsa, *Belle's New Suit* (N.Y.: Harper, 1929), 16 pp. P.
Bradshaw, Angela, *World Costumes* (N.Y.: Macmillan, 1953), 191 pp. U.
Haire, Frances H., *The Folk Costume Book* (N.Y.: Barnes, 1937), 150 pp. M.
Jupo, Frank, *Nothing to Wear But Clothes* (N.Y.: Aladdin, 1953), 48 pp. M.
Petersham, M. and M., *The Story Book of Clothing* (Philadelphia: Winston, 1933), 32 pp. M.

Filmstrips

"History of Clothing" (Society for Visual Education, 1950), 71 frames, black and white.
"Story of Clothing" (Curriculum Filmstrips, 1950), 25 frames, color.

Picture Units

"Clothing Long Ago" and "Clothing in Other Lands" (Informative Classroom Picture Publishers series).
"Clothing of Other Peoples," Parts I and II (Creative Educational Society).

Slides

"Clothes Around the World," available from the American Friends Service Committee.

DOLLS

Christopher, Catherine, *The Complete Book of Doll Making and Collecting* (N.Y.: Graystone, 1949), 288 pp. U.
Hallen, Julienne, *How to Make Foreign Dolls and Their Costumes* (N.Y.: Homecrafts, 1950), 93 pp. U.
Jordan, Nina R., *Homemade Dolls in Foreign Dress* (N.Y.: Harcourt, 1939), 246 pp. M.

Slides

"Dolls Around the World," available from the American Friends Service Committee.

FOLK TALES

Bandeira-Duarte, Margarida, *The Legend of the Palm Tree* (N.Y.: Grosset, 1940), 47 pp. P.

Bartusek, Libushka, *Happy Times in Czechoslovakia* (N.Y.: Knopf, 1940), 62 pp.

Botsford, Florence, *Picture Tales from the Italian* (Phila.: Lippincott, 1929), 106 pp. M.

Carpenter, Frances, *Tales of a Chinese Grandmother* (N.Y.: Doubleday, 1937), 261 pp. M.

———, *Tales of a Korean Grandmother* (N.Y.: Doubleday, 1947), 287 pp. M.

Eells, Elsie S., *Fairy Tales from Brazil* (N.Y.: Dodd, Mead, 1951), 210 pp. M.

Hatch, Mary C., *More Danish Folk Tales* (N.Y.: Harcourt, 1949), 248 pp. M.

Hart, Johan, *Picture Tales from Holland* (Phila.: Lippincott, 1935), 117 pp. M.

Jacobs, Joseph, *English Fairy Tales* (N.Y.: Putnam, 1943), 227 pp. M.

———, *Indian Fairy Tales* (N.Y.: Putnam, 1942), 311 pp. M.

Kalibala, Ernest, and Davis, Mary Gould, *Wakaima and the Clay Man* (N.Y.: Longmans, 1946), 145 pp. M. East Africa.

Lim, Sian-tek, *Folk Tales from China* (N.Y.: John Day, 1944), 160 pp. M.

Meeker, Charles, *Folk Tales from the Far East* (Phila.: Winston, 1927), 254 pp. M.

Metzger, Berta, *Picture Tales from India* (N.Y.: Stokes, 1942), 87 pp. M.

Storm, Dan, *Picture Tales from Mexico* (Phila.: Lippincott, 1941), 122 pp. M.

Uchida, Yoshiko, *The Dancing Kettle and Other Japanese Folk Tales* (N.Y.: Harcourt, 1949), 174 pp. M.

———, *The Magic Listening Cap* (N.Y.: Harcourt, 1955), 144 pp. M.

Filmstrips

Young America series on "Clever Manka" (Czechoslovakia), "Pinocchio" (Italy), "The Tinker and the Ghost" (Spain), "Gudbrand on the Hillside," (Scandinavia), "The Goose Girl" (Germany), "The Five Chinese Brothers" (China). Approximately 45 frames each, color, M and U.

GAMES AND DANCES

Bergman, Marion, *The Russian-American Song and Dance Book* (N.Y.: Barnes, 1947), 95 pp.

Cooperative Recreation Service pocket-size booklets:
  All Time Games (from 12 nations), *Count and Capture, Fun with Folk Lore, Having Fun the Polish Way, Puzzle Craft,* and *Swing High: Korean Folk Recreation.*
Fun and Festival series (N.Y.: Friendship Press):
  Fun and Festival from Africa, Fun and Festival from China, Fun and Festival from India, Fun and Festival from Japan, and *Fun and Festival from the Other Americas.*
"Games and Play for Children," *Childhood Education,* September 1953.
Games of the U.N. Countries (Washington: U.S. Committee for United Nations Day, undated), 28 pp.
Harbin, E. O., *Games of Many Nations* (Nashville: Abington, 1955), 160 pp.
Henius, Frank, *Songs and Games of the Americas* (N.Y.: Scribners, 1943), 56 pp.
Henry, Bill, *Approved History of the Olympic Games* (N.Y.: Putnam, 1948), 371 pp.
Jacobs, Gertrude A., *Chinese-American Song and Game Book* (N.Y.: Barnes, 1944), 96 pp.
Malverne, Gladys, *Dancing Star: The Story of Anna Pavlova* (N.Y.: Messner, 1942), 280 pp.
Millen, Nina, *Children's Games from Many Lands* (N.Y.: Friendship Press, 1951), 214 pp.
U.S. Works Projects Administration, *The Spanish-American Song and Game Book* (N.Y.: Barnes, 1942), 87 pp.

Films

Dances of India—Kathak (Govt. of India Information Services, 1945), 10 min., sound, black and white.
Dances of India—Bharatnatyam (Govt. of India Information Services, 1946), 10 min., sound, black and white.

Slides and cards

Use can be made of the UNICEF Christmas cards on games around the world, and of *Sports Illustrated* magazine.
Slides on "Games Around the World" are available from the American Friends Service Committee.

HOLIDAYS

General References

Christmas Around the World (Washington: National Education Assoc., In preparation).

Count, Earl W., *4000 Years of Christmas* (N.Y.: Abelard, 1948), 95 pp.

Eberhard, Wolfram, *Chinese Festivals* (N.Y.: Abelard, 1952), 152 pp.

Gaer, Joseph, *Holidays Around the World* (Boston: Little, Brown, 1953), 212 pp.

Gaster, Theodor, *Purim and Hanukkah: In Custom and Tradition* (N.Y.: Abelard, 1950), 134 pp.

Jordan, Nina, *Holiday Handicraft* (N.Y.: Harcourt, 1938), 245 pp.

"Special Days Around the World," *Childhood Education*, November 1954.

Spicer, Dorothy G., *Book of Festivals* (N.Y.: Woman's Press, 1946), 428 pp.

———, *Windows Open to the World* (N.Y.: Woman's Press, 1946), 127 pp.

Von Grunebaum, G. E., *Muhammedan Festivals* (N.Y.: Abelard, 1951), 107 pp.

Books for Children

Bannon, Laura, *Manuela's Birthday* (Chicago: Whitman, 1943), 46 pp. M.

Bothwell, Jean, *The Story of India* (N.Y.: Harcourt, 1952), 180 pp. Chapter on "Feasts, Fairs and Fun." U.

Broomell, Anna P., *Friendly Story Caravan* (Phila.: Lippincott, 1949), 248 pp. M.

Carigiet, Alois, *A Bell for Ursli* (N.Y.: Oxford, 1950), 44 pp. P.

Fairfax, Virginia, and Buie, Hollie, *Ke Sooni* (N.Y.: Friendship Press, 1947), 128 pp. M.

Flack, Marjorie, *Pedro* (N.Y.: Macmillan, 1940), 90 pp. M.

Fun and Festival series, see notation under games.

Goodenow, Earle, *Angelo Goes to the Carnival* (N.Y.: Knopf, 1955), 32 pp. P.

Handforth, Thomas, *Mei Li* (N.Y.: Doubleday, 1953), 52 pp. P.

Liang, Yen, *Dee Dee's Birthday* (N.Y.: Oxford, 1952), unpaged. P.

Lindman, May Jan, *Holiday Time* (Chicago: Whitman, 1952), unpaged. P.

McSpalden, Joseph W., *Book of Holidays* (N.Y.: Crowell, 1940), 461 pp. M.

Morrow, Elizabeth, *The Painted Pig* (N.Y.: Knopf, 1930), 32 pp. M.

Olcott, Virginia, *Market Day and Holiday* (N.Y.: Silver Burdett, 1941), 68 pp. M.

Rodman, Maia, *Market Day for Ti Andre* (N.Y.: Viking, 1952), 48 pp. M.

Solem, Elizabeth K., *Ushido and a Japanese Carnival* (Chicago: Encyc. hood International, 1952), 304 pp.

Film

Your Neighbor Celebrates the Jewish Holidays (Anti-Defamation League), 22 min., sound, color or black and white.

Filmstrip

"Easter Customs in Many Lands" (Society for Visual Education), black and white.

CHRISTMAS (See also entries under Holidays)

Burack, A. S., *Christmas Plays for Young Actors* (Boston: Plays, Inc., 1950), 308 pp.
Crespi, Pachita, *Gift of the Earth* (N.Y.: Scribner's, 1946), 32 pp. M.
Dalgliesh, Alice, *Christmas: A Book of Stories Old and New* (N.Y.: Scribner's, 1950), 244 pp. M.
Jones, Jessie M. O., *A Little Child* (N.Y.: Viking, 1946), 38 pp. P.
Told Under the Christmas Tree (Washington: Association for Childhood International, 1952), 308 pp.
Vetter, Ernest G., *Christmas All Year Round* (N.Y.: Abelard, 1952), 320 pp. M.
Wyckoff, Marjorie, *Christmas Carols* (N.Y.: Simon and Schuster, 1946), 41 pp. P. A Little Golden Book.

Filmstrips

"Christmas Customs in Many Lands" (Popular Science, 1952), 44 frames, color.
"Christmas" (Informative Classroom Picture Publishers, 1947), 31 frames, black and white. Christmas in various countries.

Pictures and Units

"Christmas Customs" (Instructor).
"Christmas in Many Lands" (Informative Classroom Picture Publishers).
"Christmas Music" (Instructor).

MUSIC

Bergman, Marion, *The Russian-American Song and Dance Book* (N.Y.: Barnes, 1947), 95 pp.
Boni, Margaret B., *Fireside Book of Folk Songs* (N.Y.: Simon and Schuster, 1947), 323 pp.
Coleman, Satis, *The Marimba Book* (N.Y.: John Day, 1930), 106 pp.

Commins, Dorothy B., *Lullabies of Many Lands* (N.Y.: Harper, 1941), 72 pp.

Folk Songs and Dances of the Americas Nos. 1 and 2 (Washington: Pan American Union, 1949), 24 pp.

Jacobs, Gertrude, *Chinese-American Song and Game Book* (N.Y.: Barnes, 1944), 96 pp.

Songs of Many Nations (Delaware, Ohio: Cooperative Recreation Service, 1950), 96 pp.

Thomas, Edith L., *The Whole World Singing* (N.Y.: Friendship Press, 1950), 122 pp.

Tooze, Ruth, and Krone, Beatrice P., *Literature and Music as Resources for Social Studies* (N.Y.: Prentice Hall, 1955), 457 pp.

Films

Musical Instruments of China (Scientific Film Co., 1948), 11 min., sound, color.

Musical Instruments of India (Govt. of India Information Services, 1946), 10 min., sound, black and white.

Melody of Hindustan (Govt. of India Information Services, 1947), 12 min., sound, black and white.

Recordings

A large number of recordings of the music of other lands is available from Folkway Records and Service Corporations, 117 West 46th St., N.Y.C. 36.

The Winston Song and Story Records include: "The Day the Clouds Bumped Noses," "Ireland in Story, Song, and Pictures," and "Little Bettina Make Believe—Italy in Story, Songs, and Pictures," plus others being added.

TOYS

Daiken, Leslie, *Children's Toys Throughout the Ages* (N.Y.: Praeger, 1953), 208 pp. For teachers.

Lewellen, John, *The True Book of Toys at Work* (Chicago: Children's Press, 1953), 48 pp.

The Toys of the World Club is located at 235 East 50th St., N.Y.C.

ARTS AND CRAFTS (See bibliography on Art)

Made in . . . series (N.Y.: Knopf):
    On Canada, China, India, Mexico, and Poland.

Films

Ancient Arts of Japan (Japan Travel Information Office, 1953), 10 min., sound, black and white.

Handicrafts of India (Govt. of India Information Services, 1944), 10 min., sound, black and white.

Chapter 8. An Interdependent World

Primary grades

Beim, Jerrold, *Two Is a Team* (N.Y.: Harcourt, 1945), 61 pp.
Gekiere, Madeleine, *Who Gave Us—Peacocks? Planes? and Ferris Wheels?* (N.Y.: Pantheon, 1953), 60 pp.
McKean, Elly, *It's Mine* (N.Y.: Vanguard, 1951), unpaged.

Middle grades

Batchelor, Julie F., *Communications: From Cave Writing to Television* (N.Y.: Harcourt, 1953), 116 pp.

Upper grades

Brindze, Ruth, *The Story of Our Calendar* (N.Y.: Vanguard, 1949), 64 pp.
Fox, Melvin, *The Interdependence of Nations* (N.Y.: American Association for the United Nations, undated), 8 pp.
Hyde, Margaret O., *Flight Today and Tomorrow* (N.Y.: McGraw-Hill, 1953), 140 pp.
Lucas, Jannette M., *Where Did Your Garden Grow?* (Phila.: Lippincott, 1939), 55 pp.
The Made in . . . series (listed under arts and crafts).
Ogg, Oscar, *The 26 Letters* (N.Y.: Crowell, 1948), 254 pp.
Zilliacus, Laurin, *Mail for the World* (N.Y.: John Day, 1953), 256 pp.

Films

Art Survives the Times (A. F. Films, 1946), 10 min., sound, black and white.
China's Gifts to the West (Harmon, 1936), 30 min., silent, black and white.
Congo Art (Films of the Nations, 1948), 10 min., sound, black and white.
Expanding World Relationships (United World, 1946), 11 min., sound, color.
Handicrafts of Belgium (Films of the Nations, 1949), 10 min., color or black and white.
Made in U.S.A. (International Film Bureau, 1944), 10 min., sound, black and white.
Our Shrinking World (Young America, 1946), 10 min., sound, black and white.

Rhythm of Africa (A. F. Films, 1948), 15 min., sound, black and white.
Round Trip: The U.S.A. in World Trade (International Film Bureau, 1947), 20 min., sound, black and white.
World Trade for Better Living (Ency. Brit. Films, 1951), 17 min., sound, black and white.

Filmstrips

"Keystone of Prosperity—America's Foreign Trade" (N.Y. Times, 1952), 53 frames, black and white.
"Story of Interdependence" (Manhattan Publishing Co., 1952), black and white.
"The Story of Trade" (Curriculum Films, 1950), 25 frames, color.
"What Do They Mean to Us?" (Curriculum Films, 1950), 27 frames, color.
History of Measures series (Young America, undated):
   "History of Our Calendar," "History of Number Symbols," and "History of Telling Time."

Play and picture unit

Morley, Blythe, The Story of Interdependence (Manhattan Publishing Co.), a play.
"Old World Gifts" (Instructor), a picture unit.

Chapter 9.   A World of Many Countries and Cultures

Bibliographies for teachers

A Bibliography of Books for Children (Washington: Association for Childhood Education International, 1954), 109 pp. Revised frequently.
Books Are Bridges (Phila.: American Friends Service Committee, 1953), 54 pp. Revised occasionally.
Dratz, Eva, Aids to World Understanding for Elementary School Children (Minneapolis: Minneapolis Public Schools, 1950), 47 pp.
Tooze, Ruth, and Krone, Beatrice P., Literature and Music as Resources for Social Studies (N.Y.: Prentice Hall, 1955), 457 pp.

Magazines for teachers

Focus, American Geographical Society, Broadway at 156th St., N.Y.C. 32.
Headline Series, Foreign Policy Association, 345 East 46th St., N.Y.C. 17.

Other references for teachers

Harvard American Foreign Policy Library series (Cambridge, Mass.: Harvard Univ. Press). Books on most of the countries of the world.

Kenworthy, Leonard S., "Reading Ourselves Around the World," *Clearing House*, May 1952.

————, "Global Journey Via Pamphlets," *Clearing House*, November 1953.

————, *Free and Inexpensive Materials on World Affairs* (Brooklyn College: The Author, 1953), 96 pp.

Middle grades

Bice, Clare, *Across Canada* (N.Y.: Macmillan, 1950), 119 pp.

Clark, Ann N., *Magic Money* (N.Y.: Viking, 1950), 121 pp.

Edelman, Lily, *Japan in Story and Pictures* (N.Y.: Harcourt, 1953), 56 pp.

Henry, Marguerite, *New Zealand in Story and Pictures* (Chicago: Whitman, 1945), 28 pp.

Hoffman, Gloria, *Home at Last: A Story of Children in Israel Today* (N.Y.: McKay, 1951), 48 pp.

Hutton, Clarke, *Picture History of France* (N.Y.: Watts, 1952), 62 pp.

————, *Picture History of Britain* (N.Y.: Watts, 1946), 62 pp.

McNally, Evelyn G. and Andrew, *This Is Mexico* (N.Y.: Dodd, Mead, 1948), 216 pp.

Olcutt, Virginia, *Adventures in Sweden* (N.Y.: Grosset and Dunlap, 1953), 168 pp.

Strack, Lilian H., *Crossing Canada* (N.Y.: Harper, 1940), 274 pp.

Tor, Regina, *Getting to Know Germany* (N.Y.: Coward McCann, 1954), 64 pp.

————, *Getting to Know Puerto Rico* (N.Y.: Coward McCann, 1955), 62 pp.

Upper grades

Benary-Isbert, Margot, *Rowan Farm* (N.Y.: Harcourt, 1955), 288 pp.

Bonner, Mary G., *Canada and Her Story* (N.Y.: Knopf, 1950), 179 pp.

Bothwell, Jean, *The Story of India* (N.Y.: Harcourt, 1952), 180 pp.

Bourke-White, Margaret, *Halfway to Freedom: A Report on the New India in the Words and Photographs of Margaret Bourke-White* (N.Y.: Simon and Schuster, 1949), 245 pp.

Bro, Margueritte Harmon, *Indonesia: Land of Challenge* (N.Y.: Harper, 1954), 263 pp.

Brown, B. C., and Arbuthnot, H., *The Story of England* (N.Y.: Random House, 1943), 52 pp.

Carpenter, Frances, *Canada and Her Northern Neighbors* (N.Y.: American, 1946), 448 pp.

Clifford, H. B., *Canada, My Neighbor* (N.Y.: Scribners, 1944), 313 pp.

Crespi, Panchita, *Wings Over Central America* (N.Y.: Scribners, 1947), 169 pp.

Dickson, Helen, *Up Canada Way* (Boston: Heath, 1942), 64 pp.

Follett, Helen, *Ocean Outposts* (N.Y.: Scribners, 1942), 133 pp.

Gatti, Ellen and Attilio, *Here Is Africa* (N.Y.: Scribners, 1943), 166 pp.

————, *Mediterranean Spotlights* (N.Y.: Scribners, 1944), 183 pp.

Grattan, C. Hartley, *Lands Down Under* (St. Louis: Webster, 1943), 93 pp.

Greenbie, Sydney, *An American Boy Visits the Orient* (St. Louis: Webster, 1946), 311 pp.

Hogarth, Grace, *Australia, the Island Continent* (Boston: Houghton, 1943), 59 pp.

Irwin, William and Dorothy, *Australia and New Zealand* (N.Y.: Macmillan, 1950), 312 pp.

Kelley, Eric, *The Land of Polish People* (Phila.: Stokes, 1943), 72 pp.

Kennedy, Jean, *Here Is India* (N.Y.: Scribners, 1945), 150 pp.

Kenworthy, Leonard S., *Our Neighbors in the Americas* (N.Y.: Oxford Book Co., 1956), 96 pp.

Komai, Felicia, *Cry the Beloved Country: A Verse Drama* (N.Y.: Friendship Press, 1954), 80 pp.
A dramatization of Alan Paton's novel.

Masani, Minoo, *Our India* (N.Y.: Oxford, 1943), 172 pp. Written originally for Indian schools.

Nevins, A. J., *The Adventures of Wu Han of Korea* (N.Y.: Dodd, Mead, 1951), 244 pp.

Owen, Ruth Bryan, *Denmark Caravan* (N.Y.: Dodd, Mead, 1936), 197 pp.

Russell, Mary, *Great Britain and Canada* (N.Y.: Macmillan, 1950), 312 pp.

Seredy, Kate, *The Singing Tree* (N.Y.: Viking, 1939), 247 pp.

————, *Chestry Oak* (N.Y.: Viking, 1948), 236 pp.

————, *The Good Master* (N.Y.: Viking, 1935), 210 pp.

————, *The White Stag* (N.Y.: Viking, 1937), 94 pp.

Yutang, Lin, *My Country and My People* (N.Y.: John Day, 1935), 382 pp.

Book series

Unless otherwise indicated, books in this section are primarily intended for upper grade readers. Some of the better readers in the middle grades can read them.

Adventure series (N.Y.: Grosset and Dunlap):
On France, Holland, Italy, Norway, Russia, Sweden, Switzerland, Tunisia.

American Nation series (Washington: Pan American Union) pamphlets:
On Argentina, Bolivia, Brazil, Chile, Colombia, Costa Rica, Cuba, Dominican Republic, Ecuador, El Salvador, Guatemala, Haiti, Honduras, Mexico, Nicaragua, Panama, Paraguay, Peru, Uruguay, and Venezuela.

Around the World Series (N.Y.: American Geographical Society and Nelson Doubleday). On Australia, Brazil, Cuba, France, Hawaii, Holland, Italy, Mexico, South Africa, Switzerland, and Yugoslavia.

Facts About . . . series (Cleveland: Bloch and Company), 4 pages each:
On Brazil, India, Mexico, Norway, and Turkey.

First Book series (N.Y.: Franklin Watts, Inc.):
On Canada, Hawaii, India, Israel, Japan, and Mexico.

First Geography series (Boston: Little, Brown):
My First Geography of the Americas, My First Geography of the Pacific.

The Good Neighbor series (Evanston, Ill.: Row, Peterson):
Three Island Nations (Cuba, Haiti, and the Dominican Republic), *Next Door Neighbors* (Mexico), *The Central Five* (Guatemala, Honduras, El Salvador, Nicaragua, and Costa Rica), *By Caribbean Shores* (Panama, Colombia, and Venezuela), *Between Mountains and Sea* (Chile), *Republic of the Pampas* (Argentina, Paraguay, and Uruguay).

How Did They Live Series (London: Hawthorne), through the British Book Centre:
On China, Egypt, Greece, India, Peru, and Sumer.

Land and People series (N.Y.: Holiday House):
On Arabia, Australia, Brazil, British Isles, China, Dutch East Indies, Egypt, France, Germany, India, Japan, Mexico, Oceania, Palestine, Russia, Scandinavia, Turkey, and Yugoslovia.

Let's Read About . . . series (Grand Rapids, Mich.: Fideler Company):
On Alaska, Australia, Brazil, Canada, China, France, Germany, the Hawaiian Islands, India, Italy, Mexico, the Netherlands, Norway, Russia, South America, Sweden, and Switzerland.

Made in . . . series (N.Y.: Alfred A. Knopf):
On Canada, China, India, Mexico, and Poland.

New World Neighbor series (Boston: D. C. Heath), M:
Letters from Guatemala; Kimbi, Indian of the Jungle (Ecuador); *Around the Caribbean* (Cuba, Colombia, El Salvador); *Exploring the Jungle* (British Guiana); *Children of the Sun in Hawaii; The Gaucho's Daughter* (Argentina); *Holiday in Alaska; Work and Play in the Philippines; Boys of the Andes; Pioneers of Puerto Rico; Along the Inca Highway; Six Great Men of Brazil.*

Pageant of History series (N.Y.: Longmans, Green):
    On Canada, China, India, Japan, Middle America, The Nether-
    lands, Russia, and South America.
Picture Geography series (Chicago: Albert Whitman), M:
    On Alaska, Argentina, Australia, the Bahamas, Bermuda, Brazil,
    British Honduras, Canada, Chile, Dominican Republic, Hawaii,
    Mexico, New Zealand, Panama, the Virgin Islands, and the West
    Indies.
Picture Map Geography series (Phila.: J. B. Lippincott):
    On Africa, Asia, Canada and Alaska, Mexico, Central America and
    the West Indies, the Pacific Islands, and South America.
Picture Story series (N.Y.: McKay):
    On Alaska, China, Denmark, Hawaii, Holland, Norway, Philippines,
    and Sweden.
Portraits of the Nations series (Phila.: J. B. Lippincott):
    On Brazil, Canada, China, England, France, Greece, India, Ireland,
    Israel, Italy, Japan, Mexico, The Netherlands, Poland, Russia, Spain,
    South Africa, Sweden, and Switzerland.
Roundabout series (N.Y.: Dodd, Mead):
    On Central America, Ireland, Italy, and Scandinavia.
Tales from . . . series (N.Y.: Friendship Press):
    On China, Japan, Southeast Asia.
World Geography series (Columbus, Ohio: Charles E. Merrill), Pam-
    phlets, M:
    On Alaska, Australia and New Zealand, the British Isles, Canada,
    the Caribbean Islands, China, The Congo, the East Indies, France,
    Germany, Hawaii and the Pacific Islands, India, Italy, Japan, North
    Africa, North and South Polar Regions, The Netherlands and Bel-
    gium, Norway and Sweden, and The Philippines.
Young Traveller series (N.Y.: Dutton):
    On Australia, England and Wales, France, Germany, Holland, In-
    dia, Ireland, Italy, New Zealand, Norway, Sweden, and Switzerland.

FILMS (see also notations under Chap. 5, "Two and a Half Billion
Neighbors," and Chap. 6, "Ways of Living Around the World").

Coronet series:
    Alaska: A Modern Frontier; Central America: Geography of the
    Americas; Cuba: The Land and the People; Jack's Visit to Costa
    Rica, Mexico: Geography of the Americas; Modern Hawaii; Panama:
    Crossroads of the Western World; Rural Life of Mexico; Belgium
    and the Netherlands; Lands and Peoples; The British Isles: The
    Land and the People; China: The Land and the People; The Italian
    Peninsula; Japan: The Land and the People; The Malay Peninsula:
    People and Products; Modern France: The Land and the People;

Scandinavian Lands: Norway, Sweden, Denmark; Spain: The Land and the People; Visit to Ireland; Western Europe: An Introduction; Western Germany: The Land and the People.

Encyclopedia Britannica, Children of Many Lands series:

Children of America: *Eskimo Children, French-Canadian Children, Mexican Children.* Children of Europe: *Children of the Alps, English Children, French Children, Children of Germany, Greek Children, Children of Holland, Irish Children, Italian Children, Norwegian Children, Spanish Children, Children of Switzerland.* Children of Faraway Places: *Arabian Children, Children of China, Children of Japan, South Pacific Island Children.*

McGraw-Hill, March of Time series:

Britain and Her Empire, Canada, China, Costa Rica, Crisis in Iran, Czechoslovakia, Greece, India, Indonesia, Ireland, Japan and Democracy, Moroccan Outpost, New France, Palestine, Portugal, Promise of Pakistan, Republic of Italy, South Africa, Sweden, Sweden Looks Ahead, and *Turkey.*

Several of the embassies and information offices have films for loan.

Filmstrips

American Geographical Society series, Distributed by Herbert E. Budek Co., color:

On Algeria, Costa Rica, Ethiopia, Germany, Great Britain, Greece, Honduras, Ireland, Israel, Italy, Jamaica, Lebanon, Morocco and Tangier, Philippines, Puerto Rico, Switzerland (three filmstrips), Thailand, Turkey, and Yugoslavia.

Encyclopedia Britannica series:

On Maritime Provinces of Canada, Industrial Provinces of Canada, Prairie Provinces of Canada, Pacific Provinces of Canada, Alaska, Mexico, Central America and the West Indies, Belgium, Denmark, The Netherlands, Norway and Sweden, France, Italy, Portugal, Spain, and Switzerland.

Informative Classroom Picture Publishers series:

On Alaska, Australia, Brazil, Canada, China, Hawaiian Islands, India, Mexico, South America, Soviet Union.

Life series:

On Africa, Alaska, Britain, Canada, France, Germany, Hawaii, India, Indo-China, Italy, Israel, Japan, Korea, Mexico, The New Indonesia, The People of Indonesia, Saudi Aradia, South Africa.

New York Times series:

"The Dark Continent Wakens" (Africa), "Canada: A Nation Grows," "Germany Divided," and "Pivot of Asia: India and Pakistan."

Teaching Aids Service, Profile series:
  "Profile of Pakistan," "Profile of Puerto Rico."
Society for Visual Education series:
  On Finland, France, Gold Coast of Africa, India, Ireland, Italy,
  Japan, Korea, Norway, and Spain.

Picture Units

Informative Classroom Picture Publishers series:
  On Alaska, Australia, Brazil, Canada, China, the Hawaiian Islands,
  India, Mexico, Russia, and South America.

Chapter 10. A World of Poverty and Plenty

References for Teachers

Barr, Stringfellow, *Let's Join the Human Race* (Chicago: Univ. of Chicago Press, 1950), 30 pp.
Bowles, Chester, *Ambassador's Report* (N.Y.: Harper, 1953), 415 pp. (On India.)
Douglas, William O., *Strange Lands and Friendly People* (N.Y.: Harper, 1951), 336 pp.
Hanson, Earl P., *Transformation: The Story of Modern Puerto Rico* (N.Y.: Simon and Schuster, 1955), 416 pp.

Primary grades

Bulla, Clyde R., *The Poppy Seeds* (N.Y.: Crowell, 1955), 38 pp.
Leaf, Munro, *Fair Play* (Phila.: Lippincott, 1939), 94 pp.
————, *Let's Do Better* (N.Y.: Harcourt, 1945), 61 pp.

Middle grades

Buff, Mary and Conrad, *Magic Maize* (Boston: Houghton, 1953), 76 pp.
Louden, Claire and George, *Rain in the Winds: A Story of India* (N.Y.: Scribner's, 1953), 48 pp.

Upper grades

Beckel, Graham, *Workshops for the World* (N.Y.: Abelard, 1954), 213 pp.
Borth, Christy, *Pioneers of Plenty* (Indianapolis: Bobbs-Merrill, 1939), 303 pp.
Bowles, Cynthia, *At Home In India* (N.Y.: Harcourt, 1956), 180 pp.
Bro, Margueritte Harmon, *Su-Mei's Golden Year* (N.Y.: Doubleday, 1950), 246 pp.
Goodfriend, Arthur, *The Only War We Seek* (N.Y.: Farrar, 1951), 128 pp. Largely pictorial.

Shippen, Kathline, *Pool of Knowledge: How the United Nations Share Their Skills* (N.Y.: Harpers, 1954), 148 pp.

Tarshis, Elizabeth K., *The Village That Learned to Read* (Boston: Houghton, 1941), 158 pp.

Yates, Elizabeth, *Rainbow Round the World: A Story of Unicef* (Indianapolis: Bobbs-Merrill, 1954), 174 pp.

Films

Danish Children Build Greek School (United Nations, 1950), 10 min., sound, black and white.

Daybreak in Udi (British Information Services, 1949), 45 min., sound, black and white.

Indonesia Builds a Better Life (United Nations, 1953), 10 min., sound, black and white.

A Village Awakens (United Nations, 1952), 10 min., sound, black and white.

World Without End (Brandon Films, 1953), 45 min., sound, black and white.

Filmstrip

"East Africa Tackles the Land Problem" (British Information Services, 1953), 23 frames, black and white.

Chapter 11.   A World with Many Forms of Government

Primary grades

Lowe, Edith, *Animal Parade* (Kenosha, Wis.: Samuel Lowe Co., 1951), 24 pp.

Middle grades

Kastner, Erich, and Trier, Walter, *The Animal Conference* (N.Y.: McKay, 1953), unpaged.

Leaf, Munro, *Fair Play* (Phila.: Lippincott, 1949), 44 pp.

Provenson, Alice and Martin, *The Animal Fair* (N.Y.: Simon and Schuster, 1952), 76 pp.

Turner, Mina, *Town Meeting Means Me* (Boston: Houghton, 1951), 48 pp.

Upper grades

Baker, Nina B., *Chaim Weizmann: Builder of a Nation* (N.Y.: Messner, 1950), 180 pp.

————, *Juarez, Hero of Mexico* (N.Y.: Vanguard, 1942), 316 pp.

Linton, Ralph and Adelin, *Man's Way from Cave to Skyscraper* (N.Y.: Harper, 1947), 185 pp.

Masani, Minoo, *The Growing Human Family* (N.Y.: Oxford, 1951), 127 pp.

Spencer, Cornelia, *Romulo: Voice of Freedom* (N.Y.: John Day, 1953), 256 pp.

Stratton, Randall E., and Wilson, Howard E., *Juarez of Mexico: A Leader of Democracy* (N.Y.: American, 1948), 148 pp.

Wagner, Ruth H., and Green, Ivah E., *Put Democracy to Work* (N.Y.: Schuman, 1952), 132 pp.

Chapters in Let's Read About . . . series of the Fideler Company and the Portraits of Nations series of the J. B. Lippincott Company will be helpful on governments around the world.

Films

General Election (British Information Services, 1946), 20 min., sound, black and white.

Government Is Your Business (Christophers, 1952), 27 min., sound, black and white.

Government of Japan (United World-Government, 1945), 18 min., sound, black and white.

How Britain Votes (British Information Services, 1951), 18 min., sound, black and white.

Chapter 12. A World with Many Religions and Value Systems

General references

Ansley, Delight, *The Good Ways* (N.Y.: Crowell, 1950), 214 pp.

Bainton, Roland H., *The Church of Our Fathers* (N.Y.: Scribner's, 1944), 248 pp.

Browne, Lewis, *This Believing World* (N.Y.: Macmillan, 1926), 347 pp.

Cranston, Ruth, *World Faith* (N.Y.: Harpers, 1949), 193 pp.

Fitch, Florence Mary, *Allah: The God of Islam* (N.Y.: Lothrop, 1950), 144 pp.

————, *One God: The Ways We Worship Him* (N.Y.: Lothrop, 1944), 144 pp.

————, *Their Search for God: Ways of Worship in the Orient* (N.Y.: Lothrop, 1947), 160 pp.

Gaer, Joseph, *How the Great Religions Began* (N.Y.: Signet, 1954), 240 pp.

Pyne, Mabel M., *The Story of Religion* (Boston: Houghton, 1954), 54 pp.

Smith, Ruth, *Tree of Life* (N.Y.: Viking, 1942), 496 pp.

Middle and upper grades

Blanton, Catherine, *Pedro's Choice* (N.Y.: Whittlesey, 1948), 64 pp.
Seredy, Kate, *The Good Master* (N.Y.: Viking, 1935), 210 pp.
Sperry, Armstrong, *Call It Courage* (N.Y.: Macmillan, 1940), 96 pp.
Treffinger, Carolyn, *Li Lu, Lad of Courage* (Nashville: Abingdon, 1947), 96 pp.

Biographies of religious leaders

Bainton, Roland H., *Here I Stand* (Nashville: Abingdon, 1950), 422 pp. (Luther).
Eaton, Jeanette, *Gandhi: Fighter Without a Sword* (N.Y.: Morrow, 1950), 253 pp.
Gollomb, Joseph, *Albert Schweitzer* (N.Y.: Vanguard, 1949), 249 pp.
Kenworthy, Leonard S., *Twelve Citizens of the World* (N.Y.: Doubleday, 1953), 286 pp. Includes chapters on Gandhi, Kagawa, Schweitzer, and others.
Masani, Shakuntala, *Gandhi's Story* (N.Y.: Oxford, 1950), 101 pp.
Peare, Catherine O., *Mahatma Gandhi* (N.Y.: Holt, 1950), 229 pp.
Shippen, Katherine B., *Moses* (N.Y.: Harper, 1949), 132 pp.

Novels with religious theme

Asch, Sholem, *The Apostle* (N.Y.: Putnam, 1943), 804 pp.
———, *Mary* (N.Y.: Putnam, 1949), 436 pp.
———, *The Nazarene* (N.Y.: Putnam, 1939), 698 pp.
Douglas, Lloyd, *The Big Fisherman* (Boston: Houghton, 1948), 581 pp.
———, *The Robe* (Boston: Houghton, 1942), 695 pp.
Werfel, Franz, *Song of Bernadette* (N.Y.: Viking, 1942), 575 pp.

Films

Fire Upon the Earth (Broadcasting and Film Commission, 1951), 26 min., sound, color. A history of Christianity.
One God (Association Films, 1949), 37 min., sound, black and white. Based on the book by Florence Mary Fitch.
Your Neighbor Celebrates (Broadcasting and Film Commission, 1950), 28 min., sound, color. Jewish holidays.

Filmstrip and Recordings

"One God: The Ways We Worship Him" (Association Films, 1952), 100 frames, black and white. Also available as a Kapp recording with music.

Chapter 13. A World of Conflict and Cooperation

References for Teachers

Coyle, David C., *The United Nations and How It Works* (N.Y.: Signet Key, 1955), 208 pp.

Dratz, Eva M., *Guide to Teaching about the United Nations and World Affairs* (N.Y.: American Association for the United Nations, 1955), 43 pp.

Eichelberger, Clark M., *U.N.: The First Ten Years* (N.Y.: Harper, 1955), 108 pp.

Feller, A. H., *United Nations and World Community* (Boston: Little, Brown, 1952), 193 pp.

Fisher, Aileen, and Rabe, Olive, *United Nations Plays and Programs* (Boston: Plays, Inc., 1954), 285 pp.

Goetz, Delia, *A Junior High School Looks at Unesco* (Washington: U.S. National Commission for Unesco, 1951), 26 pp.

Hill, Wilhelmina, and Mackintosh, Helen, *How Children Learn About Human Rights* (Washington: G.P.O., 1951), 16 pp.

Kenworthy, Leonard S., *Studying the United Nations and Its Specialized Agencies* (Brooklyn College: The Author, 1953), 44 pp.

McLaurin, John, *The United Nations and Power Politics* (N.Y.: Harper, 1951), 468 pp.

Reid, Robert, *Box Score of the U.N.: 1945–1955* (Washington: National Education Association, 1955), 4 pp.

———, *Planning Your Trip to the U.N.* (Washington: National Education Association, 1955), 4 pp.

Round the World with a Postage Stamp: A Booklet for Teachers and Children about the Universal Postal Union (Paris: Unesco, 1953), 38 pp. Through the Columbia University Press.

A Teacher's Guide to the Declaration of Human Rights (Paris: Unesco, 1950), 28 pp.

Zocca, Marie and Louis, *The United Nations: Action for Peace: A Layman's Guide* (New Brunswick: Rutgers University Press, 1955), 68 pp.

Primary grades

Beim, Lorraine and Jerrold, *Two Is a Team* (N.Y.: Harcourt, 1945), 61 pp.

Earle, Vana, *My Friend Johnny* (N.Y.: Lothrop, 1952), 28 pp.

A Garden We Planted Together (N.Y.: United Nations, 1951), 48 pp.

Hogan, Inez, *Nappy Has a New Friend* (N.Y.: Dutton, 1947), 48 pp.

Leaf, Munro, *Let's Do Better* (Phila.: Lippincott, 1945), 45 pp.

Nemec, L., *Let's Take Turns* (N.Y.: Macmillan, 1951), 119 pp.

Tworkov, Jack, *The Camel Who Took a Walk* (N.Y.: Aladdin, 1951), unpaged.

Middle grades

Caesar, Irving, *Sing a Song of Friendship* (N.Y.: Irving Caesar, 1946), 64 pp.

Fisher, Dorothy Canfield, *A Fair World for All: The Meaning of the Declaration of Human Rights* (N.Y.: Whittlesey, 1952), 159 pp.

Fisher, Lois, *You and the United Nations* (Chicago: Childrens Press, 1947), 42 pp.

Leaf, Munro, *Fair Play* (Phila.: Lippincott, 1939), 94 pp.

Masani, Shakuntala, *Gandhi's Story* (N.Y.: Oxford, 1950), 101 pp.

————, *Nehru's Story* (N.Y.: Oxford, 1949), 81 pp.

Wilson, Clara O., *Working Together in the United Nations* (Lincoln, Nebraska: University Publishing Company, 1947), 32 pp.

Upper grades

Beckel, Graham, *Workshops for the World* (N.Y.: Abelard, 1954), 213 pp.

de Kruif, Paul, *Hunger Fighters, Men Against Death*, and *Microbe Hunters* (N.Y.: Harcourt, various editions).

Doorly, Eleanor, *The Radium Woman: A Life of Marie Curie* (N.Y.: Roy, 1955), 181 pp.

Galt, Tom, *How the United Nations Works* (N.Y.: Crowell, 1955), 247 pp.

————, *The Story of Peace and War* (N.Y.: Crowell, 1952), 202 pp.

Gollomb, Joseph, *Albert Schweitzer: Genius in the Jungle* (N.Y.: Vanguard, 1949), 249 pp.

Gray, William S., Pooley, Robert C., and Walcott, Fred G., *Paths and Pathfinders* (Chicago: Scott Foresman, 1951), 528 pp.

Hall, Anna G., *Nansen* (N.Y.: Viking, 1940), 204 pp.

Hatch, Alden, *Young Willkie* (N.Y.: Harcourt, 1944), 224 pp.

How Peoples Work Together: The United Nations and the Specialized Agencies (N.Y.: Manhattan Publishing Company, 1956), 52 pp.

Joyce, James Avery, *World in the Making: The Story of International Cooperation* (N.Y.: Schuman, 1953), 159 pp.

Kastner, Eric and Trier, Walter, *Animals' Conference* (N.Y.: McKay, 1953), 64 pp.

Kenworthy, Leonard S., *Twelve Citizens of the World* (N.Y.: Doubleday, 1953), 286 pp.

————, "World Heroes," *Social Education*, April 1952.

Kugelmass, J. Alvin, *Ralph Bunche: Fighter for Peace* (N.Y.: Messner, 1952), 174 pp.

McClintock, Marshall, *Trygve Lie* (N.Y.: Holt, 1953), 224 pp.

McLaughlin, Kathleen, *New Life in Old Lands* (N.Y.: Dodd, 1954), 272 pp.

Masani, Minocheher, *The Growing Human Family* (N.Y.: Oxford, 1951), 127 pp.

Paths to World Peace (N.Y.: Scholastic Magazines, 1952), 32 pp.

Peare, Catherine, *Albert Einstein* (N.Y.: Holt, 1949), 152 pp.

————, *Mahatma Gandhi* (N.Y.: Holt, 1950), 229 pp.

Robinson, Donald, ·*The 100 Most Important People* (N.Y.: Pocket Books, 1953), 439 pp.

Roosevelt, Eleanor, and Ferris, Helen, *Partners: The United Nations and Youth* (N.Y.: Doubleday, 1950), 208 pp.

Shippen, Katherine, *Pool of Knowledge: How the United Nations Share Their Skills* (N.Y.: Harper, 1954), 148 pp.

Steinberg, Samuel, *Peace in the Making* (N.Y.: Oxford Book Company, 1951), 60 pp.

Sterling, Dorothy, and Ehrenberg, Myron, *United Nations, N.Y.* (N.Y.: Doubleday, 1953), 80 pp.

The United Nations: A Handbook on the U.N. (Columbus, Ohio: Merrill Books, 1949), 32 pp.

Wagner, Ruth H., and Green, Ivah E., *Put Democracy to Work* (N.Y.: Schuman, 1952), 132 pp.

Yates, Elizabeth, *Rainbow Round the World: A Story of UNICEF* (Indianapolis: Bobbs Merrill, 1954), 174 pp.

Zilliacus, Laurin, *Mail for the World: From the Courier to the Universal Postal Union* (N.Y.: John Day, 1953), 256 pp.

Films

Assignment Children (Association Films 1955), 20 min., sound, technicolor.

Border Without Bayonets (McGraw-Hill, 1948), 16 min., sound, black and white.

The Children (McGraw-Hill, 1950), 10 min., sound, black and white.

Grand Design (McGraw-Hill, 1951), 9 min., sound, black and white.

United Nations, N.Y. (McGraw-Hill, 1954), 14 min., sound, black and white.

Workshop for Peace (McGraw-Hill, 1952), 29 min., sound, black and white.

World Without End (Brandon, 1954), 45 min., sound, black and white.

Plays

Nancy's Dream, The Martian Schemers and other plays are available from the American Association for the United Nations.

Kits and other materials

American Association for the United Nations, 345 East 46th St., N.Y.C. 17.

National Citizens Committee for U.N. Day, 821 21st St., N.W., Washington 6, D.C.

Unesco Relations Staff, U.S. Department of State, Washington 25, D.C.

United Nations Book Store, United Nations, N.Y.

UNICEF, United Nations, N. Y.

"The United Nations and How It Works" (N.Y.: United Nations Bookstore, 1955). A packet for a three-dimensional model of the U.N.

Appendix C. Addresses of Organizations, Publishers, Embassies and Other Groups

SOURCES OF FLAGS

Annin and Company, 85 Fifth Ave., N.Y.C. 3.

National Flag Company, 1012 Flint St., Cincinnati 14.

New England Decorating Co., Lincoln St., Boston 11.

Paramount Flag Company, 520 Folsom St., San Francisco 5.

Sherritt Flag Company, Richmond 20, Va.

Standard Flag and Manufacturing Co., 716 Chestnut St., Phil.

A set of small paper flags may be purchased from the American Association for the United Nations, 345 East 46th St., N.Y.C. 17, or from its branch offices.

A packet for making the U.N. flag is obtainable from the National Committee on Boys and Girls Club Work, 59 East Van Buren St., Chicago 5.

SOURCES FOR INTERNATIONAL CORRESPONDENCE

(From material prepared by the writer for a Bulletin of the Commission on International Understanding of the Association for Supervision and Curriculum Development)

American Junior Red Cross, 17th and D Sts., N.W., Washington, D.C. Limited to schools and classes enrolled in the American Junior Red Cross program. Group or class correspondence only. For further information consult the local chapter of the Red Cross.

Caravan of East and West, Inc., 132 East 65th St., N.Y.C. 21. Age groups: 6–15, 15–20, and adults. Around 50 countries. Cost: $1, which includes subscription to *The Caravan* magazine.

International Friendship League, 40 Mt. Vernon St., Beacon Hill, Boston. Age groups: All school and high school ages. Practically all countries in the "free world"—about 100. 50c for pupils under 19.

International Students Society, Hillsboro, Oregon. Age groups: 12–22.

Specializes in language classes and correspondence in foreign languages. 133 countries. 20c each, but minimum order for five addresses. Prefer that teachers write for group.

Inter-Scholastic Correspondence Dept., Student Forum on International Relations, P.O. Box 733, San Francisco, Cal. Age groups: 13–19. All countries outside "Iron Curtain" area. 25c per name, except for group orders, which are 10c per name.

Pen Friends Committee, English Speaking Union, 19 East 54th St., N.Y.C. 22. Age groups: 11–15. Largely Great Britain. No charge, but teachers are urged to send in names of group of pupils, stating age and interests wherever possible.

Student Letter Exchange, Waseca, Minn. Age groups: 10–20. About 40 countries. 25c for foreign names; 10c for U.S. names.

ORGANIZATIONS, PUBLISHERS, INSTITUTIONS

Abelard-Schuman Press, 404 Fourth Ave., N.Y.C. 16.

Abingdon, 810 Broadway, Nashville 2, Tenn.

Aladdin Books (see American Book Co.)

American Association for the United Nations, 345 East 46th St., N.Y.C. 17.

American Book Co., 88 Lexington Ave., N.Y.C. 16.

American Council on Education, 1785 Mass. Ave., N.W., Washington 6.

American Field Service, 113 East 40th St., N.Y.C. 16.

American Friends of the Middle East, 237 East 48th St., N.Y.C. 17.

American Friends Service Committee, 20 South 12th St., Phila. 7.

American Geographical Society, Broadway at 156th St., N.Y.C. 32.

American Korean Foundation, 345 East 46th St., N.Y.C. 17.

American Museum of Natural History, Central Park West at 79th St., N.Y.C. 24.

American Red Cross, 17th and D Sts., N.W., Washington 13.

Anti-Defamation League, 212 Fifth Ave., N.Y.C. 10.

Art for World Friendship (see Women's International League).

Arts Cooperative Service, 340 Amsterdam Ave., N.Y.C. 24.

Bantam Books, 1007 Broadway, N.Y.C.

A. S. Barnes and Co., 232 Madison Ave., N.Y.C. 16.

Bay City Public Schools, Bay City, Michigan.

Beacon Press, 25 Beacon St., Boston 8.

Beckley-Cardy, 1900 North Narragansett Avenue, Chicago 37, Ill.

Behrmann's Book House, 1261 Broadway, N.Y.C. 1.

Bloch and Co., Room 402, 1010 Euclid Building, Cleveland 15.

Bobbs Merrill, 468 Fourth Ave., N.Y.C. 16.

Boy Scouts of America, 2 Park Ave., N.Y.C. 16.

Britannica Junior, Encyclopedia Britannica, 425 North Michigan Ave., Chicago 11.

British Book Centre, 122 East 55th St., N.Y.C. 22.
Bureau of Publications, Teachers College, Columbia University, N.Y.C. 27.
Camp Fire Girls, 16 East 48th St., N.Y.C. 17.
Canadian Citizenship Council, 46 Elgin St., Ottawa, Canada.
Canadian Institute of International Affairs, 230 Bloor St., Toronto, Canada.
Capitol Publishing Company, Irvington-on-Hudson, N.Y.
Center for Information on the Americas, Washington, Conn.
Chicago Round Table (see University of Chicago).
Children's Press, Thorp and Monroe Sts., Chicago 7.
Civic Education Project, 10 Craigie St., Cambridge 38, Mass.
Columbia University Press, Broadway at 116th St., N.Y.C. 27.
Committee on International Relations, National Education Association, 1201 16th St., N.W., Washington 6.
C.I.O. International Affairs Dept., 718 Jackson Place, N.W., Washington.
Cooperative Recreation Service, Delaware, Ohio.
Creative Education Society, Mankato, Minn.
Crowell Publishing Company, 432 Fourth Ave., N.Y.C. 16.
John Day Company, 2 West 45th St., N.Y.C. 19.
Denoyer-Geppert Map Company, 5235 Ravenswood Ave., Chicago 40.
Dodd, Mead and Co., 432 Fourth Ave., N.Y.C. 16.
Doubleday and Company, 575 Madison Ave., N.Y.C. 22.
Dryden Press, 31 West 54th St., N.Y.C. 19.
E. P. Dutton Co., 300 Fourth Ave., N.Y.C. 10.
Education Department, University of Hawaii, Honolulu, Hawaii.
Fideler Company, Grand Rapids 2, Mich.
Folkways Record and Service Corporation, 117 West 46th St., N.Y.C. 36.
Follett Publishing Company, 1247 South Wabash Ave., Chicago 5.
Foreign Policy Association, 345 East 46th St., N.Y.C. 17.
Franco-American Audio-Visual Distribution Center, 972 Fifth Ave., N.Y.C. 21.
Friendship Press, 156 Fifth Ave., N.Y.C. 10.
Gawthorn (see British Book Centre).
Ginn and Company, Statler Building, Boston 17.
Girl Scouts of the U.S.A., 155 East 44th St., N.Y.C. 17.
Grolier Society, 2 West 45th St., N.Y.C. 36.
Grosset and Dunlap, 1107 Broadway, N.Y.C. 10.
Hammond Map Company, 88 Lexington Ave., N.Y.C. 16.
Harcourt, Brace and Co., 383 Madison Ave., N.Y.C. 17.
Harper & Brothers, 49 East 33rd St., N.Y.C. 16.
Harvard University Press, Cambridge, Mass.

D. C. Heath and Co., 285 Columbus Ave., Boston 16.
Hershey Chocolate Corporation, Hershey, Pa.
Holiday House, 8 West 13th St., N.Y.C. 11.
Henry Holt and Co., 257 Fourth Ave., N.Y.C. 10.
Houghton Mifflin, 2 Park St., Boston 7.
Informative Classroom Picture Publishers, Grand Rapids, Mich.
The Instructor, Danville, N.Y.
International Publishers Co., 381 Fourth Ave., N.Y.C. 10.
Japan Society, Savoy-Plaza Hotel, 5th Ave. at 58th St., N.Y.C. 22.
Kansas State Teachers College, Pittsburg, Kansas
Leonard S. Kenworthy, Brooklyn College, Brooklyn 10, N.Y.
Alfred A. Knopf, 501 Madison Ave., N.Y.C. 22.
Korean Affairs Institute, 1507 M St., N.W., Washington.
Korean Pacific Press, 1620 Eye St., N.W., Washington.
J. B. Lippincott Co., East Washington Square, Phila. 5.
Little, Brown and Co., 34 Beacon St., Boston 6.
Longmans, Green and Co., 55 Fifth Ave., N.Y.C. 3.
Lothrop, Lee and Shephard, 419 Fourth Ave., N.Y.C. 16.
Samuel Lowe Co., Kenosha, Wis.
McBride, 200 East 37th St., N.Y.C. 16.
McGraw-Hill Book Co., 330 West 42nd St., N.Y.C. 16.
David McKay, 55 5th Ave., N.Y.C. 3.
McKinley Publishing Co., 809 North 19th St., Phila. 30.
The Macmillan Company, 60 Fifth Ave., N.Y.C. 11.
Maco Magazine Corporation, 480 Lexington Ave., N.Y.C.
Magazines for Friendship, Occidental College, Los Angeles 41.
Manhattan Publishing Company, 225 Lafayette St., N.Y.C. 12.
Melmont Publishers, Inc., 5639 Melrose Ave., Los Angeles 38.
Mentor-Signet Books, 501 Madison Ave., N.Y.C. 16.
Charles E. Merrill Co., 400 South Front St., Columbus 15, Ohio.
Messner, 8 West 40th St., N.Y.C. 18.
Middle America Information Bureau, Box 93, Lennox Hill Station, N.Y.C. 21.
The Middle East Institute, 1830 19th St., N.W., Washington 9.
Middle Eastern Affairs, 650 Palisade Ave., Jersey City 7, N.J.
Minneapolis Public Schools, Board of Education, Minneapolis.
Minnesota World Affairs Center, Univ. of Minn., Minneapolis.
William Morrow and Co., 425 Fourth Ave., N.Y.C. 16.
Museum of Modern Art, 11 West 53rd St., N.Y.C. 19.
National Citizen's Committee for United Nations Day, 816 21st St., N.W., Washington.
National Committee on Boys and Girls Club Work, 59 East Van Buren St., Chicago 5.

National Conference of Christians and Jews, 381 Fourth Ave., N.Y.C. 16.

National Council of Churches, 120 East 23rd St., N.Y.C. 10.

National Council for the Social Studies, 1201 16th St., N.W., Washington 6.

National Council of Teachers of English, 211 West 68th St., Chicago 21.

National Dairy Council, Chicago 6.

National Education Association, 1201 16th St., N.W., Washington 6.

National Geographic Society, 16th and M Sts., N.W., Washington 6.

Thomas Nelson's Sons, 19 East 47th St., N.Y.C. 17.

New York Times, School Service Dept., Times Square, N.Y.C. 18.

A. J. Nystrom Maps, 3333 Elston Ave., Chicago.

Oxford Book Co., 222 Fourth Ave., N.Y.C. 3.

Oxford University Press, 114 Fifth Ave., N.Y.C. 11.

F. A. Owen Publishing Co., Dansville, N.Y.

Pantheon Books, Inc., 333 Sixth Ave., N.Y.C. 4.

Pan American Coffee Bureau, 120 Wall St., N.Y.C. 5.

Pan American Union, 19th and Constitution Ave., N.W., Washington 6.

Penguin Books, 3300 Clipper Mill Road, Baltimore 11, Md.

Platt and Munk, 200 Fifth Ave., N.Y.C. 10.

Plays, Inc., 8 Arlington St., Boston 16, Mass.

Pocket Books, Rockefeller Center, N.Y.C. 20.

Frederick A. Praeger, 105 West 40th St., N.Y.C. 18.

Prentice Hall, 70 Fifth Ave., N.Y.C. 4.

Presbyterian Board of Missions, 156 Fifth Ave., N.Y.C. 10.

Public Affairs Committee, 22 East 38th St., N.Y.C. 16.

Public Affairs Institute, 312 Penna. Ave., S.E., Washington 3.

Public Affairs Press, 2153 Florida Ave., N.W., Washington 8.

George Putnam Sons, 210 Madison Ave., N.Y.C. 16.

Rand McNally and Co., 111 Eighth Ave., N.Y.C. 11.

Random House, 457 Madison Ave., N.Y.C. 22.

Row, Peterson and Co., 1911 Ridge Ave., Evanston, Ill.

Roy, 30 East 74th St., N.Y.C. 21.

Rutgers Univ. Press, New Brunswick, N.J.

St. Paul Public Schools, Board of Education Building, St. Paul, Minn.

Save the Children Federation, One Madison Ave., N.Y.C. 10.

Scholastic Magazines, 33 West 42nd St., N.Y.C. 36.

Science Research Associates, 57 West Grand Ave., Chicago 10.

Schuman (see Abelard)

William R. Scott, 8 West 13th St., N.Y.C. 11.

Scott, Foresman and Co., 114 East 23rd St., N.Y.C. 10.

Charles Scribner's Sons, 597 Fifth Ave., N.Y.C. 17.

Sears (see Dodd, Mead)
Signet Key, 245 Fifth Ave., N.Y.C.
Silver Burdett, 45 East 17th St., N.Y.C. 3.
Simon and Schuster, 1230 Ave. of the Americas, N.Y.C. 20.
Stokes (see Lippincott)
Studio Publications, 381 Fourth Ave., N.Y.C.
UNESCO Relations Staff, U.S. Dept. of State, Washington 25.
UNESCO, United Nations, N.Y. 17.
University of Chicago Round Table, Chicago 37.
U.S. Government Printing Office, Washington 25.
U.S. Office of Education, Washington 25.
United Fruit Company, Pier 3, North River, N.Y.C. 6.
University Publishing Company, Lincoln, Nebraska.
Vanguard Press, 424 Madison Ave., N.Y.C. 17.
Viking Press, 18 East 48th St., N.Y.C. 17.
Franklin Watts Inc., 699 Madison Ave., N.Y.C. 21.
Webster Publishing Co., 1808 Washington Ave., St. Louis 3, Mo.
Westminster Press, Witherspoon Building, Phila.
Albert Whitman and Co., 1808 West Lake St., Chicago.
Wilcox and Follett, 1255 South Wabash St., Chicago.
John C. Winston Co., 1006 Arch St., Phil. 7.
Woman's Press, 425 Fourth Ave., N.Y.C. 16.
Women's International League, 2006 Walnut St., Phila. 7.
World Book Encyclopedia Reference Library, Field Enterprises, Inc., Educational Divison, Merchandise Mart Place, Chicago 54.
World Friendship Among Children, 214 East 21st St., N.Y.C. 10.

EMBASSIES AND GOVERNMENT INFORMATION OFFICES

(Arranged alphabetically by the name of the country.)

Argentine Consulate General, 9 Rockefeller Plaza, N.Y.C. 20.
Australian News and Information Bureau, 636 Fifth Ave., N.Y.C. 20.
Information Dept. of the Austrian Consulate General, 31 East 69th St., N.Y.C.
Belgian Govt. Information Center, 630 Fifth Ave., N.Y.C. 20.
Bolivian Consulate General, 10 Rockefeller Plaza, N.Y.C. 20.
Brazilian Govt. Trade Bureau, 551 Fifth Ave., N.Y.C. 17.
British Information Services, 30 Rockefeller Plaza, N.Y.C. 20.
Bulgarian Embassy, 2841 McGill Terrace, N.W., Washington 8.
Burmese Embassy, 2228 Mass. Ave., N.W., Washington.
Canadian Embassy, Information Office, 1746 Mass. Ave., N.W., Washington.
Embassy of Ceylon, 2523 Mass. Ave., N.W., Washington 8.
Chilean Consulate General, 61 Broadway, N.Y.C.
Colombian Embassy, 1609 22nd St., N.W., Washington.

Consulate General of Costa Rica, 420 Lexington Ave., N.Y.C. 17.
Delegation of Cuba to the U.N., 405 East 42nd St., N.Y.C. 17.
Czechoslovakian Embassy, 2349 Mass. Ave., N.W., Washington.
Danish Information Office, 588 Fifth Ave., N.Y.C. 36.
Dominican Republic Information Center, 6 West 51st St., N.Y.C. 20.
Ecuador Embassy, 2125 Leroy Place, Washington.
Egyptian Embassy, 2310 Decatur Place, N.W., Washington 8.
El Salvador Embassy, 2400 16th St., N.W., Washington.
Ethiopian Legation, 2134 Kalorama Road, Washington.
Finnish National Travel Office, 41 East 50th St., N.Y.C.
French Embassy, 972 Fifth Ave., N.Y.C. 21.
Diplomatic Mission of the Federal Republic of Germany, 1742 R St.,
    N.W., Washington 9.
German Tourist Information Office, 500 Fifth Ave., N.Y.C.
Greek Embassy, 2211 Mass. Ave., N.W., Washington 6.
Greek Govt. Office of Information, 30 Rockefeller Plaza, N.Y.C. 20.
Guatemalan Consulate General, 30 Rockefeller Plaza, N.Y.C. 20.
Haitian Consulate General, 30 Rockefeller Plaza, N.Y.C. 20.
Hawaiian Press Bureau, 1040 National Press Building, Washington 4.
Embassy of Honduras, 4715 16th St., N.W., Washington 1.
Hungarian Legation, 2118 Leroy Pl., N.W., Washington 8.
Icelandic Consulate General, 50 Broad St., N.Y.C. 4.
Indonesian Republic, 10 Rockefeller Plaza, N.Y.C. 20.
Indian Government Information Services, 2107 Mass. Ave., N.W., Wash-
    ington 8.
Iranian Information Bureau, 30 Rockefeller Plaza, N.Y.C. 20.
Irish Consulate, 33 East 50th St., N.Y.C.
Israel Office of Information, 11 East 60th St., N.Y.C. 21.
Consulate General of Italy, 33 East 50th St., N.Y.C.
Consulate General of Japan, Empire State Building, Room 7112, 350
    Fifth Ave., N.Y.C.
Japanese Travel Information Office, 10 Rockefeller Plaza, N.Y.C. 20.
Korean Affairs Institute, 1029 Vermont Ave., N.W., Washington.
Lebanese Legation, Suite 400 A, Wardman Park Hotel, Washington.
Liberian Embassy, 1616 Eye St., N.W., Washington.
Luxembourg Commission of Information, 441 Lexington Ave., N.Y.C.
    17.
Mexican Consulate General, 70 Pine St., N.Y.C. 5.
Netherlands Information Service, 10 Rockefeller Plaza, N.Y.C. 20.
New Zealand Embassy, 19 Observatory Circle, N.W., Washington 8.
Nicaraguan Consulate General, 1270 Sixth Ave., N.Y.C. 20.
Norwegian Information Services, 290 Madison Ave., N.Y.C. 17.
Pakistan Embassy, 2201 R St., N.W., Washington.
Panamanian Embassy, 2862 McGill Terrace, Washington.

Paraguayan Embassy, 5500 16th St., N.W., Washington.
Peruvian Consulate General, 10 Rockefeller Plaza, N.Y.C. 20.
Philippine Embassy, 1617 Mass. Ave., N.W., Washington.
Consulate General of Portugal, 630 Fifth Ave., N.Y.C. 20.
Office of Puerto Rico, 903 16th St., N.W., Washington.
Consulate General of Spain, 630 Fifth Ave., N.Y.C. 20.
Embassy of Spain, Cultural Counselor, 2700 15th St., N.W., Washton.
Consulate General of Switzerland, 444 Madison Ave., N.Y.C.
Syrian Legation, 2215 Wyoming Ave., N.W., Washington.
Thailand Embassy, 2490 Tracy Place, N.W., Washington 8.
Information Bureau of Uruguay, 630 Fifth Ave., N.Y.C. 20.
Union of South Africa Government Information Service, 500 Fifth Ave., N.Y.C. 18.
Union of Soviet Socialist Republics Embassy, 1125 Sixteenth St., N.W., Washington.
Venezuelan Information Service, 1775 Broadway, N.Y.C. 19.
Vietnam American Friendship Association, 796 Ninth Ave., N.Y.C.
Yugoslav Embassy, 1520 16th St., N.W., Washington.

UNITED NATIONS AND SPECIALIZED AGENCIES

Food and Agriculture Organization, 1325 C Street, Washington 25.
International Bank for Reconstruction and Development, 1818 H St., N.W., Washington 25.
International Civil Aviation Organization, International Aviation Building, 1080 University St., Montreal 3, Quebec, Canada.
International Labor Organization, 345 East 46th St., N.Y.C. 17.
International Monetary Fund, 1818 H St., N.W., Washington 25.
International Telecommunications Union, Palais Wilson, Geneva, Switzerland.
UNESCO, United Nations, N.Y. 17.
Universal Postal Union, Case 15, Berne, Switzerland.
World Health Organization, United Nations, N.Y. 17.
World Meteorological Organization, Campagne Rigot, 1 Avenue de la Paix, Geneva, Switzerland.
UNICEF (not a specialized agency), United Nations, N.Y. 17.

FILM COMPANIES

A. F. Films, Room 1001, 1600 Broadway, N.Y.C. 19.
Almanac Films, 516 Fifth Ave., N.Y.C. 18.
Australian News and Information Bureau, 363 Fifth Ave., N.Y.C. 20.
Association Films, 35 West 45th St., N.Y.C. 19.
British Information Service, 30 Rockefeller Plaza, N.Y.C. 20.
Brand Film Library, 2154 K St., N.W., Washington.

Brandon Films, 1600 Broadway, N.Y.C. 17.
Broadcasting and Film Commission, National Council of Churches, 220 Fifth Ave., N.Y.C. 1.
Canadian Film Board, 1270 Avenue of the Americas, N.Y.C. 20.
Canadian Travel Film Libraries, 1270 Avenue of the Americas, N.Y.C. 20.
China Film, 165 West 46th St., N.Y.C. 18.
Christophers, 18 East 48th St., N.Y.C. 18.
Coronet Films, Coronet Building, Chicago 1.
Danish Information Office, 588 Fifth Ave., N.Y.C. 36.
Edited Pictures System, 165 West 46th St., N.Y.C. 19.
Encyclopedia Britannica Films, 20 North Wacker Drive, Chicago 6.
Eye Gate House, 2716 41st Ave., Long Island City 1, N.Y.
Films of All Nations, 55 West 45th St., N.Y.C. 19.
Film Publishers, 12 East 44th St., N.Y.C.
Filmsets, 1956 North Seminary Ave., Chicago 14.
Fitzpatrick Travel Pictures, 8624 Sunset Blvd., Hollywood 46, Cal.
Frith Films, 1816 North Highland, Hollywood 28, Cal.
Gateway Productions, 1859 Powell St., San Francisco 11.
Government of India Information Services, 2107 Mass. Ave., Washington 8.
Hadassah Film Library, 13 East 37th St., N.Y.C. 16.
Harmon Foundation, 140 Nassau St., N.Y.C. 38.
Institute of Inter-American Affairs, 499 Penna. Ave., N.W., Washington 25.
International Film Foundation, 345 East 46th St., N.Y.C. 17.
Japan Travel Information Office, 10 Rockefeller Plaza, N.Y.C. 20.
Knowledge Builders, Visual Education Building, Floral Park, N.Y.
March of Time, 369 Lexington Ave., N.Y.C. 17.
Michigan University, 4028 Administration Building, Ann Arbor, Mich.
Nu-Art Films, 112 West 48th St., N.Y.C. 19.
Pictosound Productions, 4010 Lindell Blvd., St. Louis 8, Mo.
Religious Film Associations, 220 Fifth Ave., N.Y.C. 1.
Scandia Films, 220 West 42nd St., N.Y.C. 36.
Standard Oil, 30 Rockefeller Plaza, N.Y.C. 20.
Scientific Film Co., 6804 Windsor Ave., Suite 506, Berwyn, Ill.
Teaching Film Custodians, 2 West 20th St., N.Y.C. 11.
United Airlines, United Air Lines Building, Chicago 38.
United Fruit Company, Pier 3, North River, N.Y.C. 6.
United World Films, 30 Rockefeller Plaza, N.Y.C. 17.
Young America Films, 8 West 41st St., N.Y.C. 17.

FILMSTRIP PUBLISHERS

American Geographical Society (see Budek)

Anti-Defamation League of B'nai B'rith, 212 Fifth Ave., N.Y.C. 10.
Audio-Visual Associates, Bronxville, N.Y.
Baptist North, 152 Madison Ave., N.Y.C. 16.
Brandon Films, 200 West 57th St., N.Y.C. 19.
Budek Co., 324 Union St., Hackensack, N.J.
CARE, 20 Broad St., N.Y.C. 5.
Curriculum Films, 358 West 44th St., N.Y.C. 36.
Encyclopedia Britannica Films, 20 North Wacker Drive, Chicago 6.
Eye Gate House, 2716 41st Ave., Long Island City 1.
Film Alliance of America, 1600 Broadway, N.Y.C.
Film Publishers, 12 East 44th St., N.Y.C. 10.
Informative Classroom Picture Publishers, Grand Rapids, Mich.
Jam Handy Organization, 2821 East Grand Blvd., Detroit 11.
Life Filmstrips, 9 Rockefeller Plaza, N.Y.C. 20.
Manhattan Publishing Co., 225 Lafayette St., N.Y.C. 12.
McGraw-Hill Book Co., Text-Film Dept., 330 West 42nd St., N.Y.C. 36.
Methodist Publishing House, 810 Broadway, Nashville 2, Tenn.
New York Times, School Service Dept., Times Square, N.Y.C. 18.
New Zealand Embassy, Washington 8, D.C.
Photolab, 3825 Georgia Ave., N.W., Washington 11.
Popular Science (see McGraw-Hill).
Public Affairs Committee, 22 East 38th St., N.Y.C. 16.
Society for Visual Education, 100 East Ohio St., Chicago.
Stillfilm, 8443 Melrose Ave., Hollywood 46, Cal.
Teaching Aids Laboratory, Ohio State University, Columbus 10.
Teaching Aids Service, 31 Union Square West, N.Y.C.
Teaching Films, 2 West 20th St., N.Y.C. 11.
Telecurve, 5620 Hollywood Blvd., Hollywood 28, Cal.
U.S. Department of Agriculture, Washington 25.
Yale Divinity School, 400 Prospect St., New Haven 11.
Young America Films, 18 East 41st St., N.Y.C. 17.

INDEX